Story and Art
Terry Moore

Publisher
Robyn Moore

Color
Brian Miller

Strangers In Paradise: Ever After
Copyright ©2007 Terry Moore
All Rights Reserved

ISBN 978-1-892597-35-9

Published by
Abstract Studio, Inc.
P. O. Box 271487
Houston, Texas 77277-1487
StrangersInParadise.com
sipnet@StrangersInParadise.com

Printed in Canada

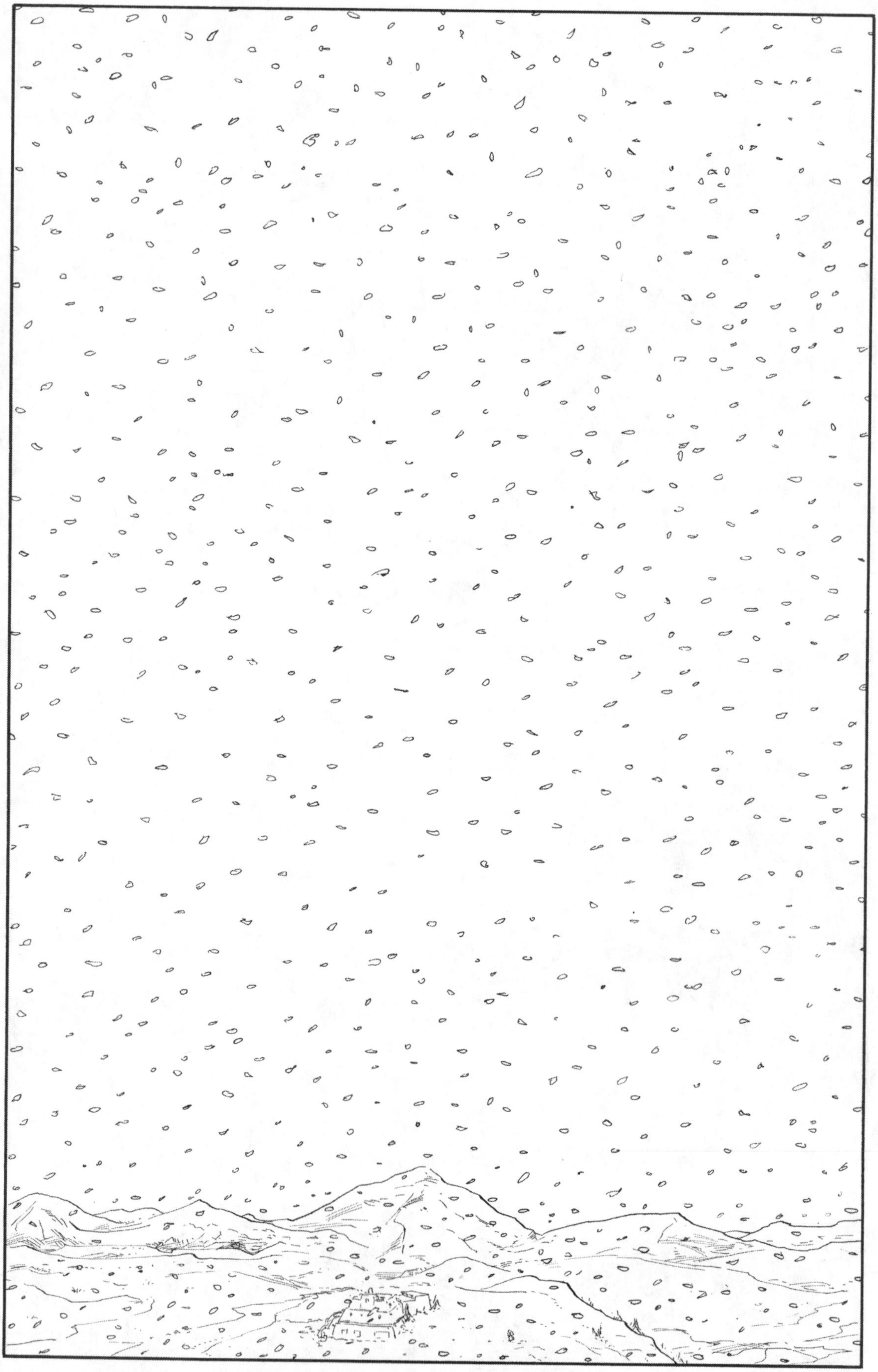

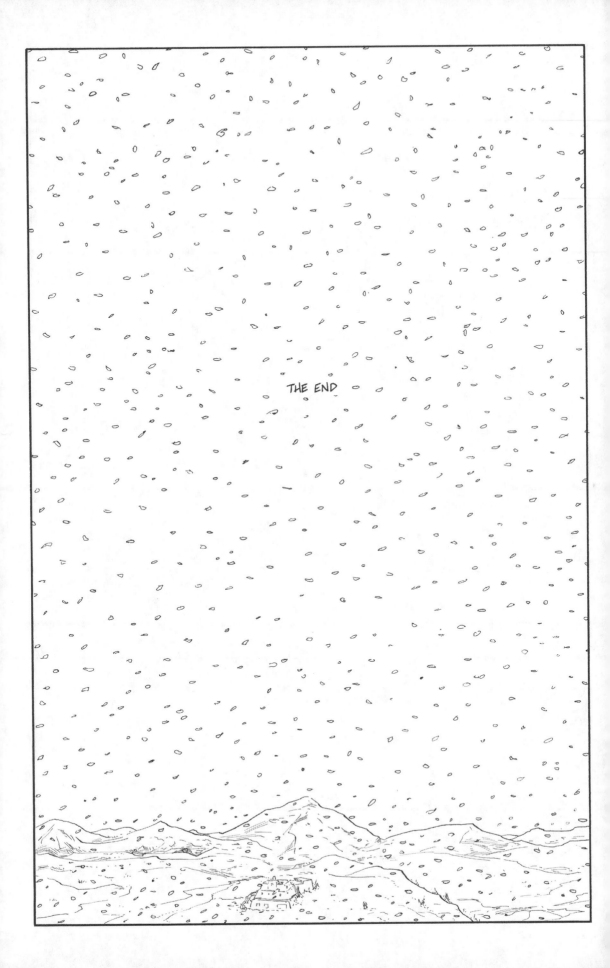

THE END

Ever After

GRIFFIN SILVER
1963 - 2006

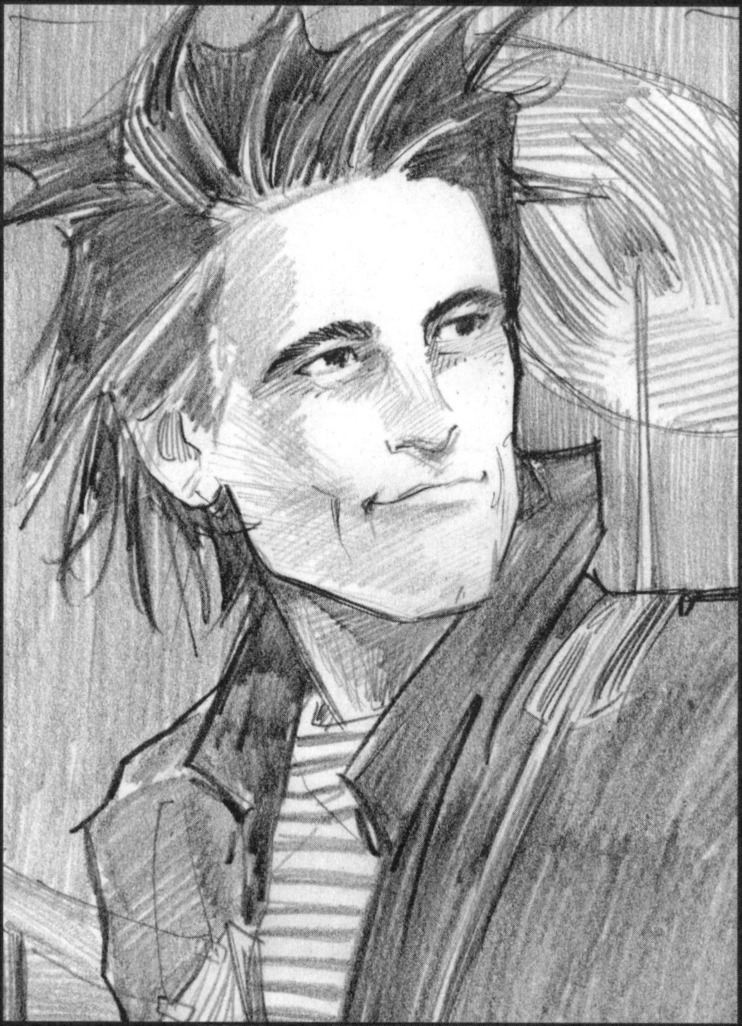

Where were you the night Griffin Silver was shot? For years, maybe decades, people will ask each other that question and shake their heads. Like Kennedy, King, and Lennon, Griffin Silver was more than a public figure, he was an American icon — the last rocker left from the days when bands lived or died by the strength and ingenuity of their songcraft and musicianship. No video girls or studio tricks for this guy, he was the real thing. And now he's gone, dead at the hands of a crazed fan who claimed killing Silver would make him immortal. For Silver, who never seemed comfortable with his fame, the irony is tragic.

Griffin Silver's career began at the age of 17, playing the bars of Washington D.C. with his band Silvershot. Silver's band was playing the B Lounge when David Bowie stopped by for an after-concert drink and, so the story goes, was so impressed by the young musician that he offered Silver a job on the spot. Silver declined in order to finish high school, but his reputation was made in the DC area, allowing him to record a demo that ultimately landed him a recording contract with Torrent.

Torrent released Griffin's first album, Silver Rush, to modest sales but Silver toured extensively, opening for big name

cont. pg 52

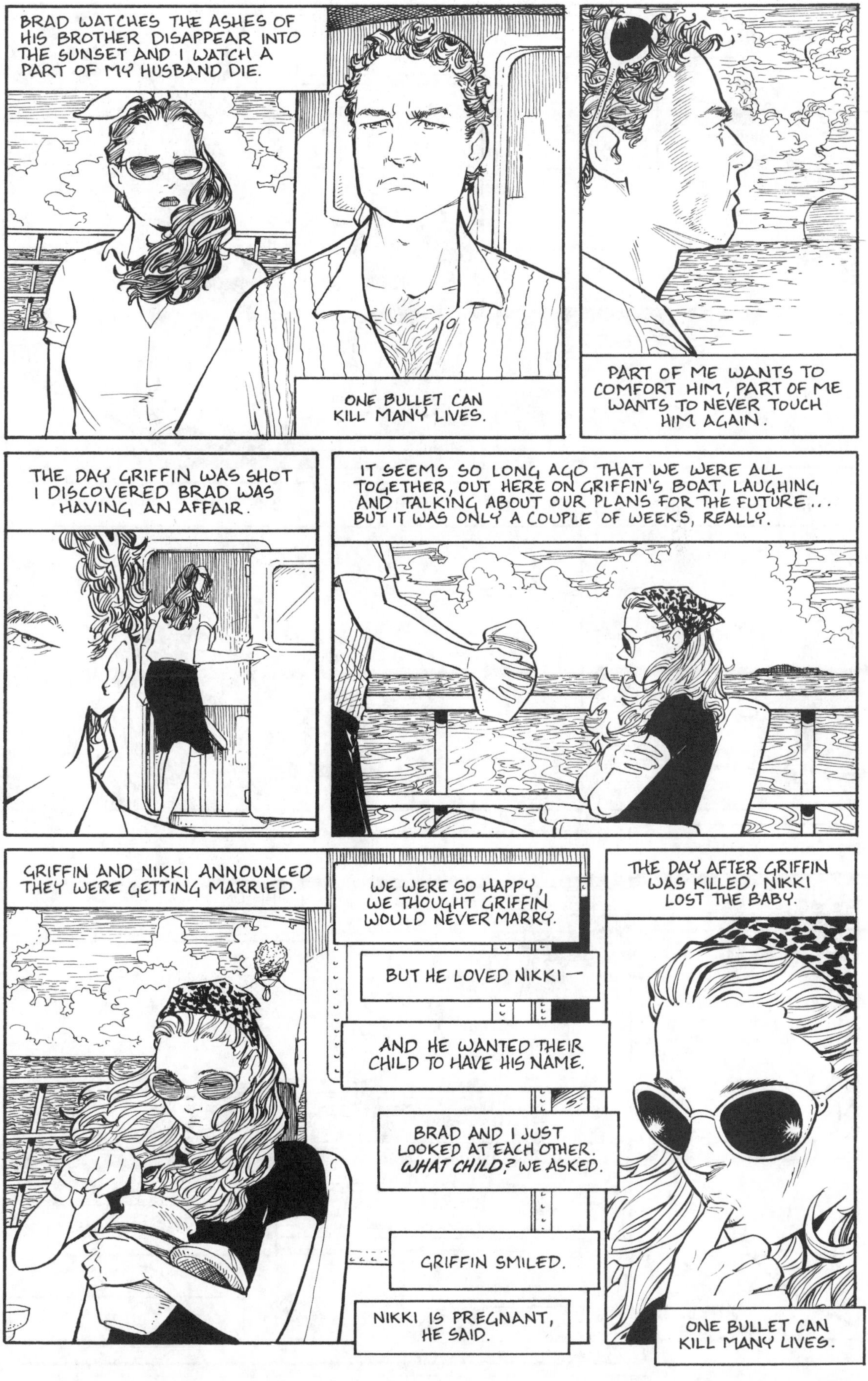

BRAD WATCHES THE ASHES OF HIS BROTHER DISAPPEAR INTO THE SUNSET AND I WATCH A PART OF MY HUSBAND DIE.
ONE BULLET CAN KILL MANY LIVES.
PART OF ME WANTS TO COMFORT HIM, PART OF ME WANTS TO NEVER TOUCH HIM AGAIN.
THE DAY GRIFFIN WAS SHOT I DISCOVERED BRAD WAS HAVING AN AFFAIR.
IT SEEMS SO LONG AGO THAT WE WERE ALL TOGETHER, OUT HERE ON GRIFFIN'S BOAT, LAUGHING AND TALKING ABOUT OUR PLANS FOR THE FUTURE... BUT IT WAS ONLY A COUPLE OF WEEKS, REALLY.
GRIFFIN AND NIKKI ANNOUNCED THEY WERE GETTING MARRIED.
WE WERE SO HAPPY, WE THOUGHT GRIFFIN WOULD NEVER MARRY.
BUT HE LOVED NIKKI—
AND HE WANTED THEIR CHILD TO HAVE HIS NAME.
BRAD AND I JUST LOOKED AT EACH OTHER. *WHAT CHILD?* WE ASKED.
GRIFFIN SMILED.
NIKKI IS PREGNANT, HE SAID.
THE DAY AFTER GRIFFIN WAS KILLED, NIKKI LOST THE BABY.
ONE BULLET CAN KILL MANY LIVES.

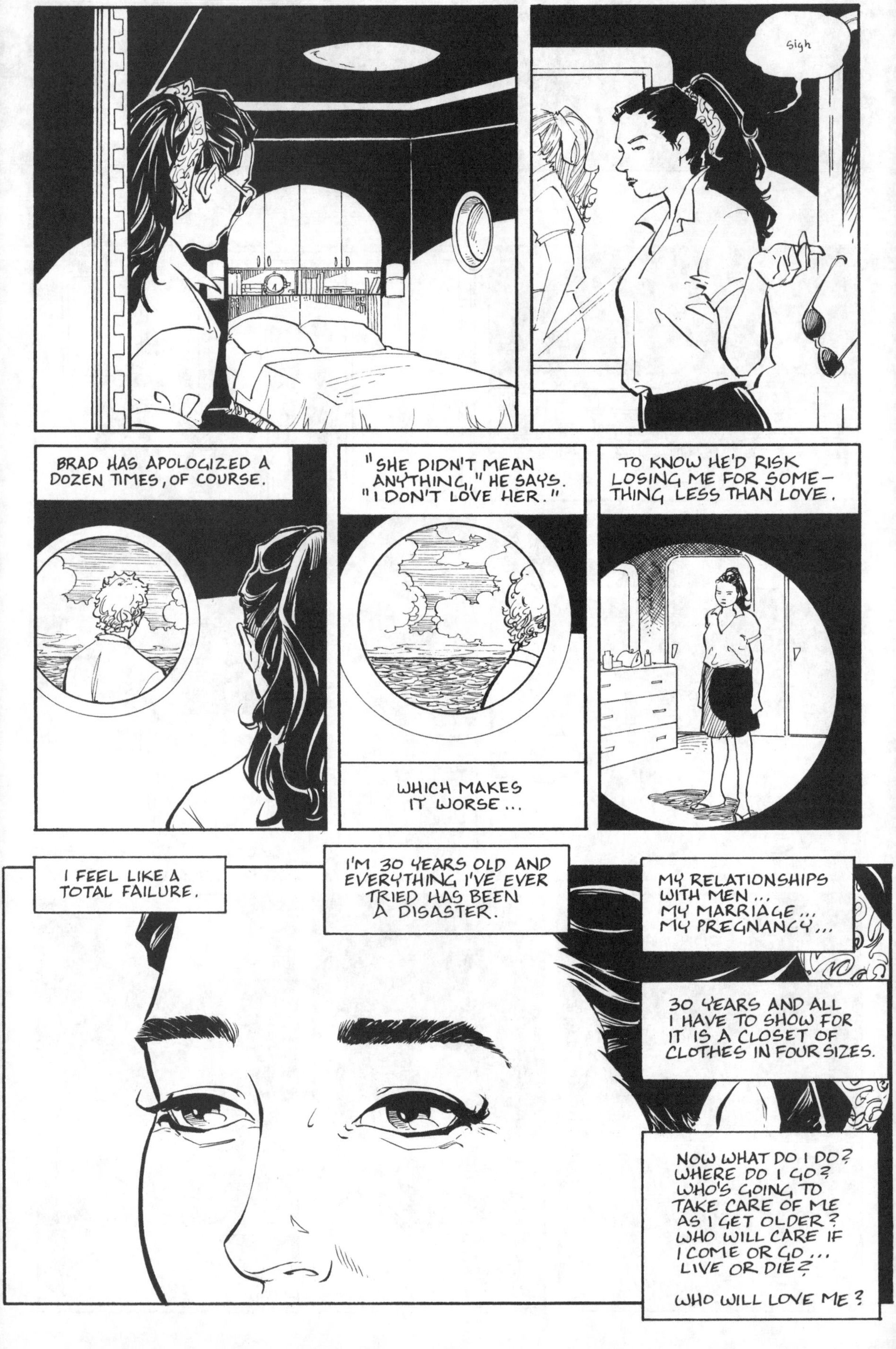
Sigh
BRAD HAS APOLOGIZED A DOZEN TIMES, OF COURSE.
"SHE DIDN'T MEAN ANYTHING," HE SAYS. "I DON'T LOVE HER."
WHICH MAKES IT WORSE...
TO KNOW HE'D RISK LOSING ME FOR SOMETHING LESS THAN LOVE.
I FEEL LIKE A TOTAL FAILURE.
I'M 30 YEARS OLD AND EVERYTHING I'VE EVER TRIED HAS BEEN A DISASTER.
MY RELATIONSHIPS WITH MEN... MY MARRIAGE... MY PREGNANCY...
30 YEARS AND ALL I HAVE TO SHOW FOR IT IS A CLOSET OF CLOTHES IN FOUR SIZES.
NOW WHAT DO I DO? WHERE DO I GO? WHO'S GOING TO TAKE CARE OF ME AS I GET OLDER? WHO WILL CARE IF I COME OR GO... LIVE OR DIE?
WHO WILL LOVE ME?

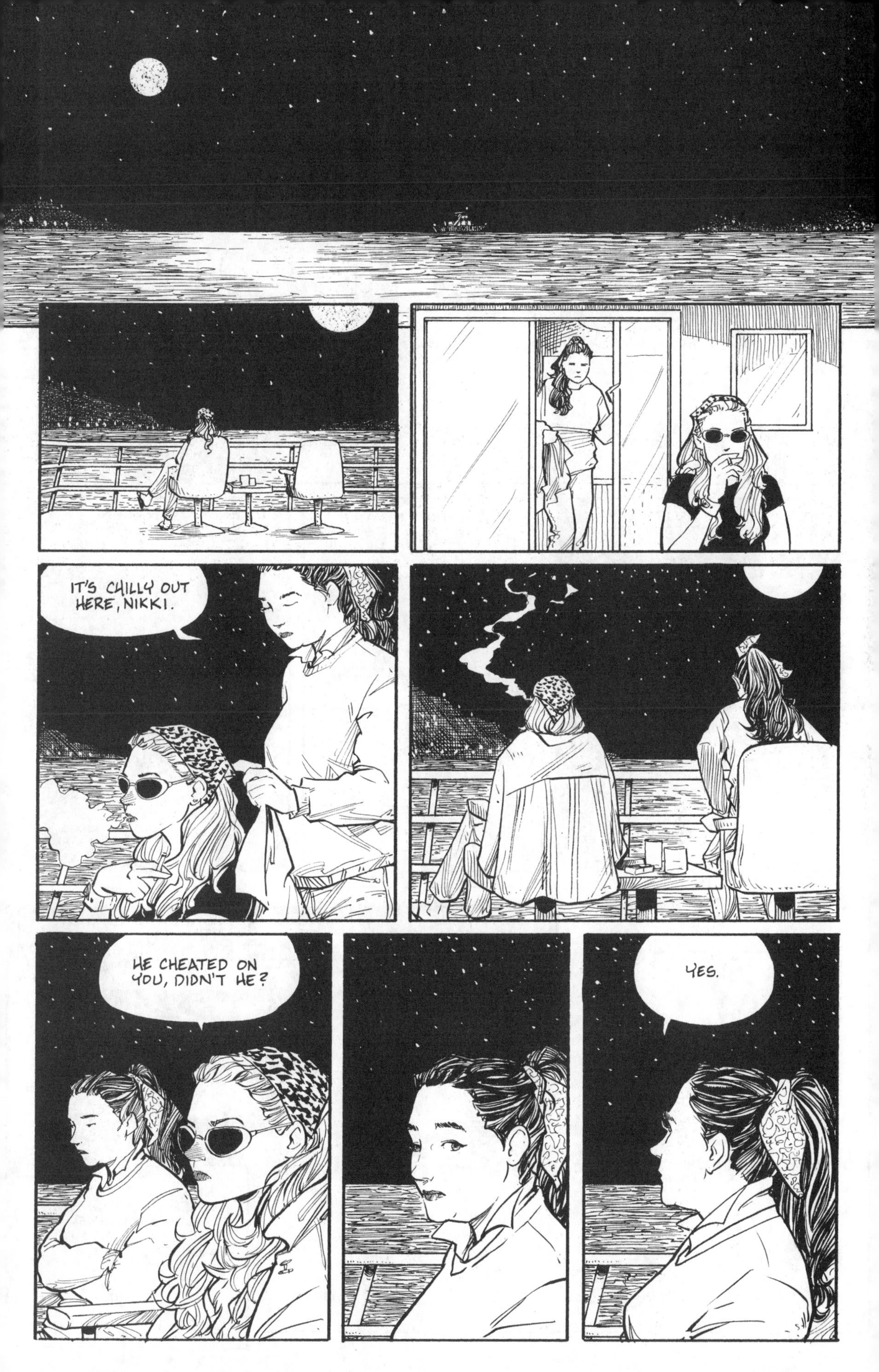
IT'S CHILLY OUT HERE, NIKKI.
HE CHEATED ON YOU, DIDN'T HE?
YES.

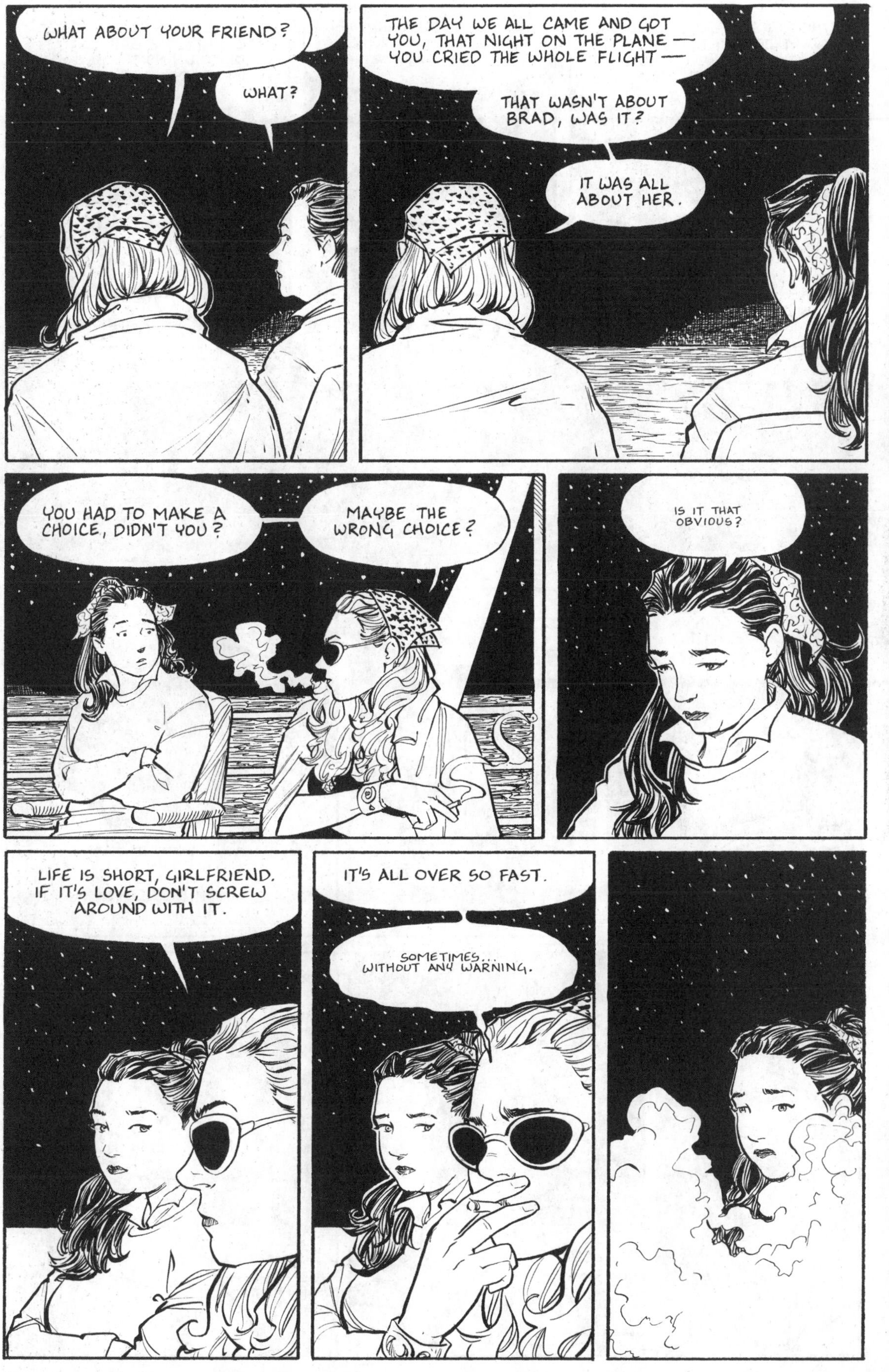
WHAT ABOUT YOUR FRIEND?
WHAT?
THE DAY WE ALL CAME AND GOT YOU, THAT NIGHT ON THE PLANE — YOU CRIED THE WHOLE FLIGHT —
THAT WASN'T ABOUT BRAD, WAS IT?
IT WAS ALL ABOUT HER.
YOU HAD TO MAKE A CHOICE, DIDN'T YOU?
MAYBE THE WRONG CHOICE?
IS IT THAT OBVIOUS?
LIFE IS SHORT, GIRLFRIEND. IF IT'S LOVE, DON'T SCREW AROUND WITH IT.
IT'S ALL OVER SO FAST.
SOMETIMES... WITHOUT ANY WARNING.

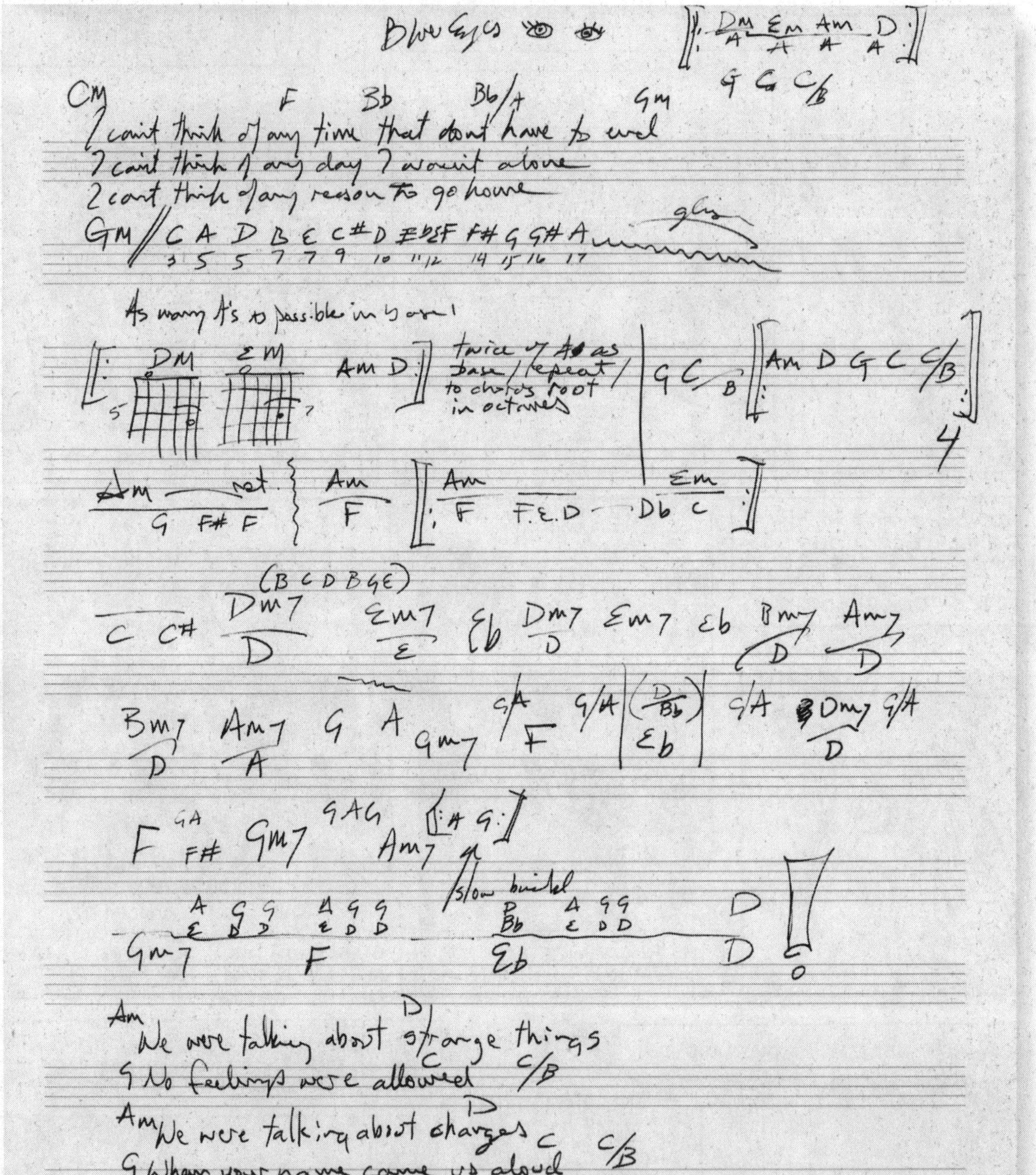

Blue Eyes 👁 👁

[: Dm/A Em/A Am/A D/A :]
G G C/B

Cm   F   Bb   Bb/A   Gm
I can't think of any time that don't have to end
I can't think of any day I wouldn't alone
I can't think of any reason to go home

GM//C A D B E C# D Eb F F# G G# A   gliss
    3 5 5 7 7 9 10 11 12 14 15 16 17

As many A's as possible in 5 on!

[: Dm   Em   Am D :] twice of A# as | G C/B [: Am D G C C/B :]
5   base / repeat
                         to chords root   4
                         in octaves

Dm ——— rest } Am   [: Am   Em
G F# F   F   F F E D   Db C :]

                (B C D B G E)
C C# Dm7   Em7   Eb   Dm7   Em7   Eb   Bm7   Am7
       D   E   D   D   D   D

Bm7 Am7 G A Gm7 G/A   G/A (D/Bb) G/A   Dm7 G/A
D   A   F   Eb   D

F G/A Gm7 G A G Am7 [: A G :]
   F#   G

—Gm7— A G G —A G G— slow build Bb A G G   D
 Eb D D Eb D D   Bb E D D   D
Gm7   F   Eb   0

Am   D
We were talking about strange things
G No feelings were allowed   C/B
Am   D
We were talking about changes C C/B
G When your name came up aloud   C/B

Am
Oh — D   my blue eyes   G
What went wrong C/B [: Fortissimo
                       Em7 A D :]

Blue Eyes by Griffin Silver ©1984 Ma Malai Music

WHAT HAPPENED TO GRIFFIN SILVER WAS JUST WRONG.

I MEAN, IT DOESN'T *FEEL* RIGHT—LIKE, *THAT* WASN'T SUPPOSED TO HAPPEN, AND THE EVENT ITSELF DOESN'T RESONATE WITH THE PLANET.

IS *THAT* POSSIBLE?

IT'S SO SAD.

I KNEW HIM, BACK IN MY DARCY PARKER DAYS.

▶ Now Playing
4 of 95
I Am Waiting
Griffin Silver
Silversongs
2:20   -3:05
menu

HE CAME TO A FEW OF HER PARTIES.

HE WAS A NICE MAN—REALLY GORGEOUS BACK THEN, BEFORE THE SUN AND CIGARETTES TOOK THEIR TOLL.

IS IT REALLY YOU? HOLY CRAP! I DON'T BELIEVE IT!

● REPLAY

HE RECOGNIZED ME AT FRANCINE'S WEDDING.

"BABY JU..."!

WHAK

● REPLAY

I FELT BAD ABOUT PUNCHING HIM OUT BUT HE WAS ABOUT TO BLURT OUT MY PARKER NICKNAME AND, WELL, *THAT* CAN'T HAPPEN.

DAVID'S HEALTH IS COME AND GO.

AT THIS STAGE WITH HIS GLIOBLASTOMA HE HAS GOOD DAYS AND BAD—BUT HE NEVER COMPLAINS.

THE ANIMAL CHANNEL SAYS HUMAN BEINGS ARE THE ONLY CREATURES WHO FEEL SORRY FOR THEMSELVES.

IF DAVID'S FEELING SOMETHING LIKE THAT HE'S DOING A GOOD JOB OF HIDING IT.

I'M SURE IF I ASKED HIM HOW HE COPES DAVID WOULD SAY SOMETHING ABOUT FAITH. AND MAYBE THERE'S SOMETHING TO THAT. WHAT THE HELL DO I KNOW?

AS THE YEARS GO BY I'VE NOTICED I HAVE LOTS OF OPINIONS BUT VERY FEW ANSWERS, Y'KNOW?

IF OPINIONS WERE NICKELS, I'D BE RICH.

BUT I'M NOT RICH...NOT ANYMORE. SO I'VE DECIDED TO GO TO SWITZERLAND AND PULL MY STASH OUT OF THE BANK — $850,000 — THE MAD MONEY I TOOK FROM DARCY WHEN I ESCAPED...ER, LEFT.

DARCY, THE FERRARI'S BEEN REPORTED ABANDONED ON DOHENY, WITH THE KEYS LOCKED IN IT.

● REPLAY

MRS. PARKER! WOULD YOU CARE TO EXPLAIN WHY A UNITED STATES SENATOR IS HANDCUFFED NAKED TO A CEILING FAN IN YOUR BEDROOM?!!

KATINAAA!!

I WAS SAVING THAT MONEY TO BUY A HOME WITH FRANCINE WHEN SHE CAME TO HER SENSES, BUT LOOKS LIKE THAT WAS A STUPID DREAM. BETTER TO SPEND IT ON SOMEBODY WHO REALLY NEEDS IT.

FOR SALE
SOLD

THERE'S NO WAY I'M GOING TO LET DAVID SIT AROUND HERE AND WAIT TO DIE.

WHATEVER TIME HE HAS LEFT, HE SHOULD BE IN A BETTER PLACE — SOMEPLACE GOOD FOR THE SPIRIT —

CASEY TOO, OF COURSE. WE'RE A THREESOME NOW SO...

I KNOW, SOUNDS WEIRD...

BUT FOR US...

FOR RIGHT NOW...

IT WORKS.

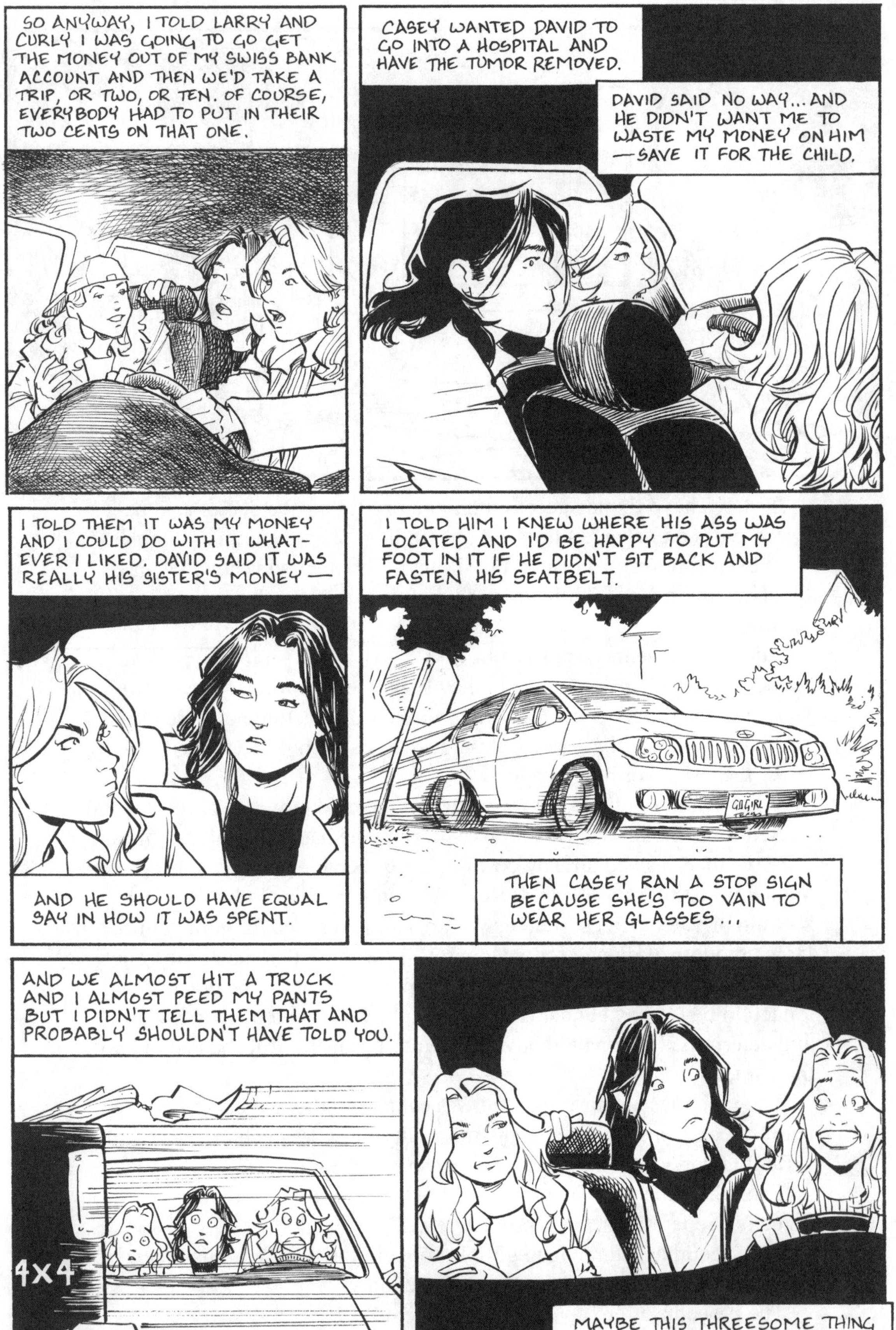
SO ANYWAY, I TOLD LARRY AND CURLY I WAS GOING TO GO GET THE MONEY OUT OF MY SWISS BANK ACCOUNT AND THEN WE'D TAKE A TRIP, OR TWO, OR TEN. OF COURSE, EVERYBODY HAD TO PUT IN THEIR TWO CENTS ON THAT ONE.
CASEY WANTED DAVID TO GO INTO A HOSPITAL AND HAVE THE TUMOR REMOVED.
DAVID SAID NO WAY... AND HE DIDN'T WANT ME TO WASTE MY MONEY ON HIM —SAVE IT FOR THE CHILD.
I TOLD THEM IT WAS MY MONEY AND I COULD DO WITH IT WHAT-EVER I LIKED. DAVID SAID IT WAS REALLY HIS SISTER'S MONEY —
AND HE SHOULD HAVE EQUAL SAY IN HOW IT WAS SPENT.
I TOLD HIM I KNEW WHERE HIS ASS WAS LOCATED AND I'D BE HAPPY TO PUT MY FOOT IN IT IF HE DIDN'T SIT BACK AND FASTEN HIS SEATBELT.
THEN CASEY RAN A STOP SIGN BECAUSE SHE'S TOO VAIN TO WEAR HER GLASSES...
AND WE ALMOST HIT A TRUCK AND I ALMOST PEED MY PANTS BUT I DIDN'T TELL THEM THAT AND PROBABLY SHOULDN'T HAVE TOLD YOU.
4X4
MAYBE THIS THREESOME THING ISN'T GOING TO BE AS EASY AS I THOUGHT. OR AS SAFE.

"Yes, we have found success in laboratory tests," the doctor said between puffs on his cigarette, "but our findings with the human samples have been limited, promising, but limited. The method is new. We have much testing to do. It will take years before we are ready to publish our findings."

"I don't have years," said Tambi.

They were playing a game and they both knew it. *You sniff me, I sniff you*, thought Tambi. She was asking him to do something outside the ethics of medicine; he was checking to see if she could be trusted and make the risks worth his while.

Tambi stared out the window, watching the cold gray sky of Berlin, and waited for Dr. Sturzbacher's reply. She knew he had to be careful, his aggressive theories had already cost him a respectable position at the Kaiser-Wilhelm Institute for Cerebral Research. Funding his work now meant seeking private sources, sources with personal reasons for giving him large amounts of money for a dangerous procedure that may or may not work. Tambi played the role of prospective benefactor. The doctor pretended to be torn by ethical issues. If Tambi was found to be trustworthy and determined, she would have her request granted. But she had to play the game.

"The variables are case specific. We cannot predict the outcome. The neurological consequences… the morbidity rates are uncharted."

Tambi nodded. *I understand. He may die. Let's move on.*

"Even the expense is an unknown. Each case is unique, requiring a wide range of preparations, tests, procedures…"

"My friend has a three inch glioblastoma in the middle of his brain. He has been given a year to live. We must act now."

"The procedures are taxing on the system."

"He is strong."

"We could lose much time establishing a baseline."

"I can have all his records sent to you."

"Technically I am not allowed to request his records."

"I will deliver them personally."

"You must understand… I can make no guarantees."

"I understand."

"And… the expenses…"

Finally, thought Tambi.

The doctor paused, studying his prospective client, waiting for an uncomfortable shift in the chair that did not come. He continued. "Each attempt adds to the costs as we refine the process. It is the preparation that costs so much…the labwork, the DNA…"

"How much are we talking about?" Tambi said.

"Our last patient was unable to complete the payment before she died. Now we must predict our costs before work."

"How much"

"5 million euro… cash. Before we begin."

And the mask drops, Tambi smiled to herself. "And if he dies?"

"I will be very sorry, but no refunds."

"When can you begin?"

The doctor smiled. The game was over. "You are fortunate, we have an opening in two weeks. You may reserve the opportunity with 1 million euro."

Tambi shot the doctor a look but said nothing. *And you will probably pay off your worst creditor and have enough left over to be a big shot in Monte Carlo for a few days before we begin*, she thought. Tambi reached into her left coat pocket and pulled out a thick envelope, tossing it onto the desk between them.

"1 million euro," she said.

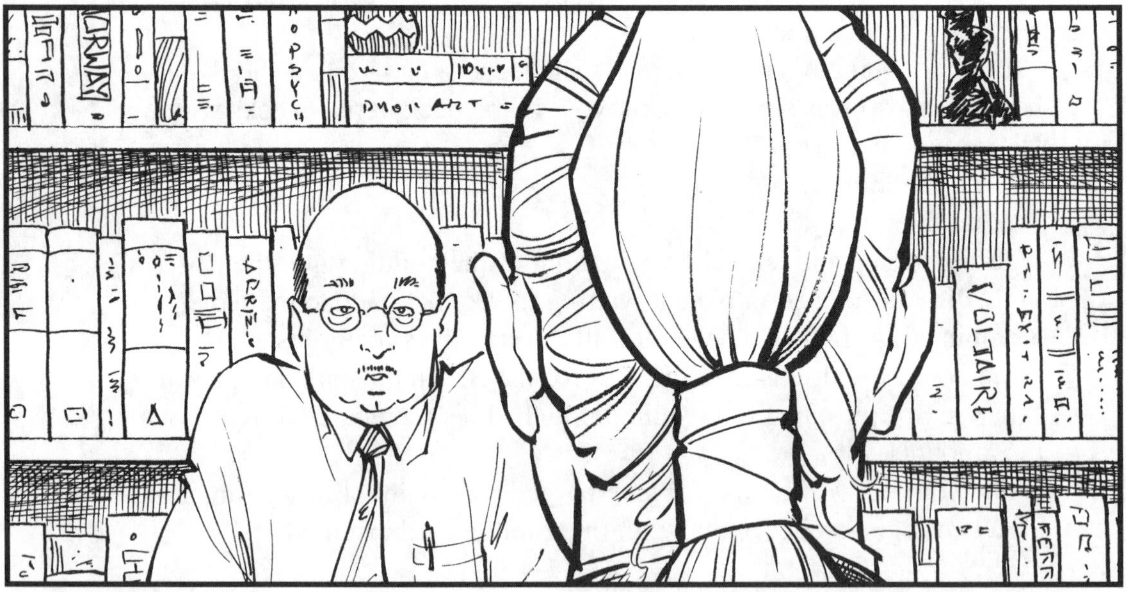
NORWAY
VOLTAIRE

If things had gone badly Tambi would have reached into her right hand pocket and produced a packet of photographs showing the noble doctor at a local night club, kissing a fifteen year old male prostitute. Tambi didn't like to use such cheesy tactics, but she always had a Plan B for these types of meetings. Knowing that the doctor was in the middle of a nasty divorce, the pictures might have been necessary to persuade him to work for her on her timetable. And if the meeting had been a disaster, with threats of legal action and police, there was always Plan C, known throughout the American crime community as The Baker Refund. Or, in short: Kill The Bastard.

Tambi stood from her chair. The doctor did not look at the envelope on his desk, but smiled at Tambi and offered his hand. "It will be a pleasure to work with you, Miss Baker. I will make all the necessary arrangements." He did not stand.

Tambi towered over the doctor as she leaned forward and shook his hand. His grip was weak. "Thank you. I'll be back in two weeks with my friend and his records."

"And the money."

"And the money."

Tambi turned and left. She walked out of the building into the frosty night air and stepped into a car waiting to take her back to the Hotel Kempinski. A light rain began to fall through the streetlights as the car turned onto Freidrichstraße, headed for the B2. In the dark and private sanctuary of the car, Tambi smiled. She had been prepared to pay twice the amount.

They turned west on the B2 and merged calmly into traffic. Tambi dialed two digits on her phone with the satellite card installed and

waited. 5500 miles away Cherry Hammer answered the call.

"Hey boss." As always, Cherry's voice was husky and quiet, despite the crowd sounds in the background.

"Where are you?"

"Eh… I'm not sure how to pronounce it… the Omotesando café… in Tokyo. Man, this is some place, let me tell you. Futurama. They have this drink here called the Dublin Peach… pretty sure it's illegal in the states."

"That's nice. I'm glad you're having a good time and getting liquored up on my dime."

"Jealousy becomes you, boss. Before you fire me you might want to ask me why I'm here."

"Let me guess, they have an Elvis impersonator."

"Now that would be too good to be true. I did hear the Brian Setzer Orchestra is playing somewhere in town this weekend. I might check them out if there's time."

"Where's David's sister?"

"About 50 feet in front of me, at the table by the window."

Tambi paused, silently taken aback. Cherry could be trying at times, but she was the best bloodhound in the business. "Is she alone?"

"She's not a customer, boss, she's a waitress."

Tambi watched the lights of Berlin streak and flicker across her tinted window. The daughter of the most powerful Yakuza leader in recent history was a cocktail waitress. *She probably doesn't even know*, thought Tambi.

"Don't engage her," Tambi said. "Just… stay on her. Don't lose her. I'll get back to you."

"No problem"

"Cherry…"

"Yeah?"

"How… how does she look?"

"Ah… short, pretty…"

"That's not what I mean."

"Oh. She looks clean, boss. Nice kid."

Tambi breathed a sigh of relief that surprised her. "Thanks," she said, and ended the call just as the car pulled up to the entrance of the hotel.

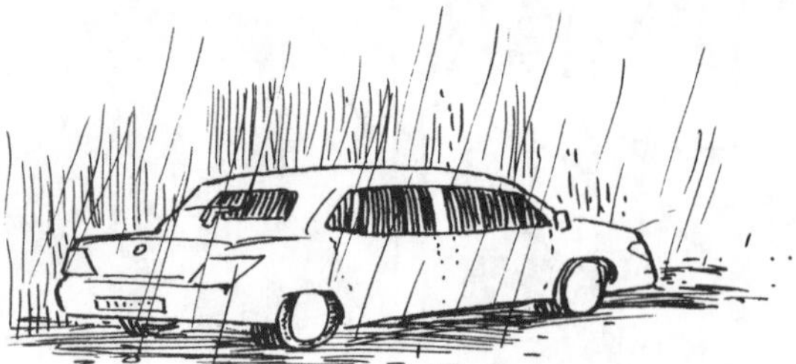

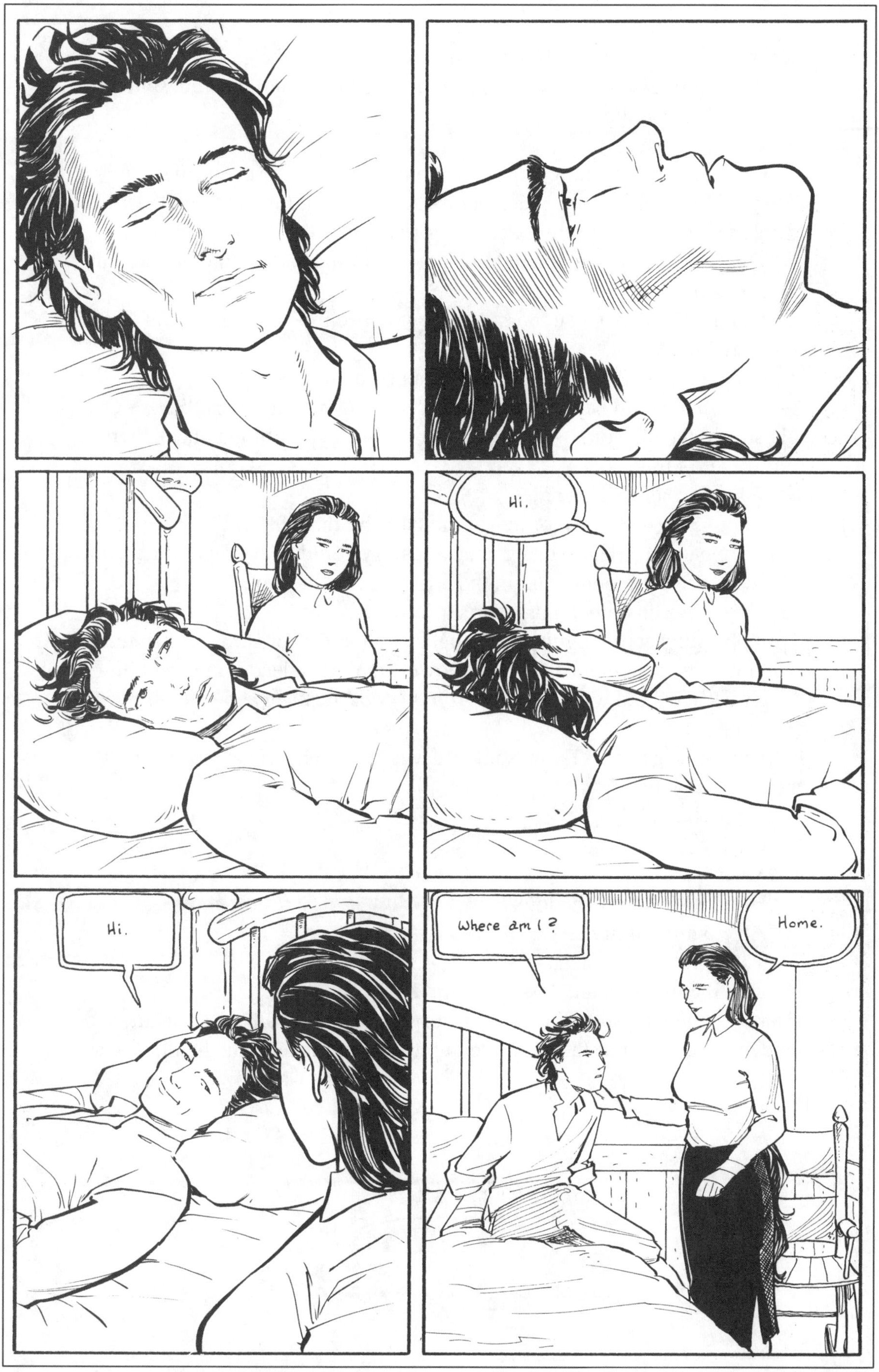
Hi.
Hi.
Where am I?
Home.

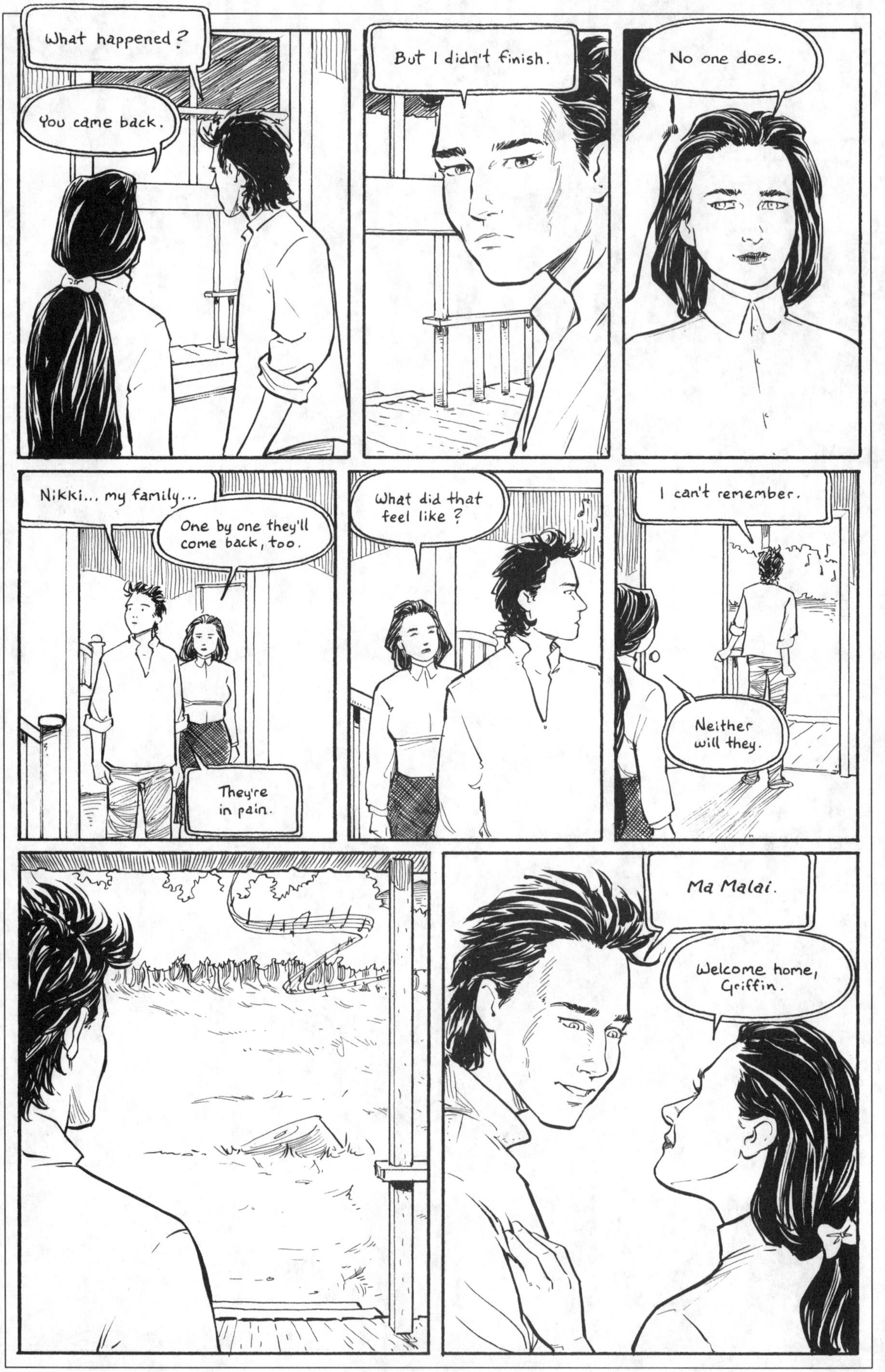
What happened?
You came back.
But I didn't finish.
No one does.
Nikki... my family...
One by one they'll come back, too.
They're in pain.
What did that feel like?
I can't remember.
Neither will they.
Ma Malai.
Welcome home, Griffin.

ABSTRACT STUDIO

84

US $2.95
CAN $4.50

TERRY MOORE

STRANGERS IN PARADISE

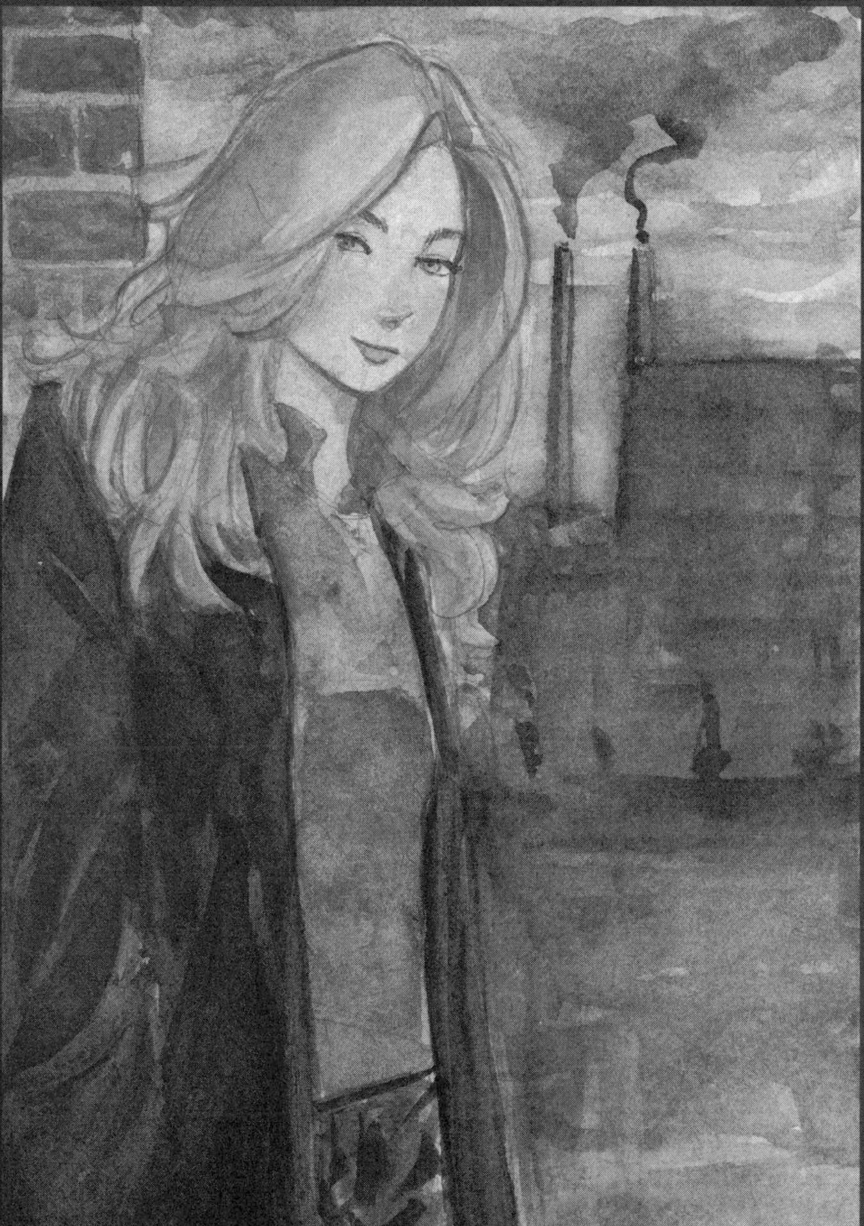

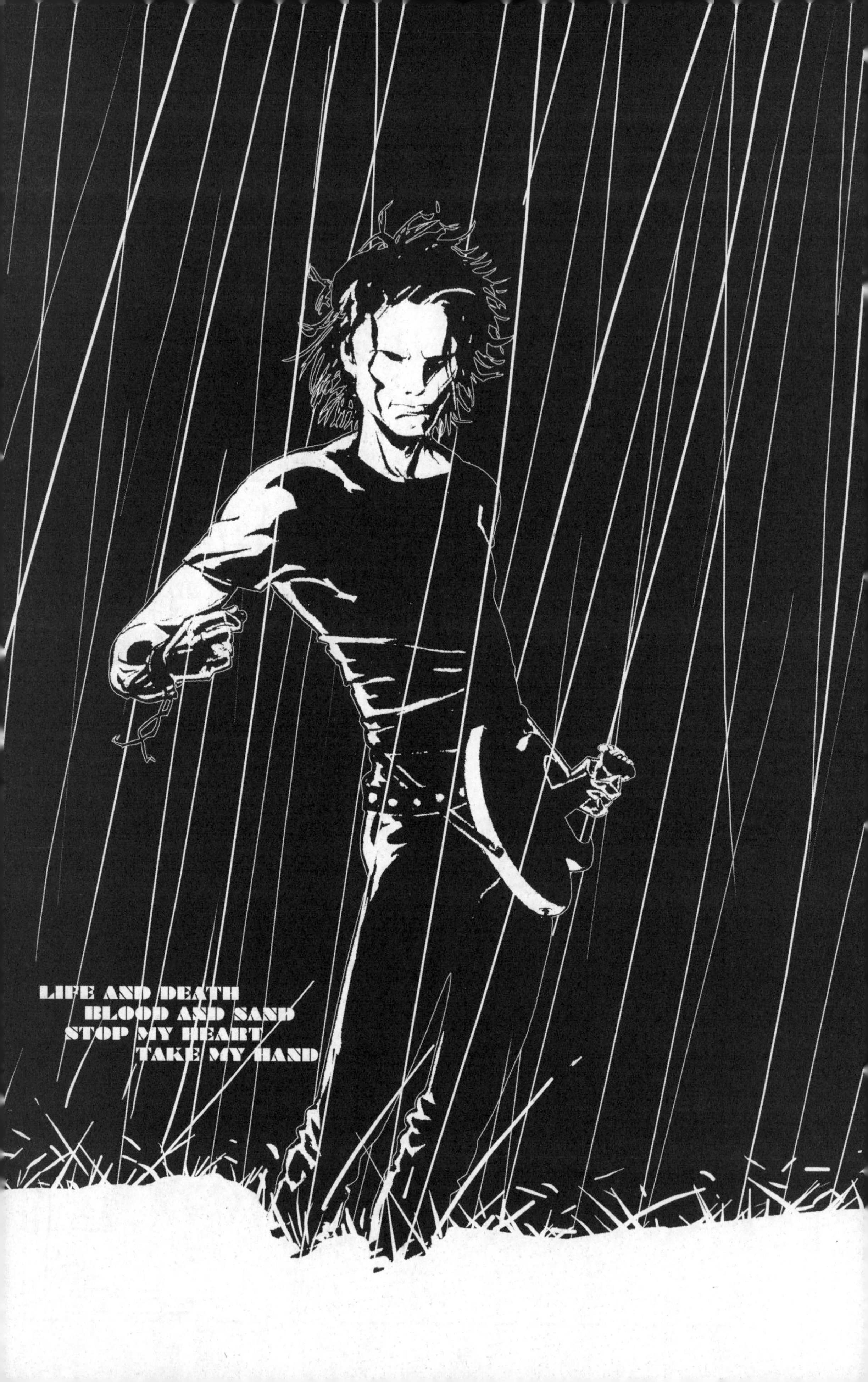
LIFE AND DEATH
BLOOD AND SAND
STOP MY HEART
TAKE MY HAND

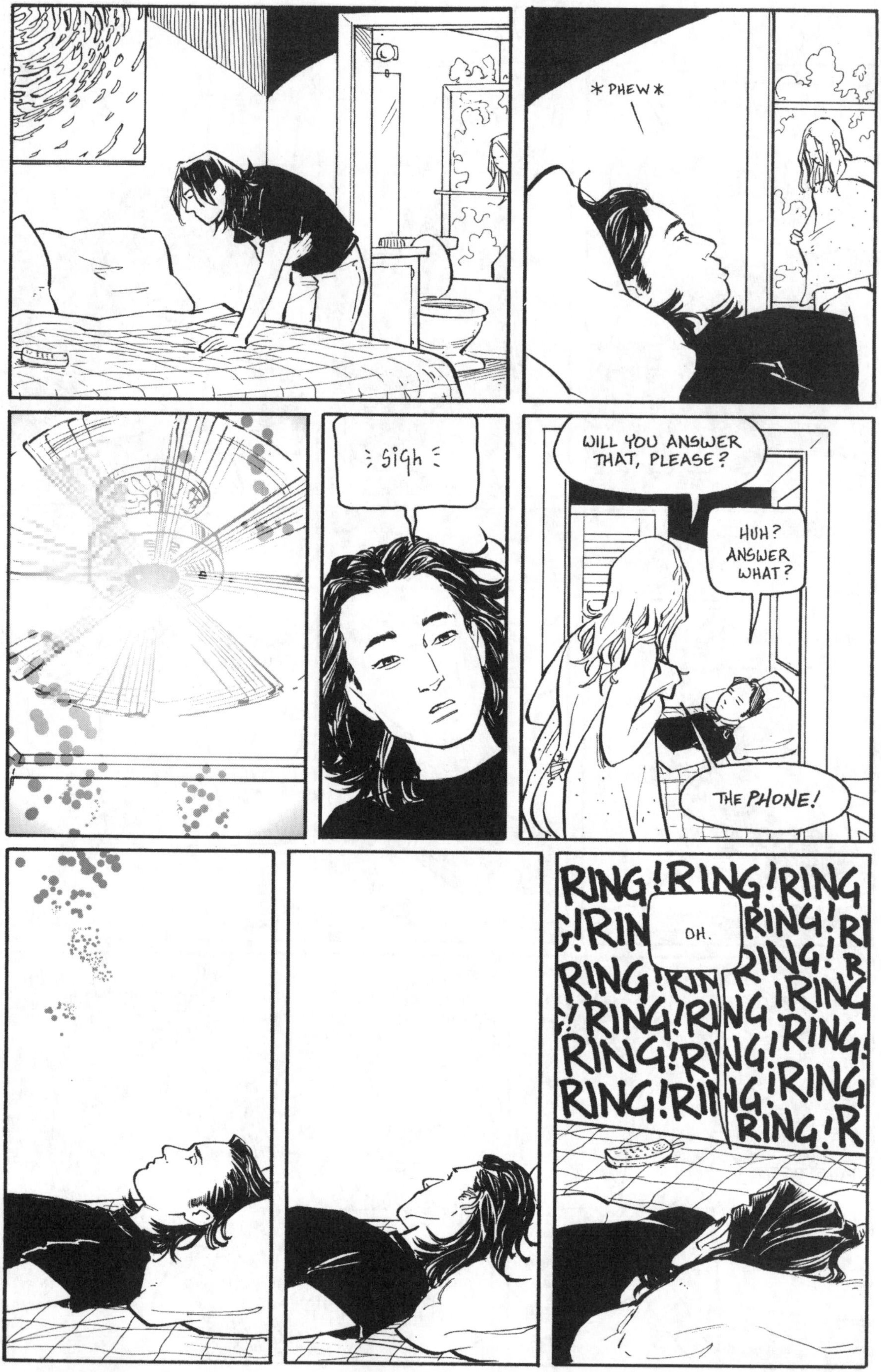
PHEW
SIGH
WILL YOU ANSWER THAT, PLEASE?
HUH? ANSWER WHAT?
THE PHONE!
OH.
RING! RING! RING! RING! RING! RING!

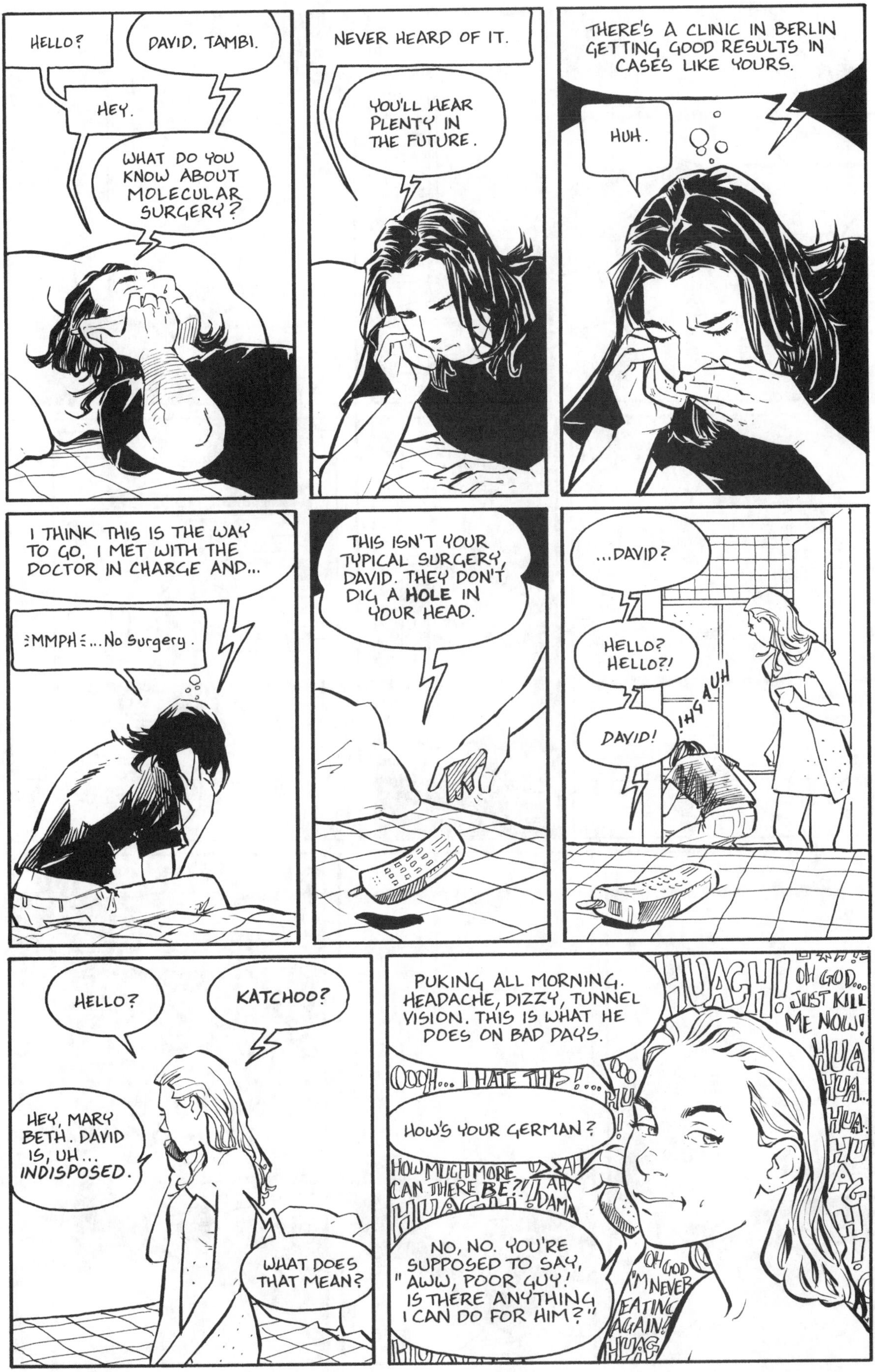

HELLO?
DAVID. TAMBI.
HEY.
WHAT DO YOU KNOW ABOUT MOLECULAR SURGERY?
NEVER HEARD OF IT.
YOU'LL HEAR PLENTY IN THE FUTURE.
THERE'S A CLINIC IN BERLIN GETTING GOOD RESULTS IN CASES LIKE YOURS.
HUH.
I THINK THIS IS THE WAY TO GO, I MET WITH THE DOCTOR IN CHARGE AND...
MMPH ...No Surgery.
THIS ISN'T YOUR TYPICAL SURGERY, DAVID. THEY DON'T DIG A **HOLE** IN YOUR HEAD.
...DAVID?
HELLO? HELLO?!
DAVID!
HELLO?
KATCHOO?
HEY, MARY BETH. DAVID IS, UH... **INDISPOSED.**
WHAT DOES THAT MEAN?
PUKING ALL MORNING. HEADACHE, DIZZY, TUNNEL VISION. THIS IS WHAT HE DOES ON BAD DAYS.
HUACH!
OH GOD... JUST KILL ME NOW!
OOOH... I HATE THIS!...
HOW'S YOUR GERMAN?
HOW MUCH MORE CAN THERE BE?!
NO, NO. YOU'RE SUPPOSED TO SAY, "AWW, POOR GUY! IS THERE ANYTHING I CAN DO FOR HIM?"
OH GOD I'M NEVER EATING AGAIN!

Griffin Silver's east coast house was hidden in the middle of sixty acres of prime Long Island real estate. Billy Joel and Paul McCartney had homes nearby. After a sad trip to the Caribbean to disperse Griffin's ashes, Brad and I accompanied Nikki back to the Long Island house. Brad met with Griffin's accountants and lawyers because Griffin's will stipulated that his music catalog would be left to his brother to manage. Turns out that even though Griffin's personal career had dimmed, the popularity of his music hadn't. Funny how that works. Maybe that's why Judy Garland drank. Anyway, Griffin's company, Ma Malai Music, was worth a lot of money. With no other immediate family to share the spoils, Brad was rich. He didn't seem very happy about it, though. He and Griffin had been very close.

I didn't like staying at the house after Griffin died; it just wasn't the same. Brad spent several days in meetings and some general planning sessions that had nothing to do with me, so I wandered the grounds and poked through the library. A full time staff of four ran the house and I spent a lot of time just hanging out in the kitchen, talking to the chef, who taught me how to make gravy.

After three days I decided I didn't need to be there any longer. I hardly saw Brad, we slept in separate bedrooms, and when we did see each other we barely spoke. Nikki kept to herself, sleeping late and taking one meal a day alone on a private balcony. Griffin had left the business to Brad, but he left this house to Nikki, along with a management fund to keep it going for the rest of her days. She wasn't sure if she was going to keep it, but for now it was home and every room reminded her of Griffin and better days.

The chauffeur was putting my bags in the car to take me to the airport when Nikki came to say goodbye. She asked me to walk with her. We strolled the gardens behind the house talking about nothing in particular. The air was chilly but the sun was warm and bright. A butterfly danced above the flowers and birds chattered in the trees, resting on their way south.

At the far end of the garden, Nikki took my hand and led me into the trees and over a hill. On the other side was a small cottage, sitting peacefully in a clearing. It looked to me like something in a fairy tale. "Griffin's hideaway," Nikki smiled. I followed her to the front door.

"Griffin left me too much," she said. "I don't know what to do with it all."

"Most people would say that's a nice problem to have," I replied.

"I'd rather have Griffin."

"We need to watch the time, Nikki. I don't want to miss the plane."

"It's a private plane, Francine. He'll wait. This will only take a minute." Nikki took a key from her pocket. "Griffin liked art, you know. He bought a lot of it over the years. Matisse, Frazetta…you ever heard of Frazetta?"

"No."

"Neither had I until I met Griffin. This lock is…" She fidgeted with the door a moment before the key finally turned. "There, got it."

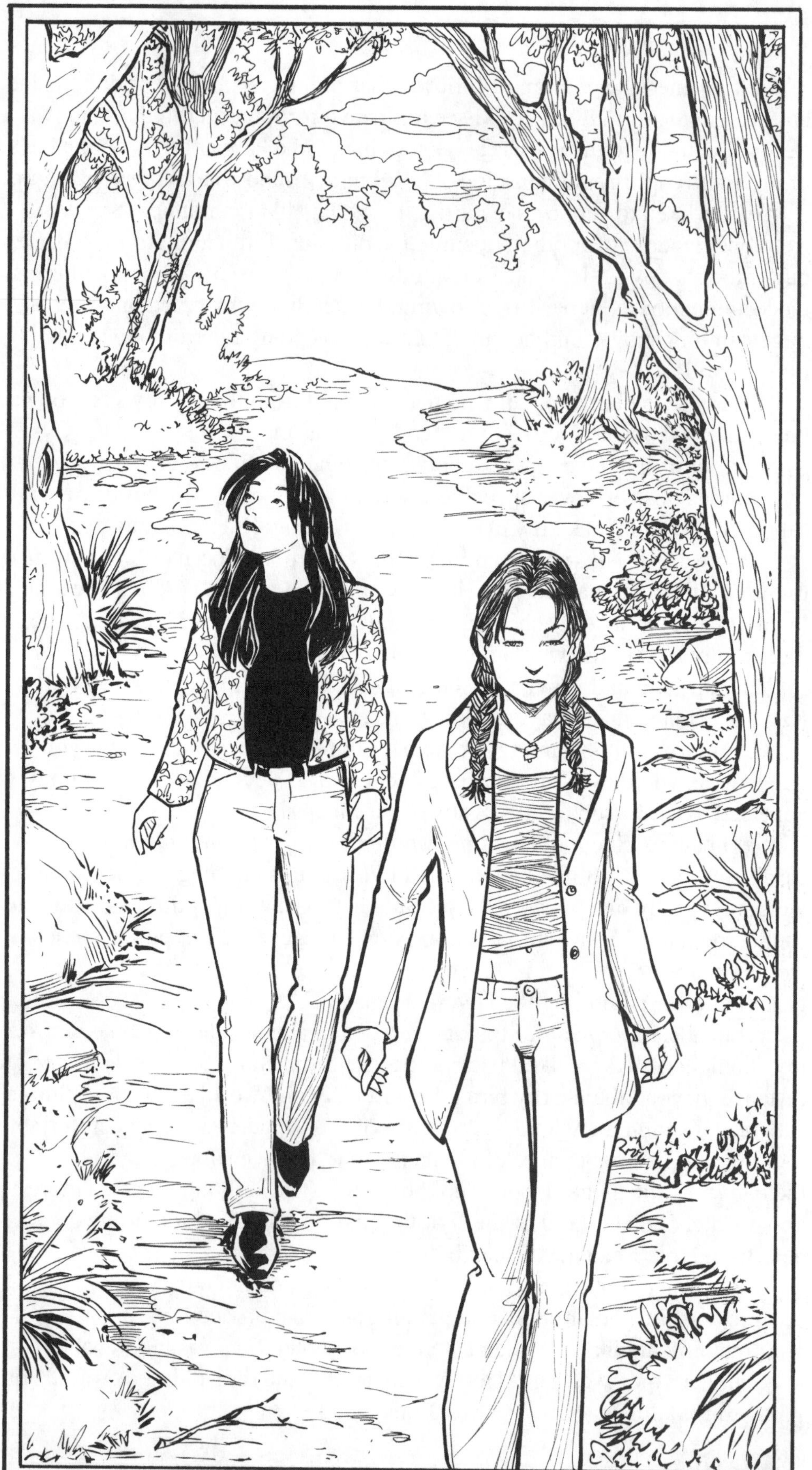

Nikki opened the door and I followed her into the room. It was dark inside, but even in the dim light I could see a massive form lurking in the shadows. Before I could recognize what I was looking at, the hair stood up on the back of my neck, as if my subconscious knew but my mind was trying to catch up.

"Griffin liked to support new artists as well," Nikki continued. She went from one window to another, opening the curtains, forcing the form to come out of the shadows. "He'd heard good things about this artist and bought this piece anonymously at her first showing. I asked him why he bought such a huge painting and he said he didn't know it was going to be so big, he just liked the title."

I stared at the giant woman who had emerged from the shadows and owned one entire wall of the room. Oh my god... it was me.

"'Portrait of Francine', by Katchoo. You've heard of her, right?"

I couldn't answer. I was speechless. I felt the arm of a chair beside me and sat down. I couldn't take my eyes from the painting. Katchoo...my god.

I was aware of Nikki watching me. "Fills the room, doesn't it?" She turned to the painting and walked up to it the way a child might approach a resting locomotive. Her hand reached out and touched the edge of the canvas. She looked tiny next to the woman, next to me, as I sat naked, legs crossed, arms folded, hair long and flowing in the breeze. I had never posed for this but Katchoo painted it anyway; she knew me so well.

"Griffin loved this painting, Francine. I think he felt something for you. Not that he would ever say anything because of Brad, and me, but I think you appealed to the Byron in him. Know what I mean?"

Nikki paused. She looked at me, waiting for my response but no words came. She smiled. "Some people would look at this painting and see a naked woman. A really big, naked woman. But Griffin saw something else. He was such a romantic." I saw Nikki's expression change; a weight pulled the joy from her face. "Griffin and I loved each other, but we never had this," she gestured to the painting. "We never had magic."

I remembered to breath. I took a deep breath and felt the tension ease from my shoulders. Nikki walked back across the room and stood beside me. In the distance, beyond the nearby birds, I heard a lawnmower. The alarm within me subsided, leaving me with a shaky sense of awe. I mean, I wasn't comfortable looking at a gigantic picture of me naked, but the sheer impact and... and... the *beauty* of the painting could not be denied. The painting revealed more about Katchoo than it did of me. For the first time I saw a side of my once dear friend that I had never seen before: genius.

Nikki's voice broke the silence. "Look," she said, in a quiet voice, "The artist loves this woman. It's not a painting, it's an embrace."

Something in Nikki's voice made me look at her. She was talking about love but her voice was hard. Her eyes met mine and didn't blink. "You're not going to find this twice in one life, Francine."

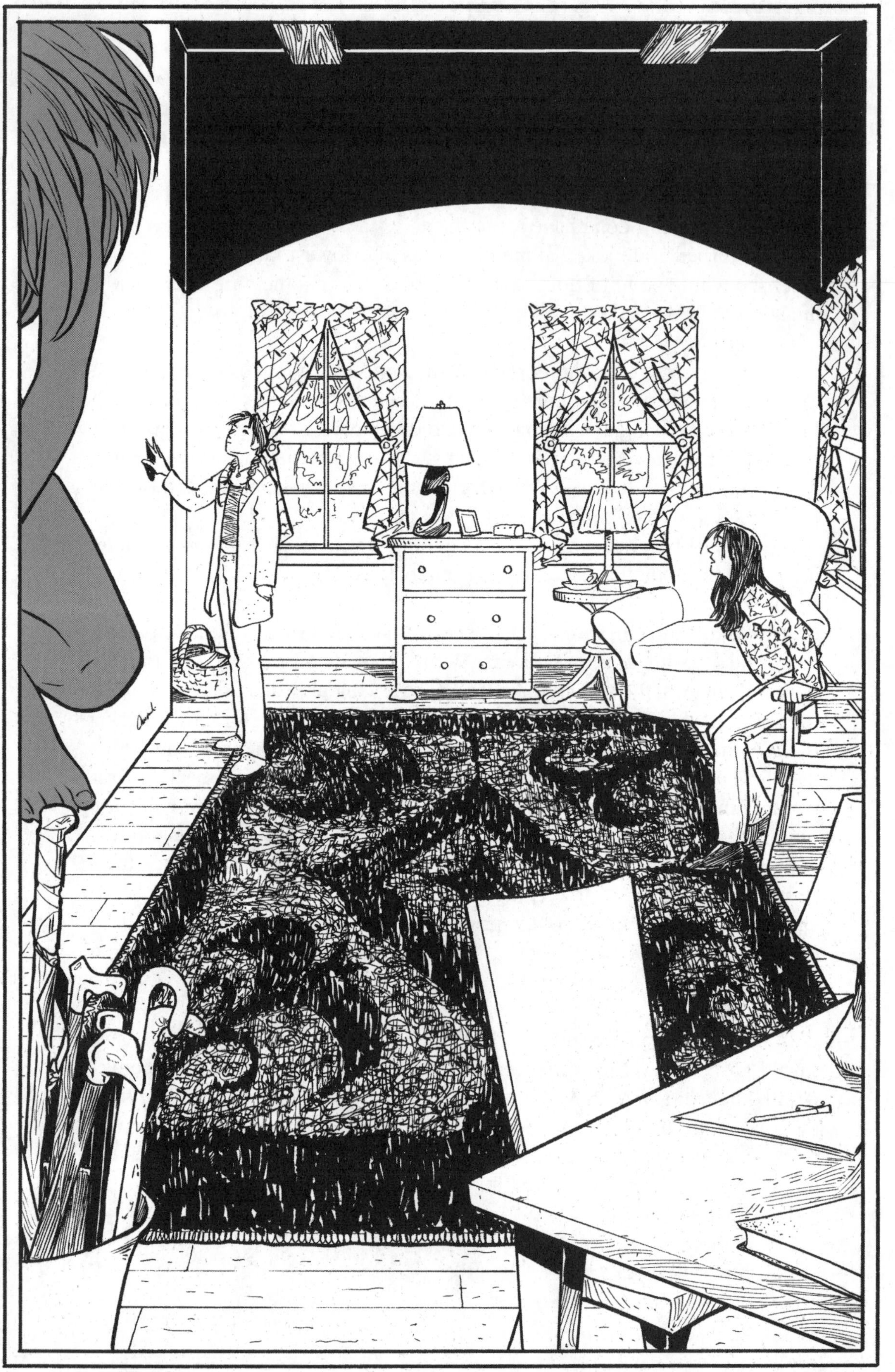

Nikki stepped back to the window and studied the painting. "Anyway, I thought you might like to have it. Griffin paid a lot of money for it, but it's yours if you want it."

"Oh Nikki, I couldn't."

"Sure you could."

"I... it's so big. I don't have room for it."

Nikki turned and looked at me like I was the slowest kid in class. "But that's the whole point of things like this, isn't it? For something like this... you *make room* in your life."

I blinked.

Something about the sight of her by the window, trying to get me to see a fact of life too big to be ignored, while the sun and shadows fought across her face... this wasn't a game anymore. We didn't have a lifetime to work things out, we had whatever was left, remnants. We were getting older. We were dying, one by one. It was possible for me to spend whatever was left of my life doing the wrong thing, or worse, nothing.

I asked Griffin once what it was like, being famous. He said most people don't lead lives, they accept them. Sitting between the towering image of Katchoo's dream girl and the disappointment on Nikki's face, I saw myself clearly for the very first time. It was as if I had been sleepwalking all these years and a spell had been broken. My life flashed before my eyes—high school, Katchoo, the school play, the college scandal, Katchoo's return to my life, Freddie, David, our little rent house above the garage, Katchoo's Parker trouble, the night we almost had sex, the arguments, the fights, running away, the plane crash, nursing David, the year at my mother's house, meeting Brad, being kidnapped, trying to get back with Katchoo and finding her with Casey, running back to Brad, our wedding day and saying goodbye to Katchoo for what I thought was the last time. All the awkwardness, the uncertainty, the indecision, the awful act of keeping Katchoo at arm's length for years while I enjoyed the attention but not the price—I saw it all as if it had been written down and shown to me in a book. Then that night in the studio when we made up... or rather, she forgave me.

I'd been a fool.

If I died today and found myself facing God tonight, He'd look at me and say, "I gave you all those chances at happiness. Why didn't you take them?" And I'd have no answer. My reasons all looked like excuses now. I had forced the love of my life to live without me. Meanwhile, I was drifting through the lives of other people, alone, unhappy, losing the inner joy that once defined me. And I had no one to blame but myself.

I'd been a fool.

I stood up.

I took my life back.

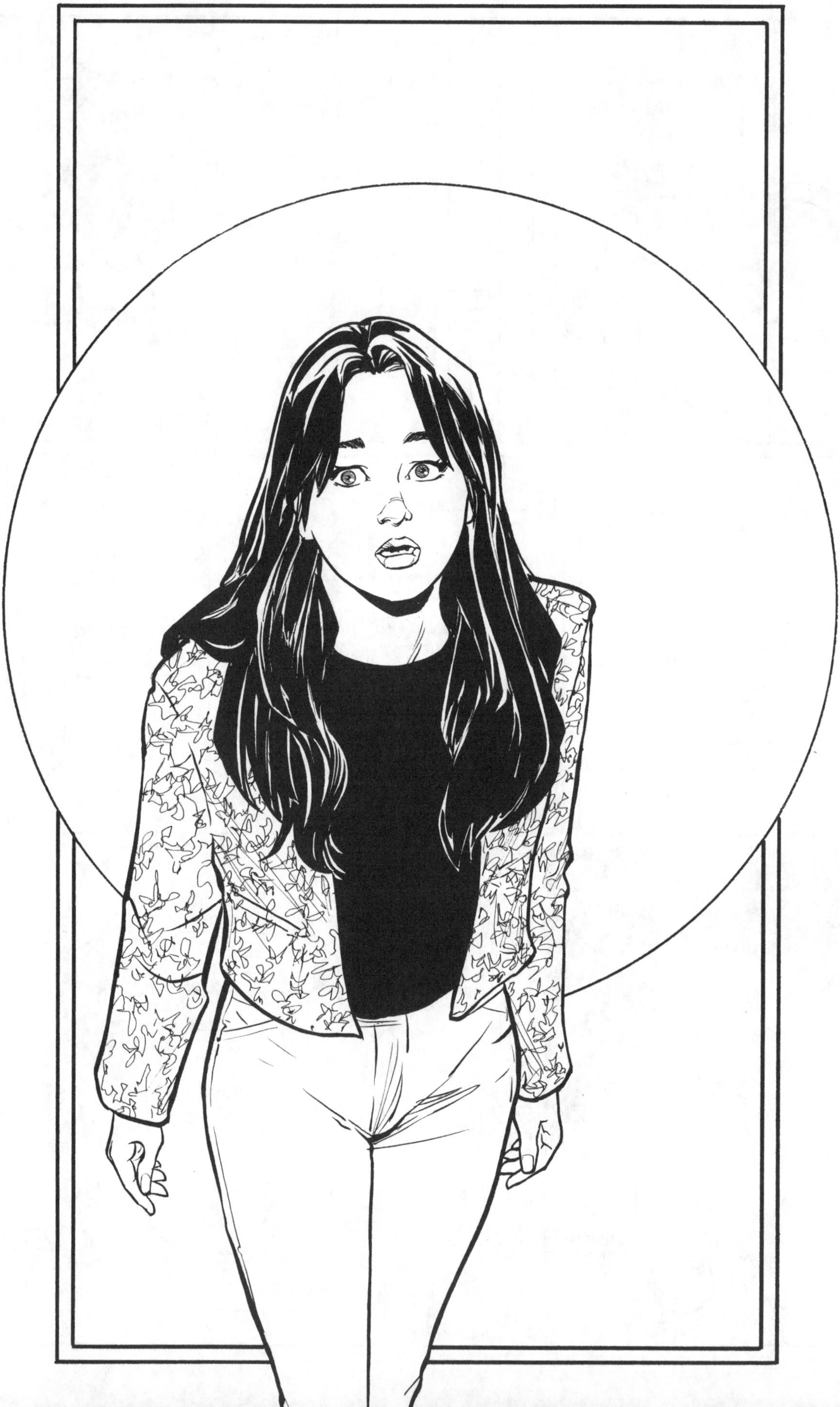

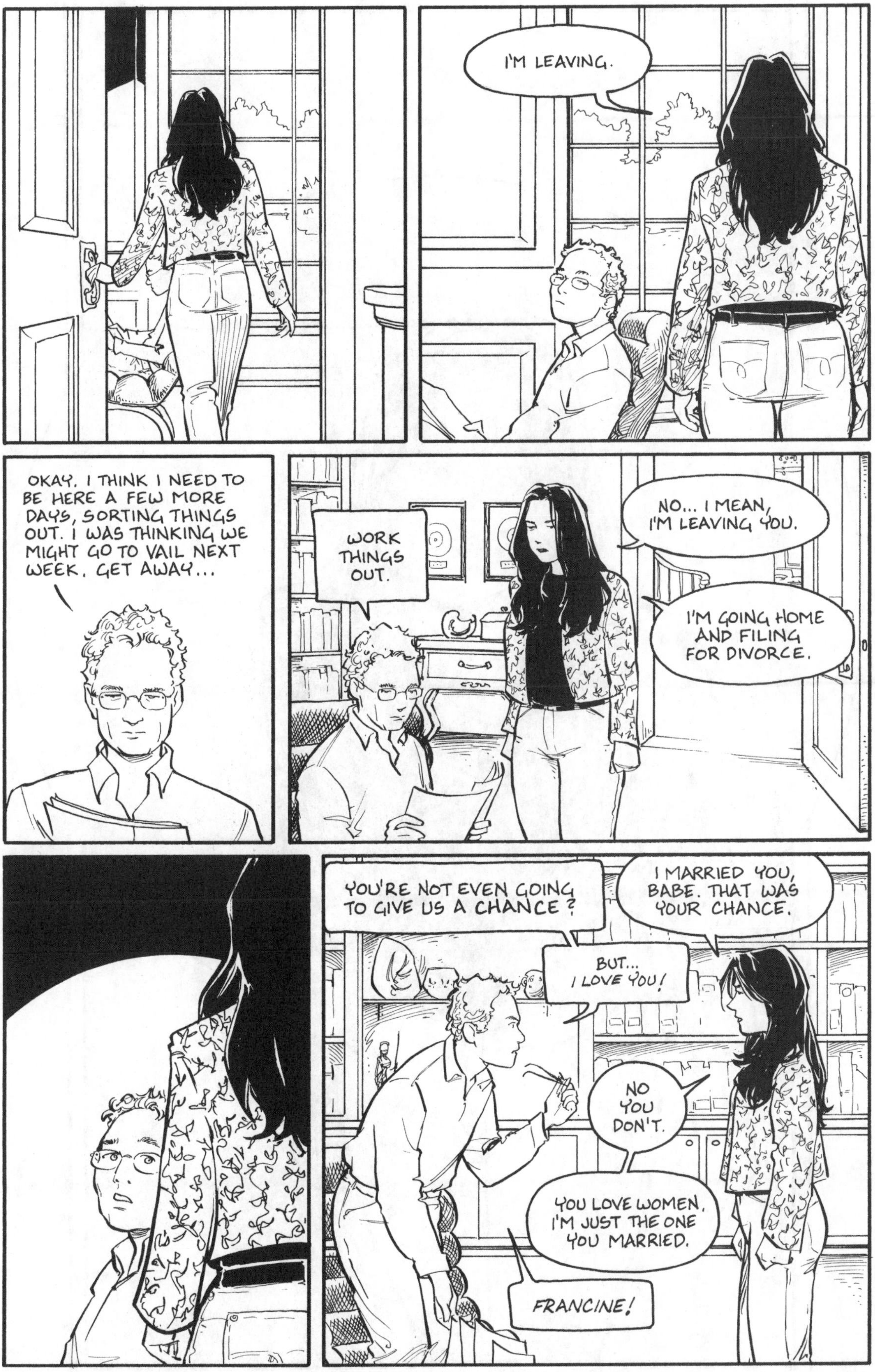
I'M LEAVING.
OKAY. I THINK I NEED TO BE HERE A FEW MORE DAYS, SORTING THINGS OUT. I WAS THINKING WE MIGHT GO TO VAIL NEXT WEEK. GET AWAY...
WORK THINGS OUT.
NO... I MEAN, I'M LEAVING YOU.
I'M GOING HOME AND FILING FOR DIVORCE.
YOU'RE NOT EVEN GOING TO GIVE US A CHANCE?
I MARRIED YOU, BABE. THAT WAS YOUR CHANCE.
BUT... I LOVE YOU!
NO YOU DON'T.
YOU LOVE WOMEN. I'M JUST THE ONE YOU MARRIED.
FRANCINE!

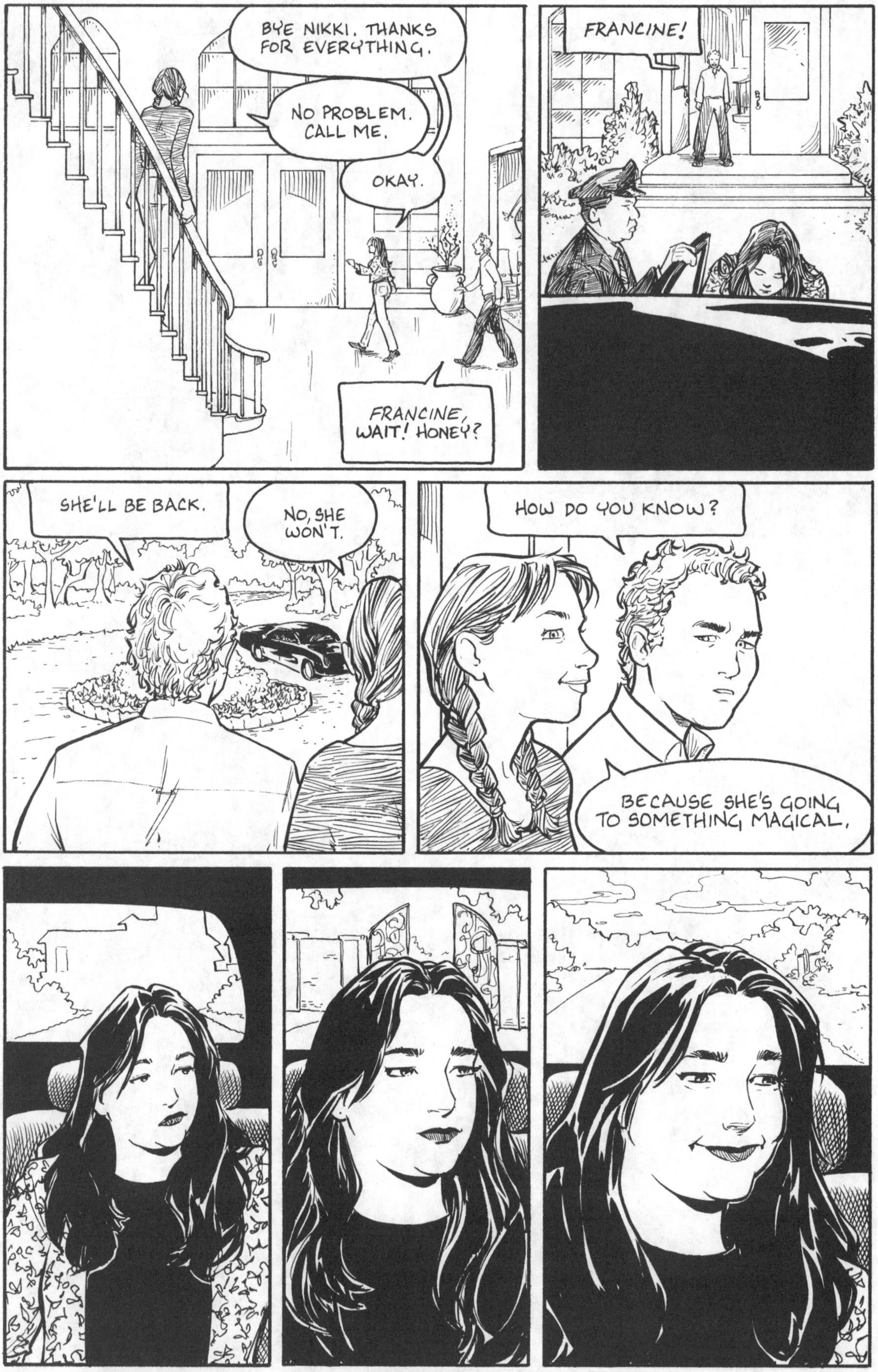
BYE NIKKI. THANKS FOR EVERYTHING.
NO PROBLEM. CALL ME.
OKAY.
FRANCINE, WAIT! HONEY?
FRANCINE!
SHE'LL BE BACK.
NO, SHE WON'T.
HOW DO YOU KNOW?
BECAUSE SHE'S GOING TO SOMETHING MAGICAL.

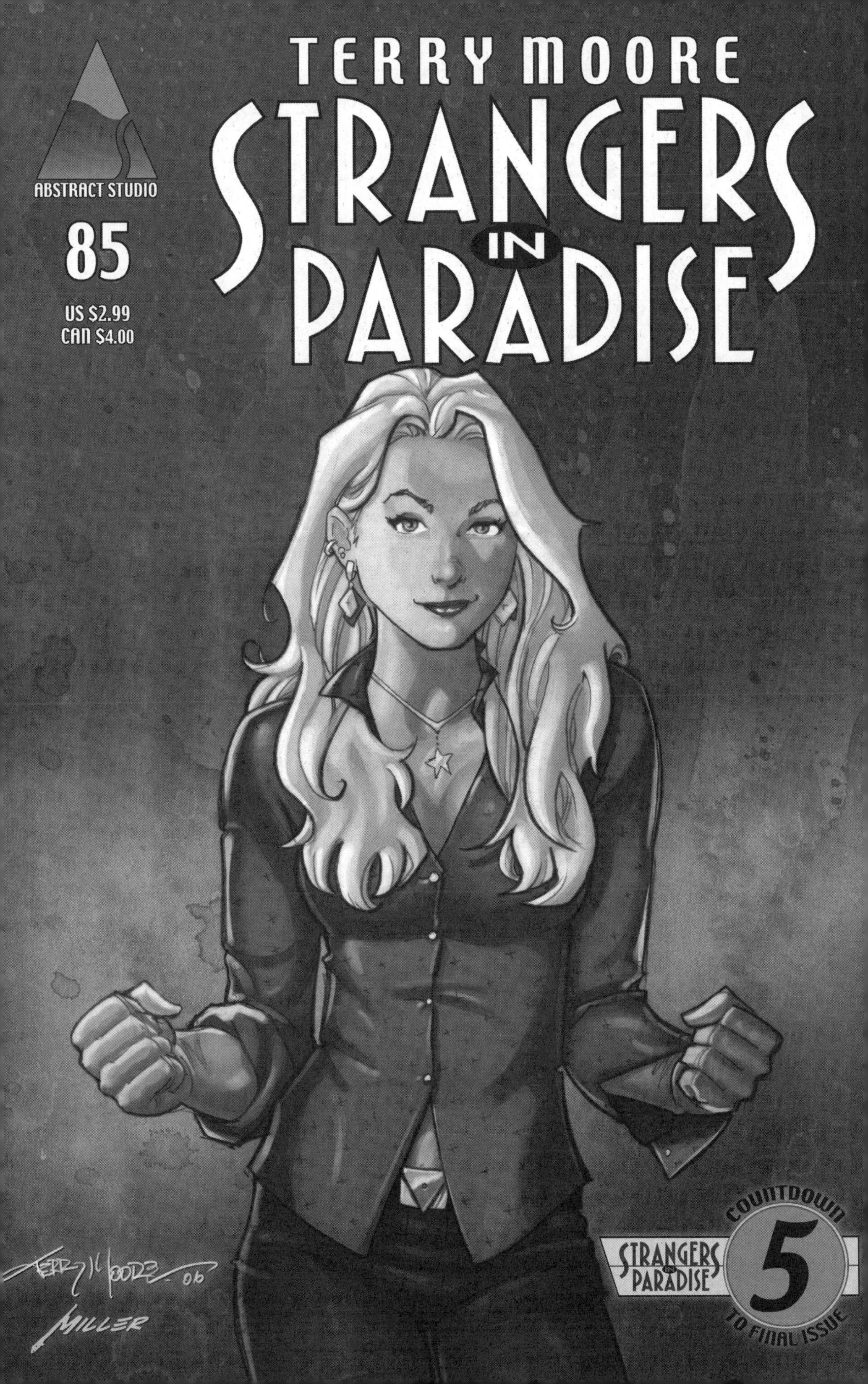
ABSTRACT STUDIO
85
US $2.99
CAN $4.00
TERRY MOORE
STRANGERS IN PARADISE
COUNTDOWN
STRANGERS IN PARADISE
5
TO FINAL ISSUE
TERRY MOORE 06
MILLER

Fool me once, shame on you.
Fool me twice, shame on me.
Try it again and I'll kick your ass and trash your car and spam your email and post your phone number on myspace and write your unauthorized biography and train your dog to poop when the phone rings then sign you up for every call list in the country.

—Katchoo

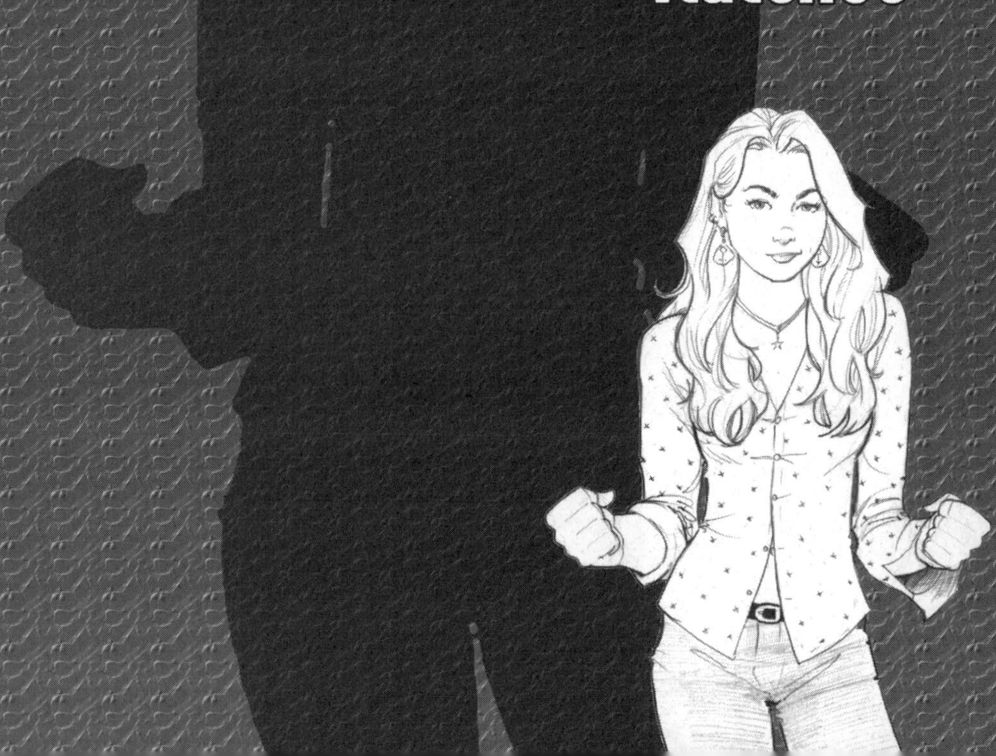

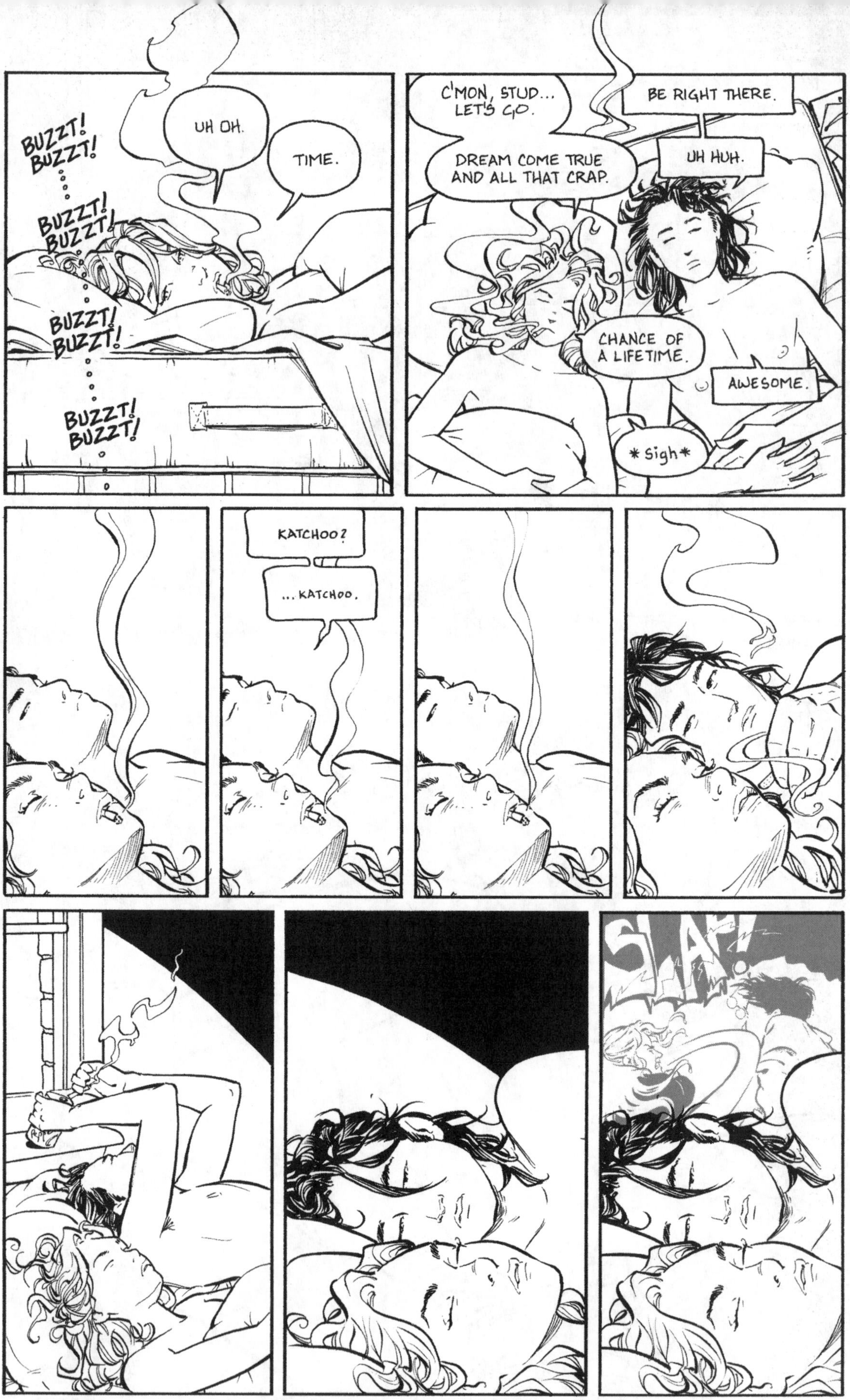
BUZZT! BUZZT!
BUZZT! BUZZT!
BUZZT! BUZZT!
BUZZT! BUZZT!
UH OH.
TIME.
C'MON, STUD... LET'S GO.
BE RIGHT THERE.
DREAM COME TRUE AND ALL THAT CRAP.
UH HUH.
CHANCE OF A LIFETIME.
AWESOME.
sigh
KATCHOO?
...KATCHOO.
SLAP!

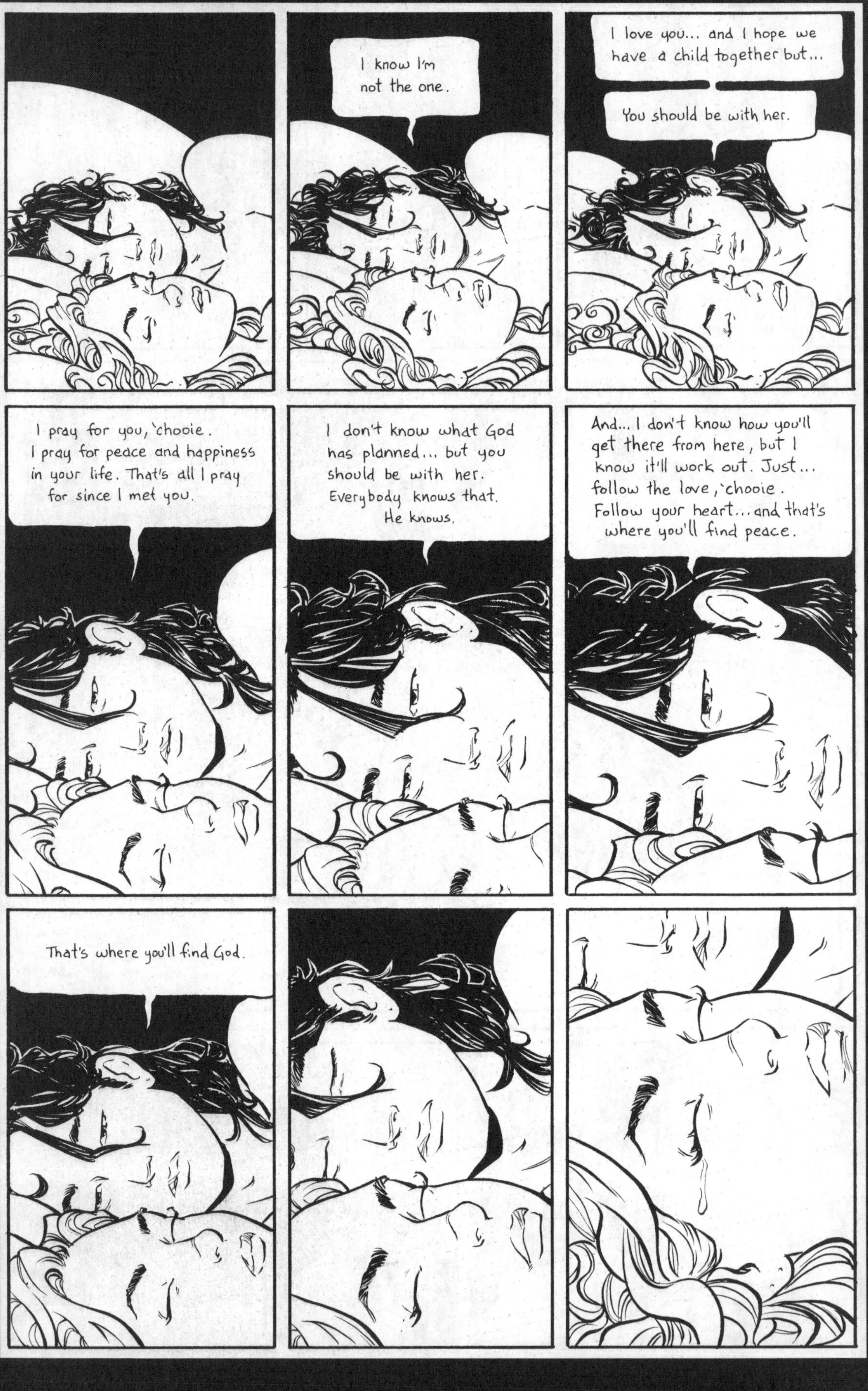
I know I'm not the one.
I love you... and I hope we have a child together but...
You should be with her.
I pray for you, `choozie. I pray for peace and happiness in your life. That's all I pray for since I met you.
I don't know what God has planned... but you should be with her. Everybody knows that. He knows.
And... I don't know how you'll get there from here, but I know it'll work out. Just... follow the love, `choozie. Follow your heart... and that's where you'll find peace.
That's where you'll find God.

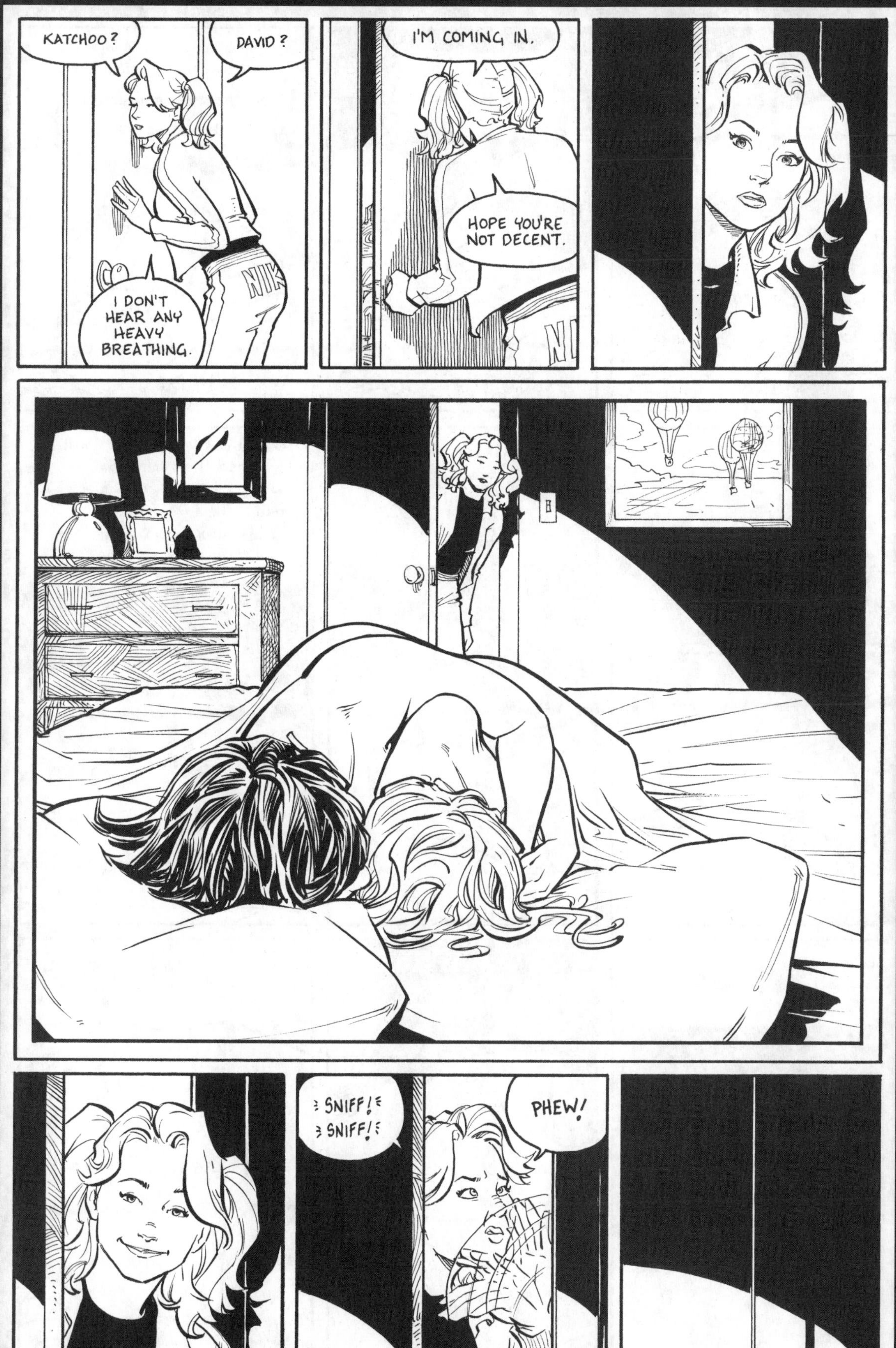
KATCHOO?
DAVID?
I DON'T HEAR ANY HEAVY BREATHING.
I'M COMING IN.
HOPE YOU'RE NOT DECENT.
SNIFF! SNIFF!
PHEW!

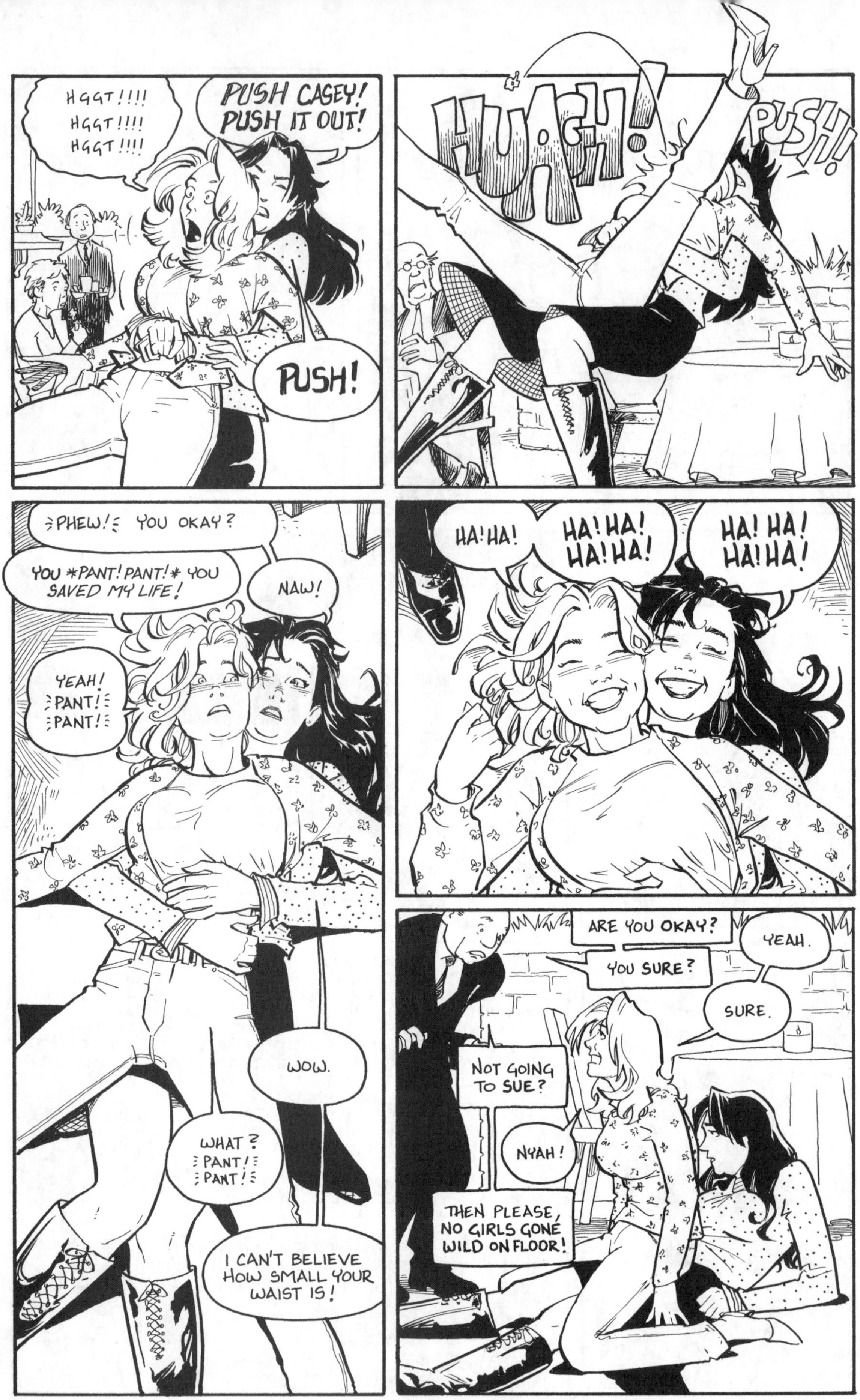

HGGT!!!!
HGGT!!!!
HGGT!!!!
PUSH CASEY! PUSH IT OUT!
PUSH!
HUAGH!
PUSH!
PHEW! YOU OKAY?
YOU *PANT! PANT!* YOU SAVED MY LIFE!
NAW!
YEAH! PANT! PANT!
HA! HA!
HA! HA! HA! HA!
HA! HA! HA! HA!
WOW.
WHAT? PANT! PANT!
I CAN'T BELIEVE HOW SMALL YOUR WAIST IS!
ARE YOU OKAY?
YEAH.
YOU SURE?
SURE.
NOT GOING TO SUE?
NYAH!
THEN PLEASE, NO GIRLS GONE WILD ON FLOOR!

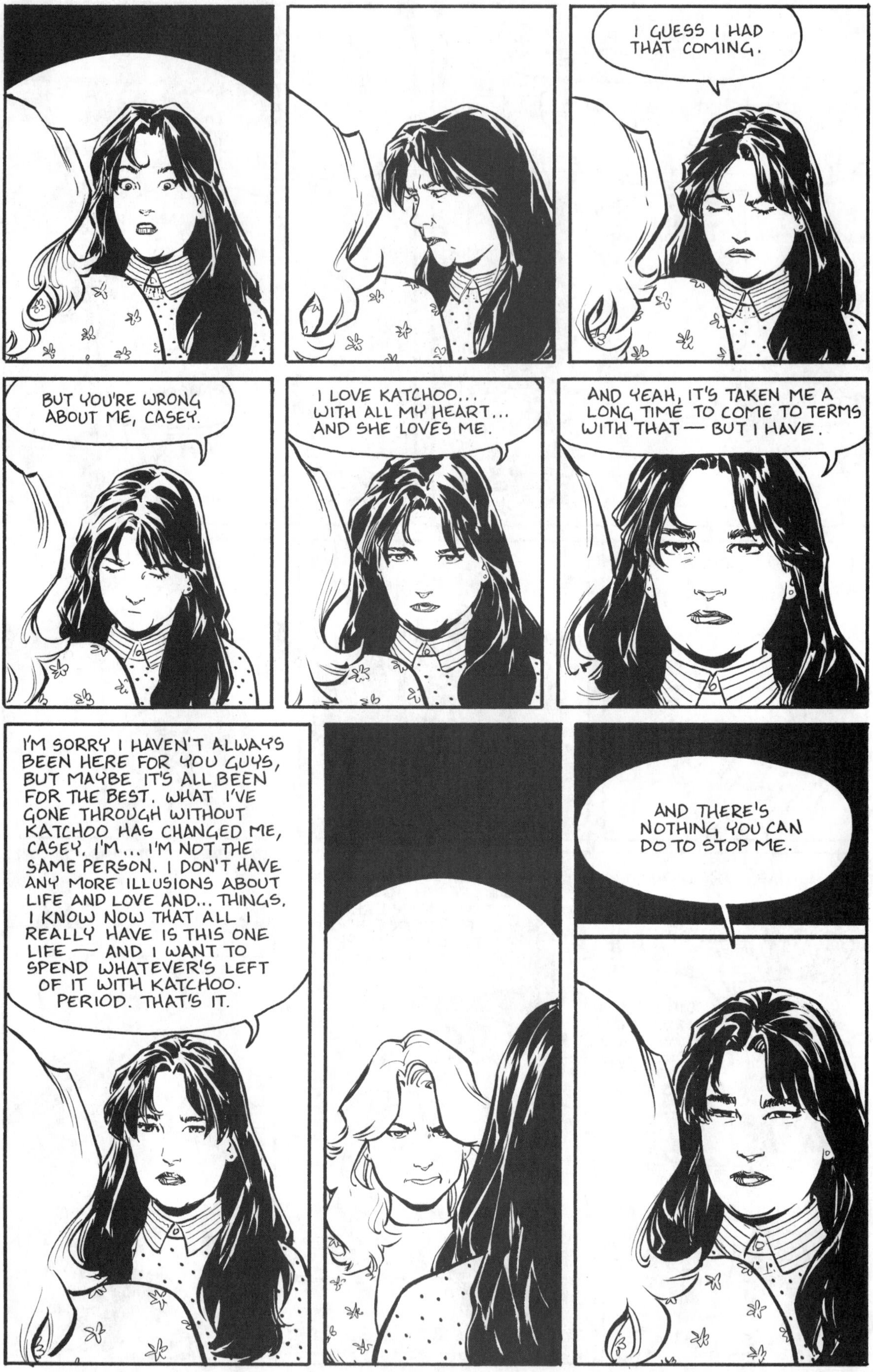
I GUESS I HAD THAT COMING.
BUT YOU'RE WRONG ABOUT ME, CASEY.
I LOVE KATCHOO... WITH ALL MY HEART... AND SHE LOVES ME.
AND YEAH, IT'S TAKEN ME A LONG TIME TO COME TO TERMS WITH THAT — BUT I HAVE.
I'M SORRY I HAVEN'T ALWAYS BEEN HERE FOR YOU GUYS, BUT MAYBE IT'S ALL BEEN FOR THE BEST. WHAT I'VE GONE THROUGH WITHOUT KATCHOO HAS CHANGED ME, CASEY. I'M... I'M NOT THE SAME PERSON. I DON'T HAVE ANY MORE ILLUSIONS ABOUT LIFE AND LOVE AND... THINGS. I KNOW NOW THAT ALL I REALLY HAVE IS THIS ONE LIFE — AND I WANT TO SPEND WHATEVER'S LEFT OF IT WITH KATCHOO. PERIOD. THAT'S IT.
AND THERE'S NOTHING YOU CAN DO TO STOP ME.

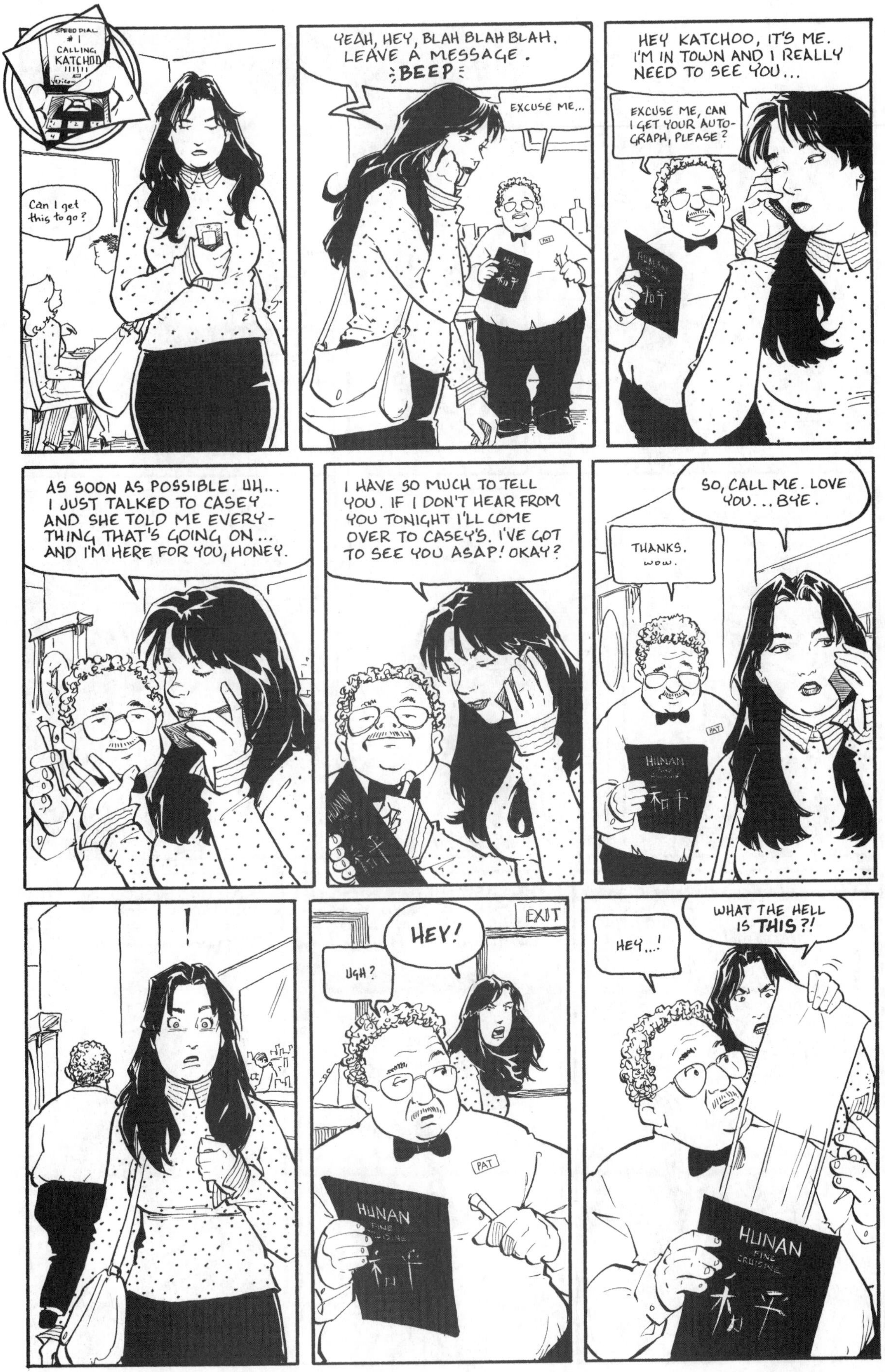
SPEED DIAL # 1 CALLING KATCHOO
Can I get this to go?
YEAH, HEY, BLAH BLAH BLAH. LEAVE A MESSAGE. BEEP
EXCUSE ME...
HEY KATCHOO, IT'S ME. I'M IN TOWN AND I REALLY NEED TO SEE YOU...
EXCUSE ME, CAN I GET YOUR AUTOGRAPH, PLEASE?
AS SOON AS POSSIBLE. UH... I JUST TALKED TO CASEY AND SHE TOLD ME EVERYTHING THAT'S GOING ON... AND I'M HERE FOR YOU, HONEY.
I HAVE SO MUCH TO TELL YOU. IF I DON'T HEAR FROM YOU TONIGHT I'LL COME OVER TO CASEY'S. I'VE GOT TO SEE YOU ASAP! OKAY?
SO, CALL ME. LOVE YOU... BYE.
THANKS. WOW.
PAT
HUNAN
!
EXIT
HEY!
UGH?
PAT
HUNAN FINE CUISINE
HEY...!
WHAT THE HELL IS THIS?!
HUNAN FINE CUISINE

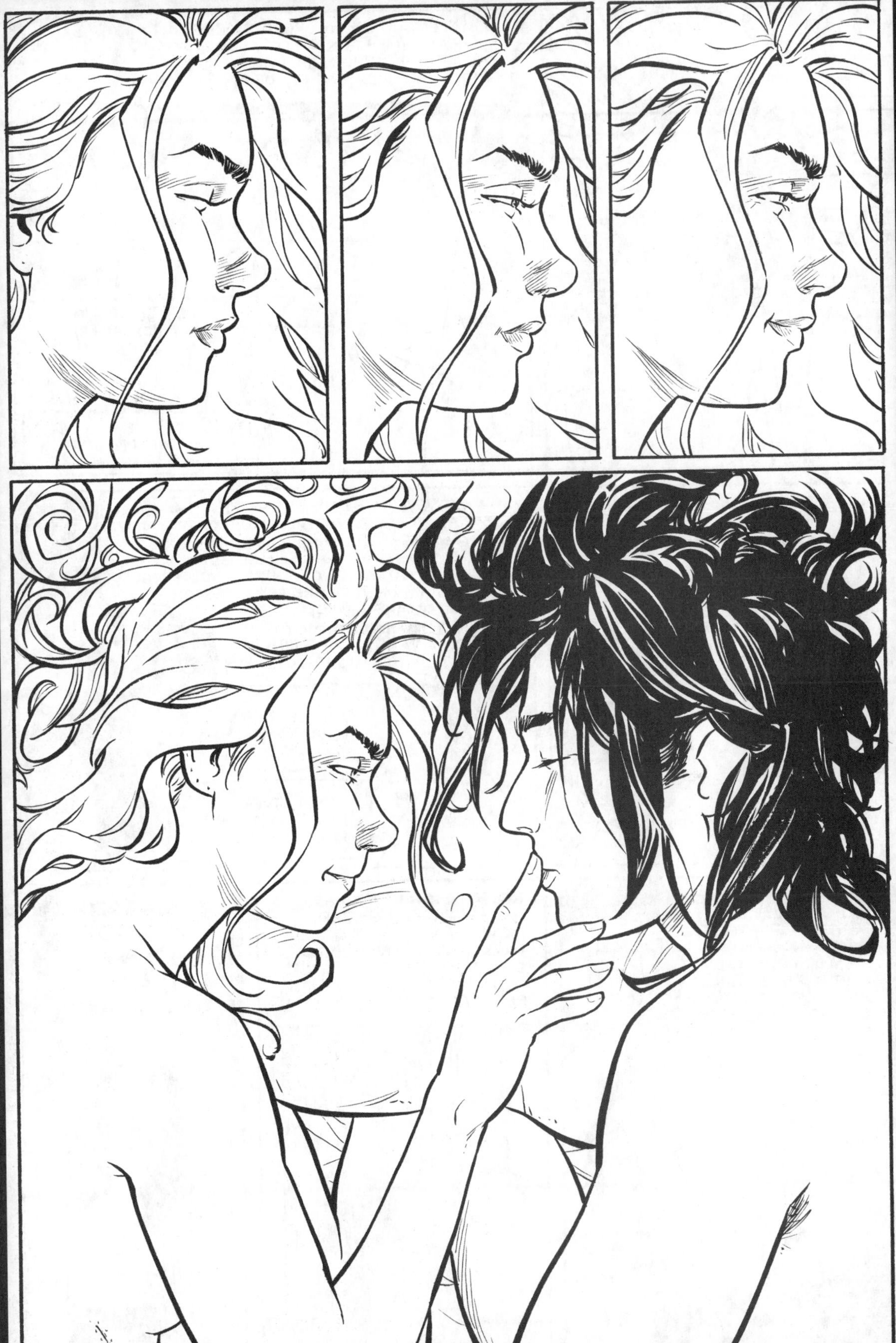

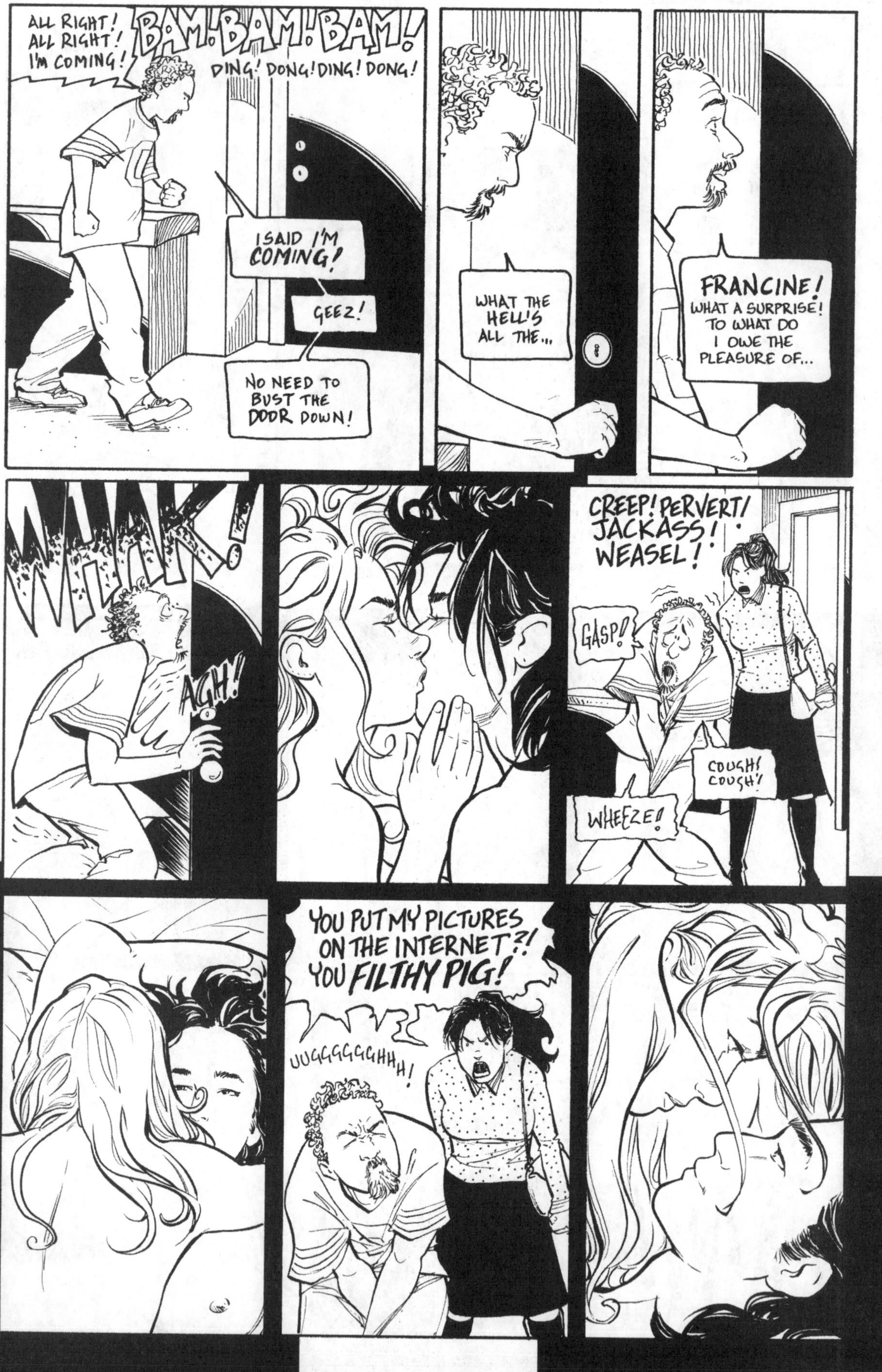
ALL RIGHT! ALL RIGHT! I'M COMING!
BAM! BAM! BAM!
DING! DONG! DING! DONG!
I SAID I'M COMING!
GEEZ!
NO NEED TO BUST THE DOOR DOWN!
WHAT THE HELL'S ALL THE...
FRANCINE! WHAT A SURPRISE! TO WHAT DO I OWE THE PLEASURE OF...
AGH!
CREEP! PERVERT! JACKASS! WEASEL!
GASP!
COUGH! COUGH!
WHEEZE!
YOU PUT MY PICTURES ON THE INTERNET?! YOU FILTHY PIG!
UUGGGGGGHHH!

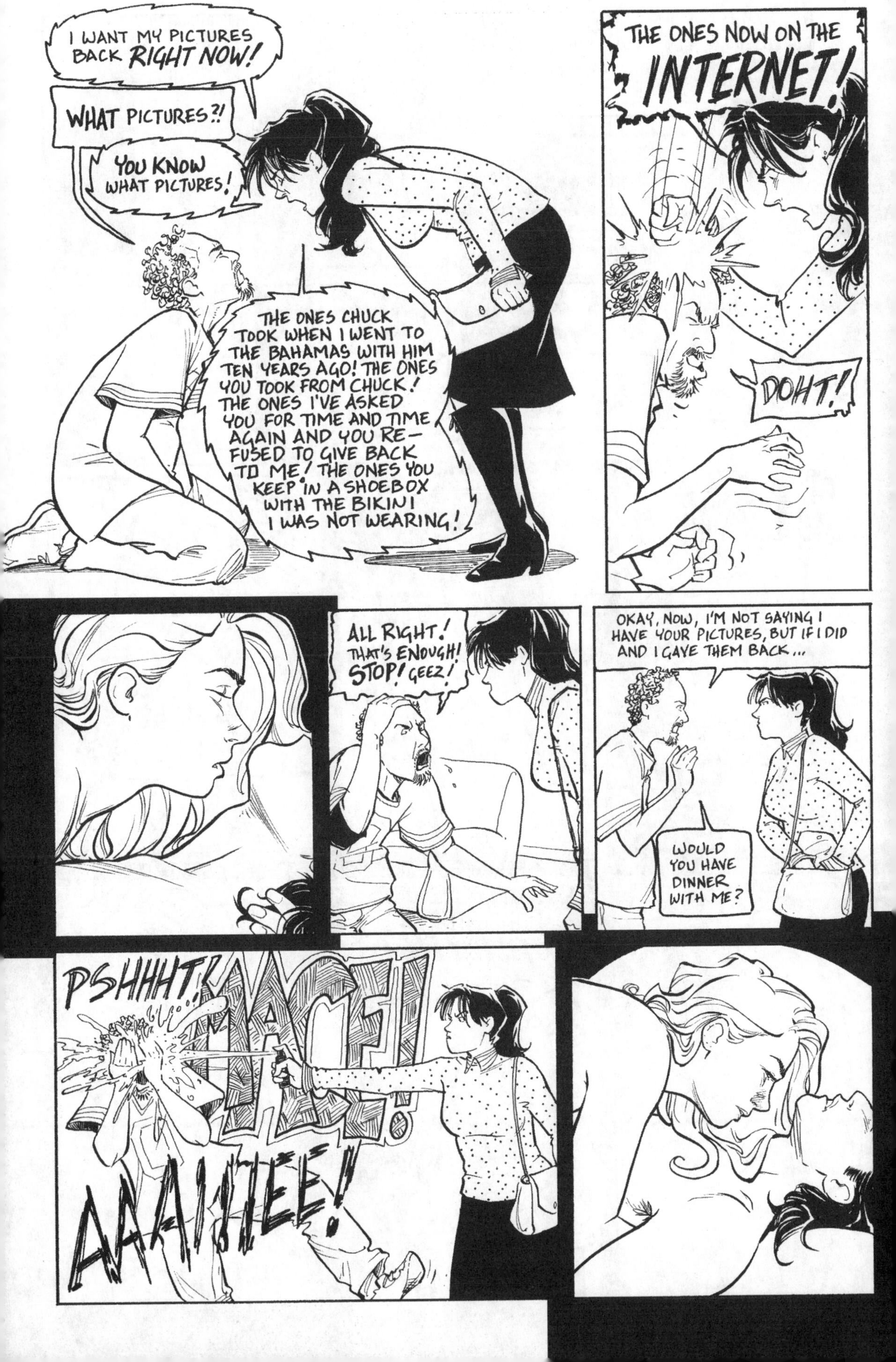
I WANT MY PICTURES BACK RIGHT NOW!
WHAT PICTURES?!
YOU KNOW WHAT PICTURES!
THE ONES CHUCK TOOK WHEN I WENT TO THE BAHAMAS WITH HIM TEN YEARS AGO! THE ONES YOU TOOK FROM CHUCK! THE ONES I'VE ASKED YOU FOR TIME AND TIME AGAIN AND YOU RE-FUSED TO GIVE BACK TO ME! THE ONES YOU KEEP IN A SHOEBOX WITH THE BIKINI I WAS NOT WEARING!
THE ONES NOW ON THE INTERNET!
DOHT!
ALL RIGHT! THAT'S ENOUGH! STOP! GEEZ!
OKAY, NOW, I'M NOT SAYING I HAVE YOUR PICTURES, BUT IF I DID AND I GAVE THEM BACK...
WOULD YOU HAVE DINNER WITH ME?
PSHHHT!
MACE!
AAAIIIEE!

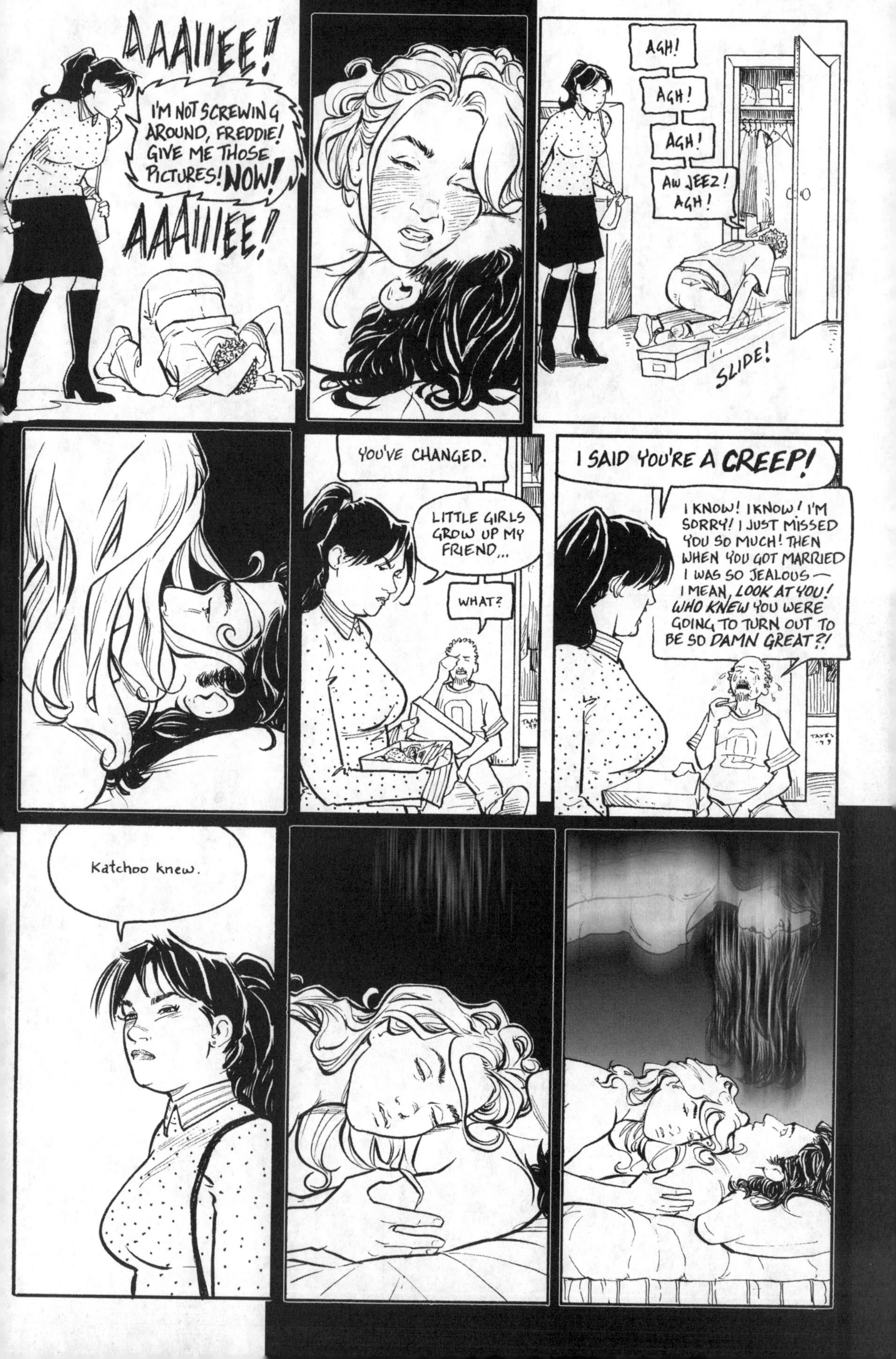
AAAIIEE!!
I'M NOT SCREWING AROUND, FREDDIE! GIVE ME THOSE PICTURES! NOW!
AAAIIEE!
AGH!
AGH!
AGH!
AW JEEZ! AGH!
SLIDE!
YOU'VE CHANGED.
LITTLE GIRLS GROW UP MY FRIEND...
WHAT?
I SAID YOU'RE A CREEP!
I KNOW! I KNOW! I'M SORRY! I JUST MISSED YOU SO MUCH! THEN WHEN YOU GOT MARRIED I WAS SO JEALOUS— I MEAN, LOOK AT YOU! WHO KNEW YOU WERE GOING TO TURN OUT TO BE SO DAMN GREAT?!
Katchoo knew.

TERRY MOORE

STRANGERS IN PARADISE

ABSTRACT STUDIO

86

US $2.99
CAN $4.00

I promise you tomorrow
I promise you the moon
I promise no more sorrow
As if promises come true

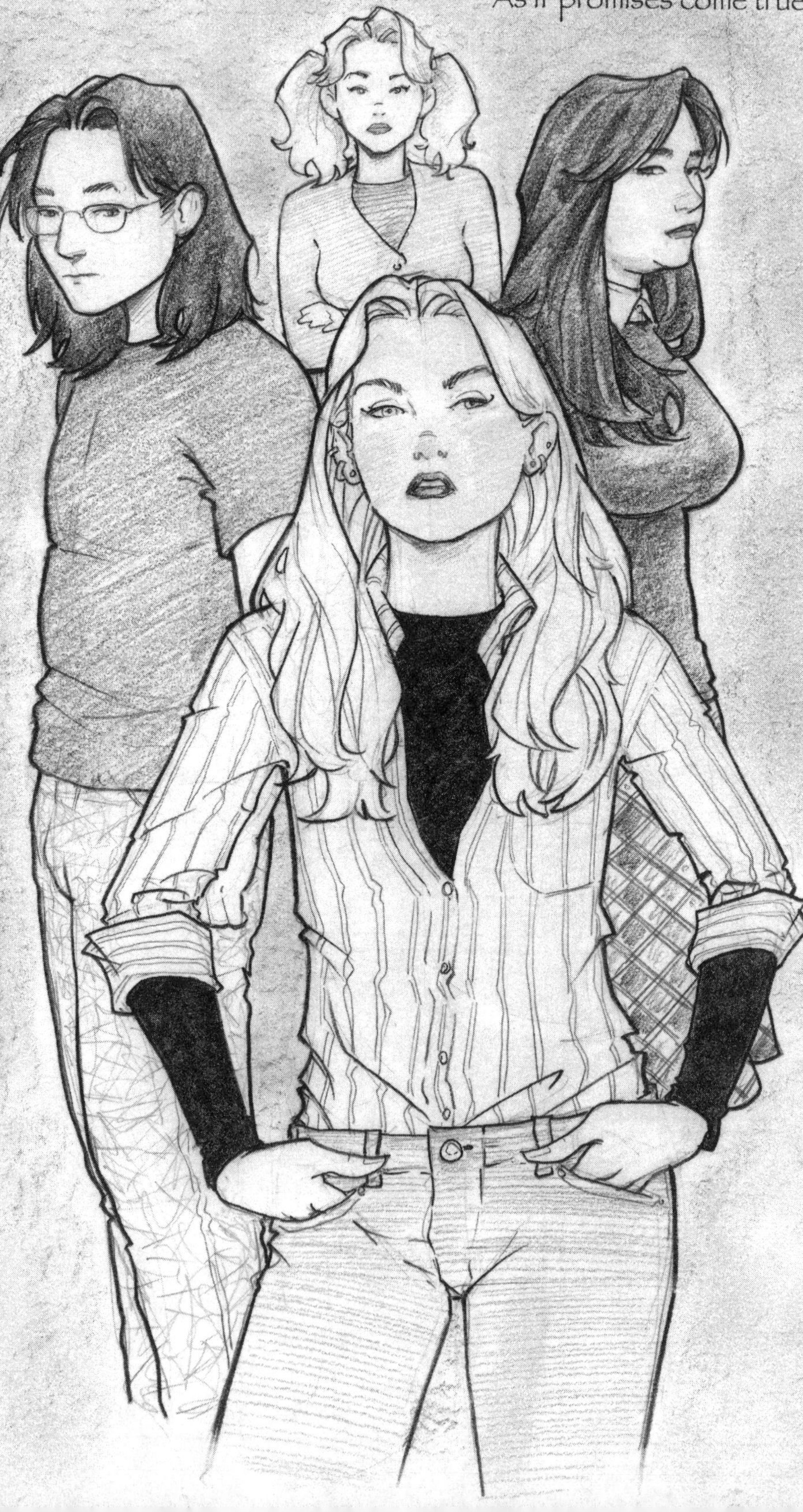

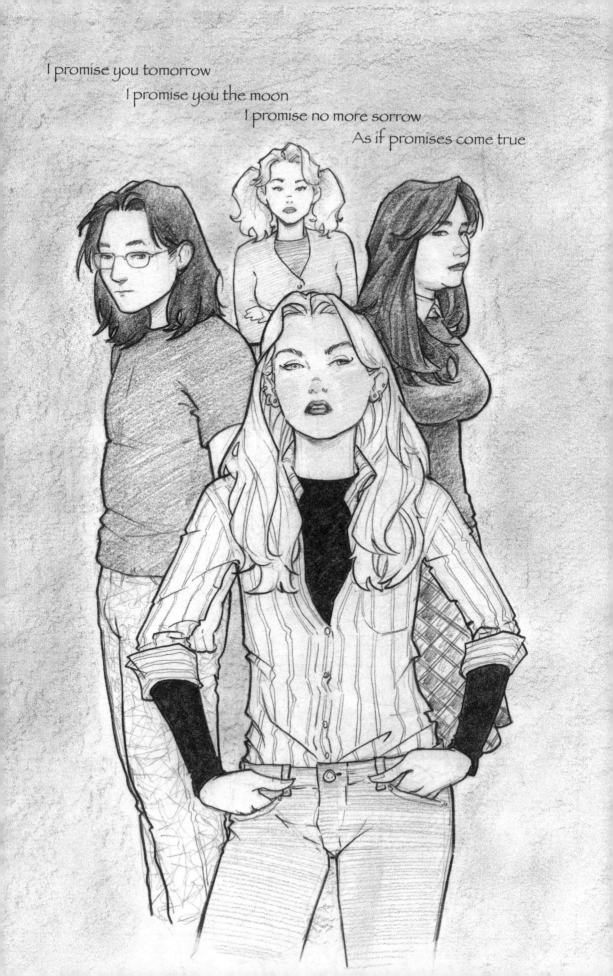

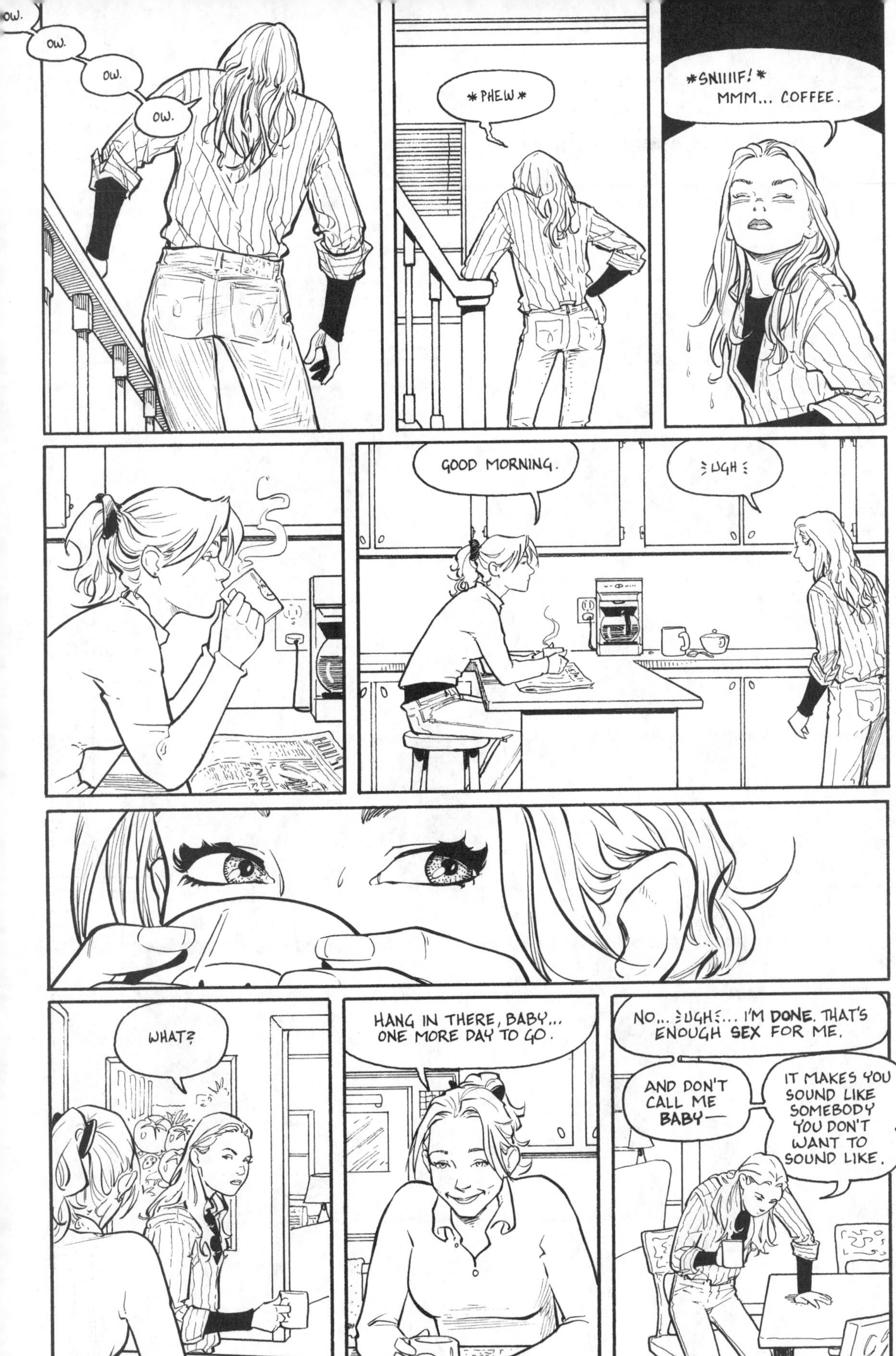
OW.
OW.
OW.
OW.
PHEW
SNIIIIF! MMM... COFFEE.
GOOD MORNING.
UGH
WHAT?
HANG IN THERE, BABY... ONE MORE DAY TO GO.
NO... UGH... I'M DONE. THAT'S ENOUGH SEX FOR ME.
AND DON'T CALL ME BABY—
IT MAKES YOU SOUND LIKE SOMEBODY YOU DON'T WANT TO SOUND LIKE.

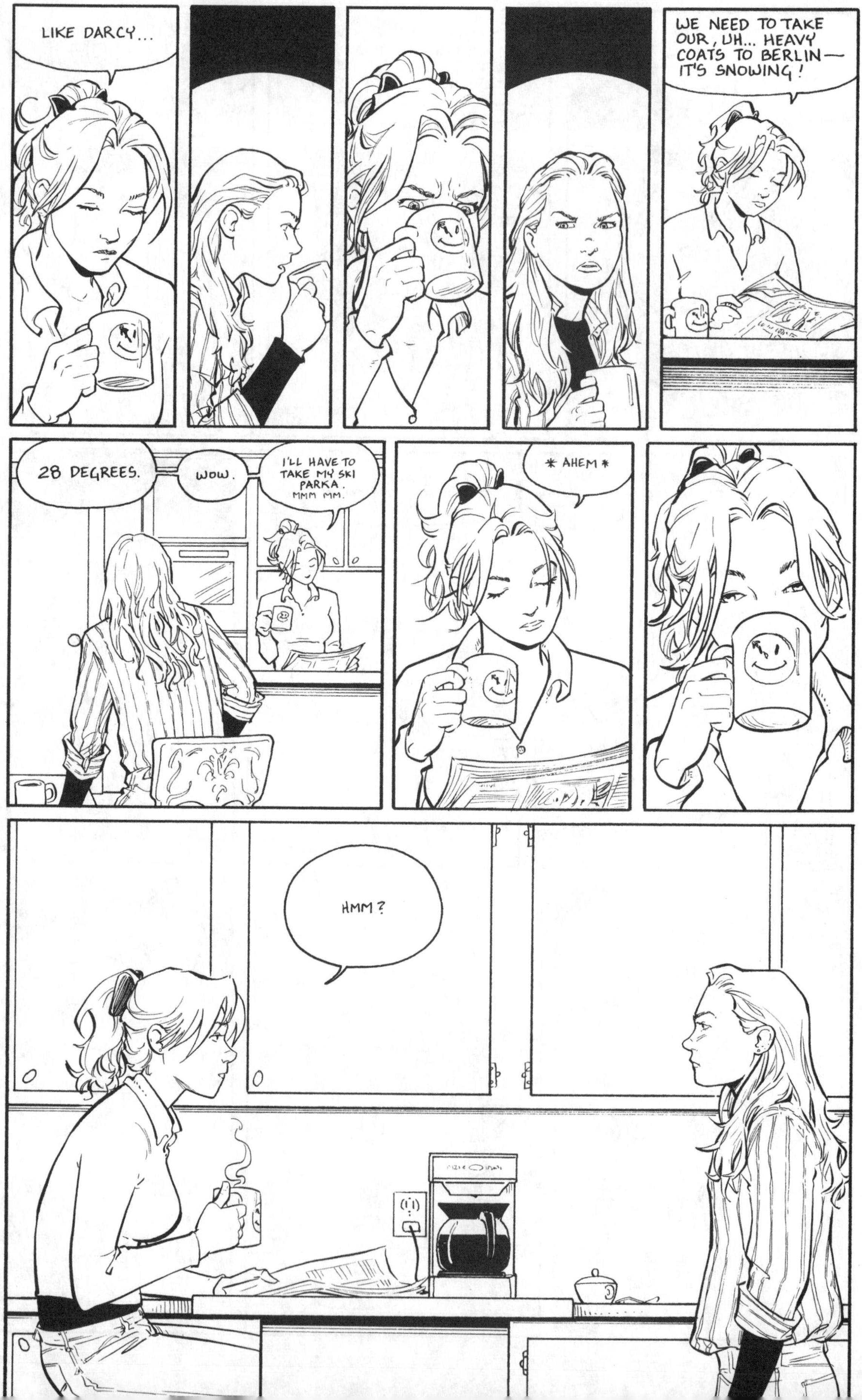
LIKE DARCY...
WE NEED TO TAKE OUR, UH... HEAVY COATS TO BERLIN— IT'S SNOWING!
28 DEGREES.
WOW.
I'LL HAVE TO TAKE MY SKI PARKA. MMM MM.
* AHEM *
HMM?

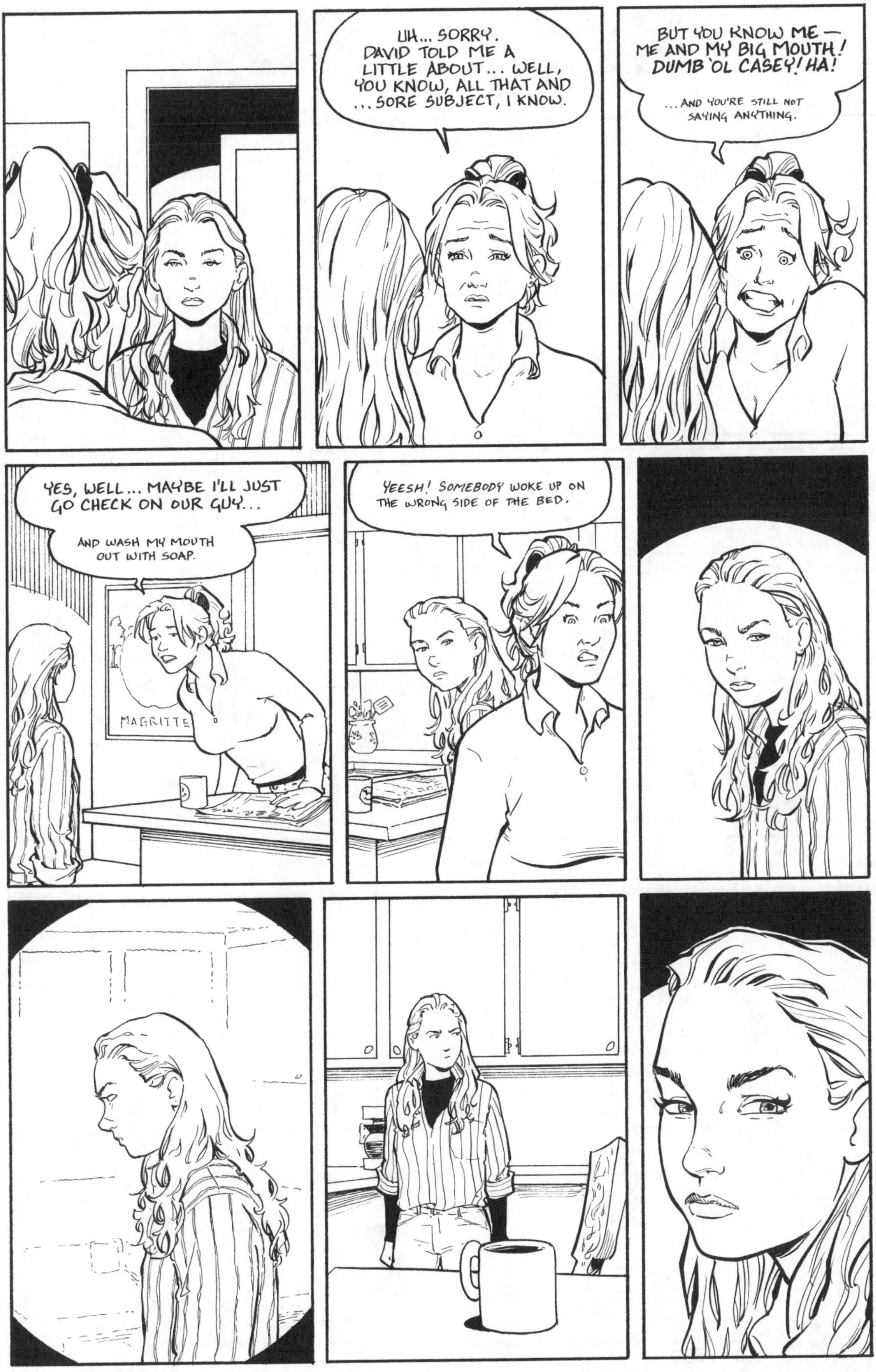
UH... SORRY. DAVID TOLD ME A LITTLE ABOUT... WELL, YOU KNOW, ALL THAT AND ...SORE SUBJECT, I KNOW.
BUT YOU KNOW ME — ME AND MY BIG MOUTH! DUMB 'OL CASEY! HA!
...AND YOU'RE STILL NOT SAYING ANYTHING.
YES, WELL... MAYBE I'LL JUST GO CHECK ON OUR GUY...
AND WASH MY MOUTH OUT WITH SOAP.
MAGRITTE
YEESH! SOMEBODY WOKE UP ON THE WRONG SIDE OF THE BED.

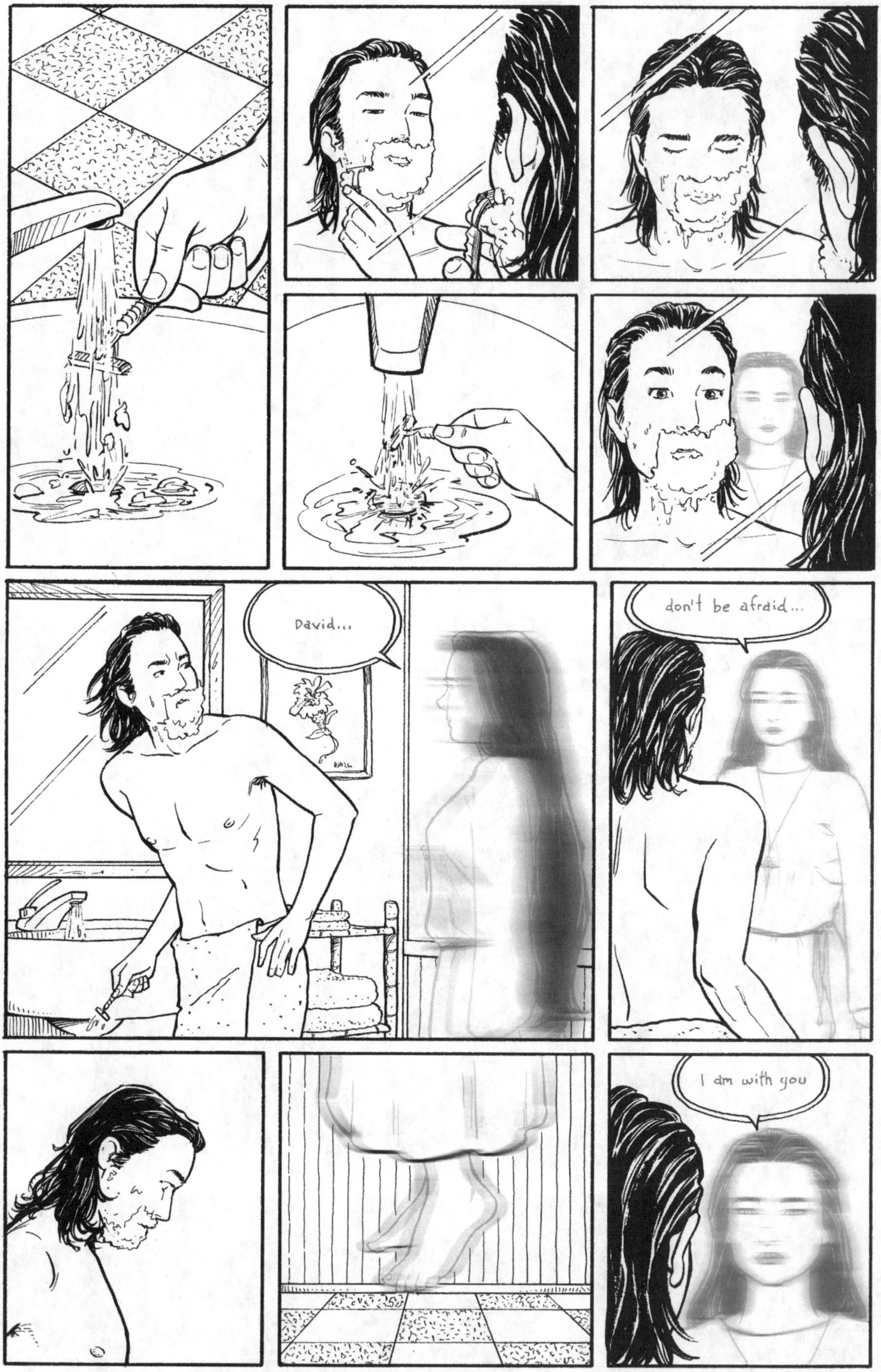
David...
don't be afraid...
I am with you

as if promises come true...

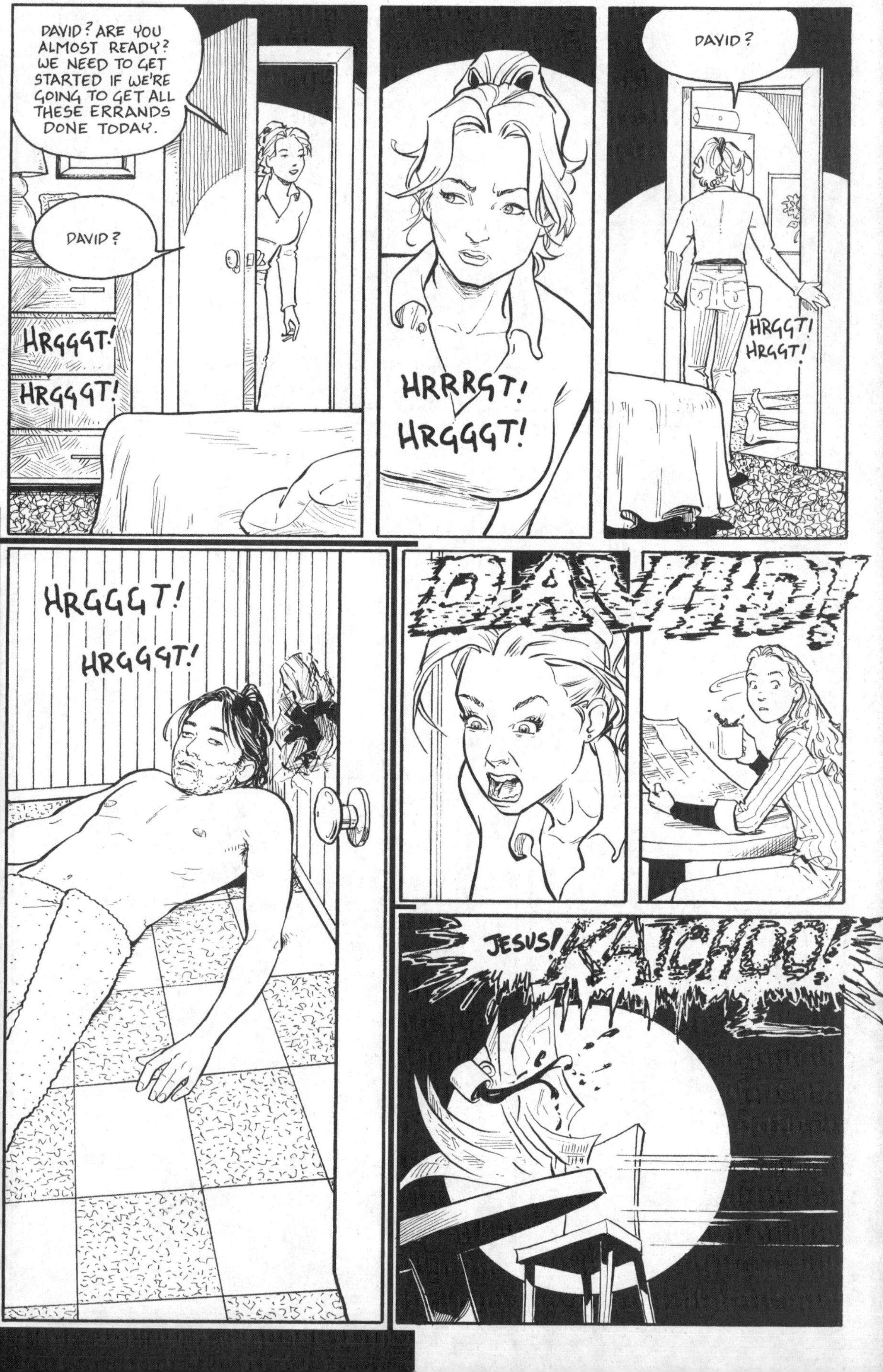
DAVID? ARE YOU ALMOST READY? WE NEED TO GET STARTED IF WE'RE GOING TO GET ALL THESE ERRANDS DONE TODAY.
DAVID?
HRGGGT!
HRGGGT!
HRRRGT!
HRGGGT!
DAVID?
HRGGT!
HRGGT!
HRGGGT!
HRGGGT!
DAVID!
JESUS!
KATCHOO!

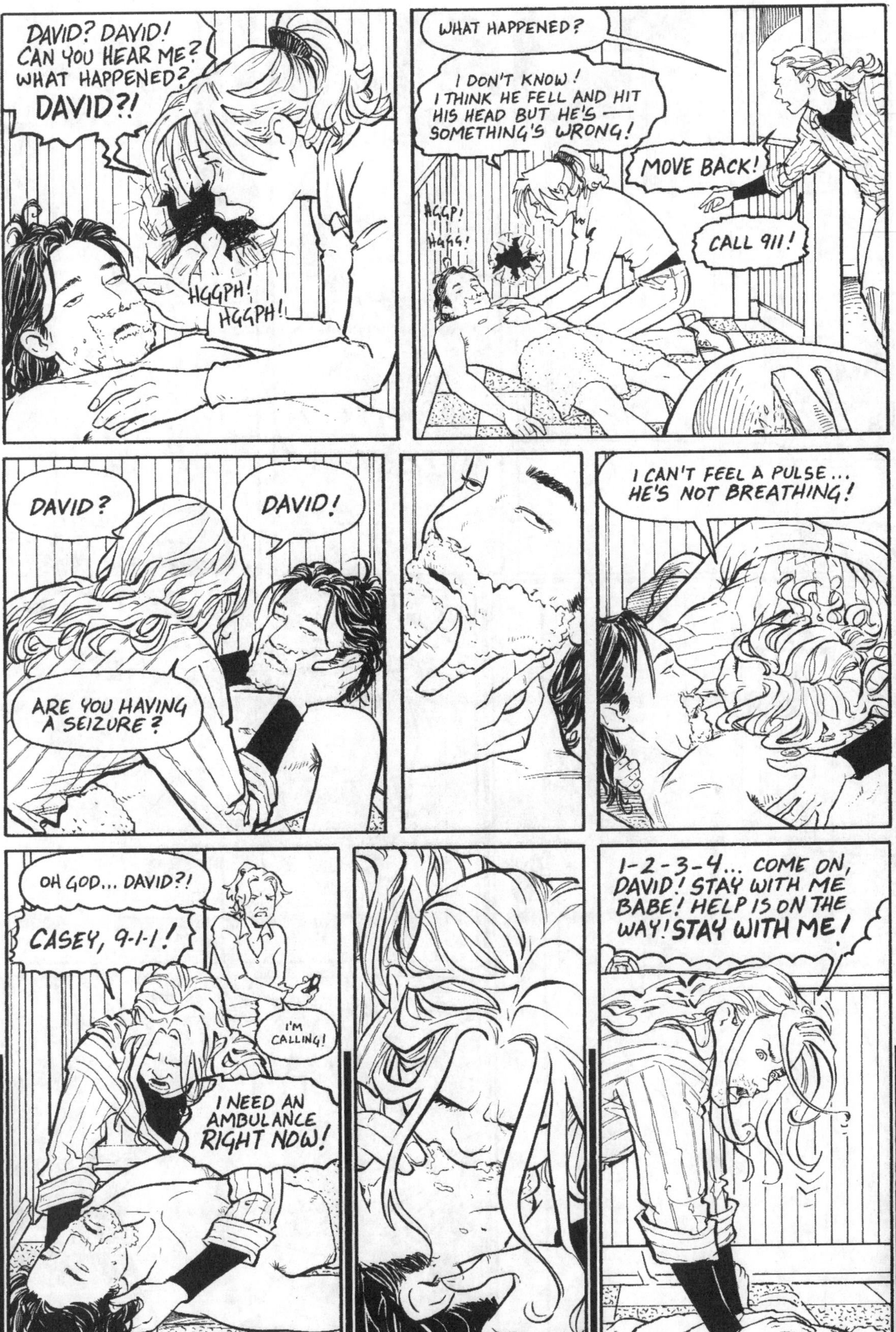

DAVID? DAVID! CAN YOU HEAR ME? WHAT HAPPENED? DAVID?!
HGGPH! HGGPH!
WHAT HAPPENED?
I DON'T KNOW! I THINK HE FELL AND HIT HIS HEAD BUT HE'S — SOMETHING'S WRONG!
MOVE BACK!
HGGP! HGGG!
CALL 911!
DAVID?
DAVID!
ARE YOU HAVING A SEIZURE?
I CAN'T FEEL A PULSE... HE'S NOT BREATHING!
OH GOD... DAVID?!
CASEY, 9-1-1!
I'M CALLING!
I NEED AN AMBULANCE RIGHT NOW!
1-2-3-4... COME ON, DAVID! STAY WITH ME BABE! HELP IS ON THE WAY! STAY WITH ME!

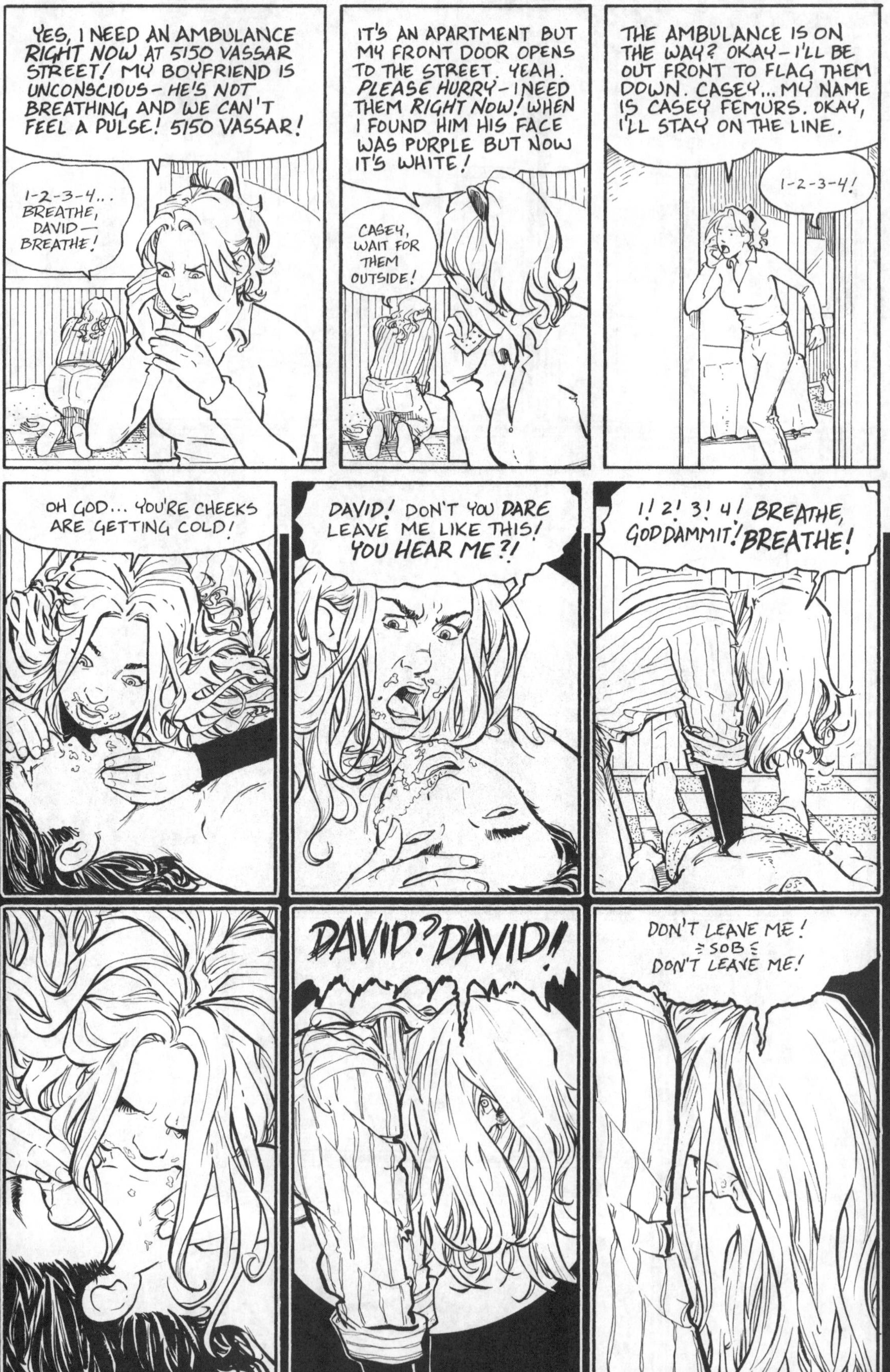
YES, I NEED AN AMBULANCE RIGHT NOW AT 5150 VASSAR STREET! MY BOYFRIEND IS UNCONSCIOUS - HE'S NOT BREATHING AND WE CAN'T FEEL A PULSE! 5150 VASSAR!
1-2-3-4... BREATHE, DAVID - BREATHE!
IT'S AN APARTMENT BUT MY FRONT DOOR OPENS TO THE STREET. YEAH. PLEASE HURRY - I NEED THEM RIGHT NOW! WHEN I FOUND HIM HIS FACE WAS PURPLE BUT NOW IT'S WHITE!
CASEY, WAIT FOR THEM OUTSIDE!
THE AMBULANCE IS ON THE WAY? OKAY - I'LL BE OUT FRONT TO FLAG THEM DOWN. CASEY... MY NAME IS CASEY FEMURS. OKAY, I'LL STAY ON THE LINE.
1-2-3-4!
OH GOD... YOU'RE CHEEKS ARE GETTING COLD!
DAVID! DON'T YOU DARE LEAVE ME LIKE THIS! YOU HEAR ME?!
1! 2! 3! 4! BREATHE, GODDAMMIT! BREATHE!
DAVID? DAVID!
DON'T LEAVE ME! SOB DON'T LEAVE ME!

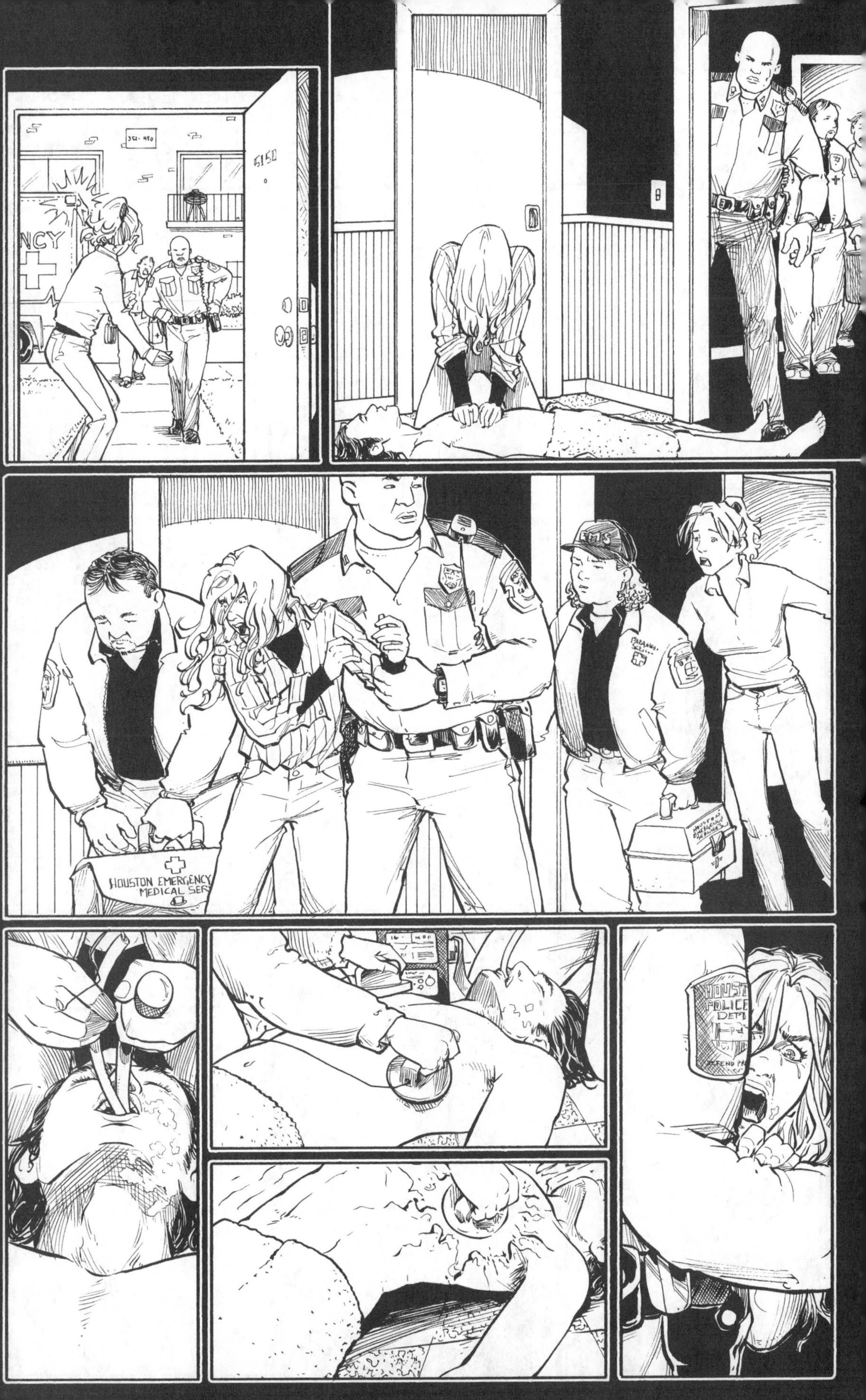
NCY
5150
HOUSTON EMERGENCY
MEDICAL SER
EMS
POLICE
DEPT

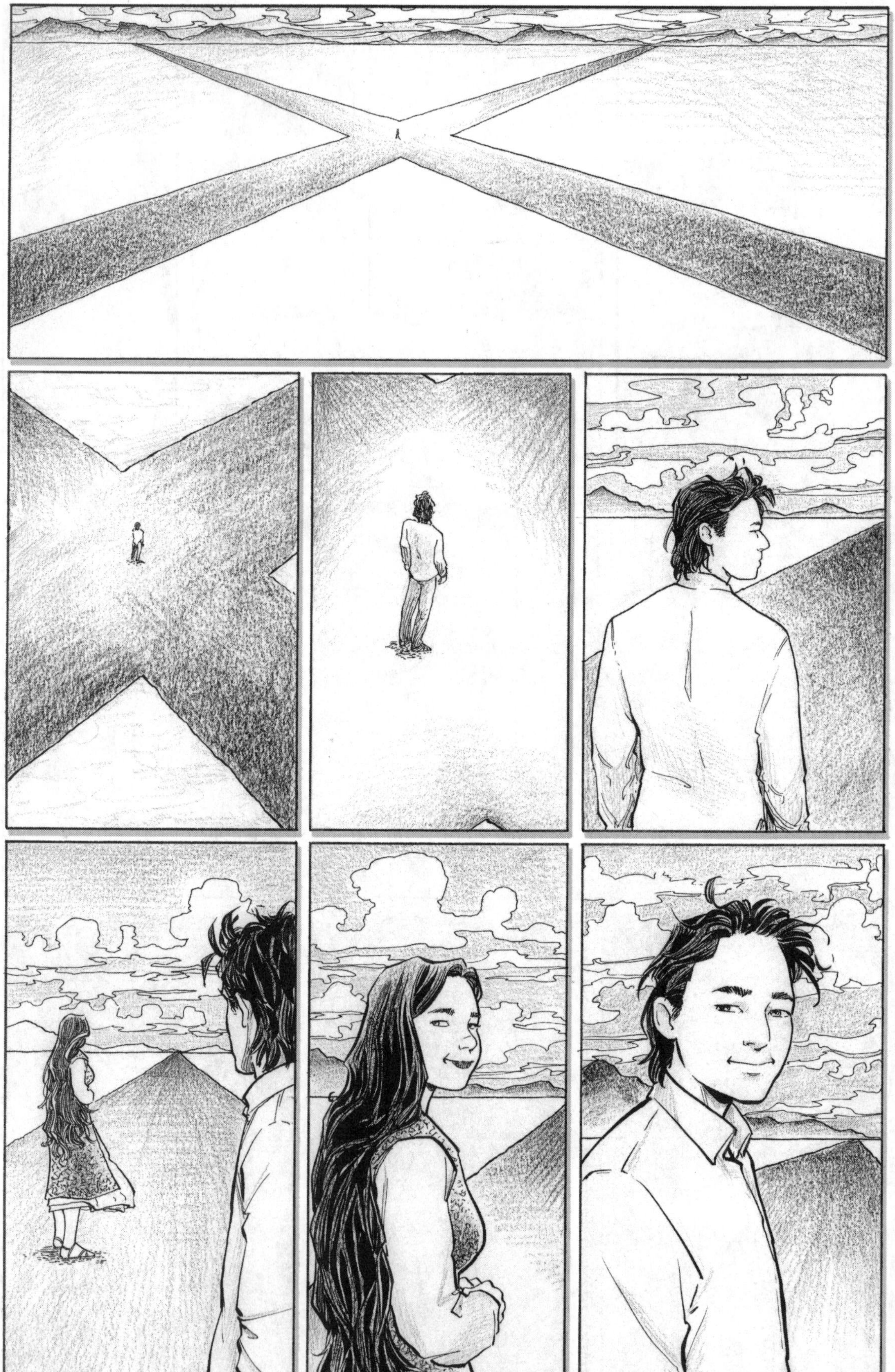

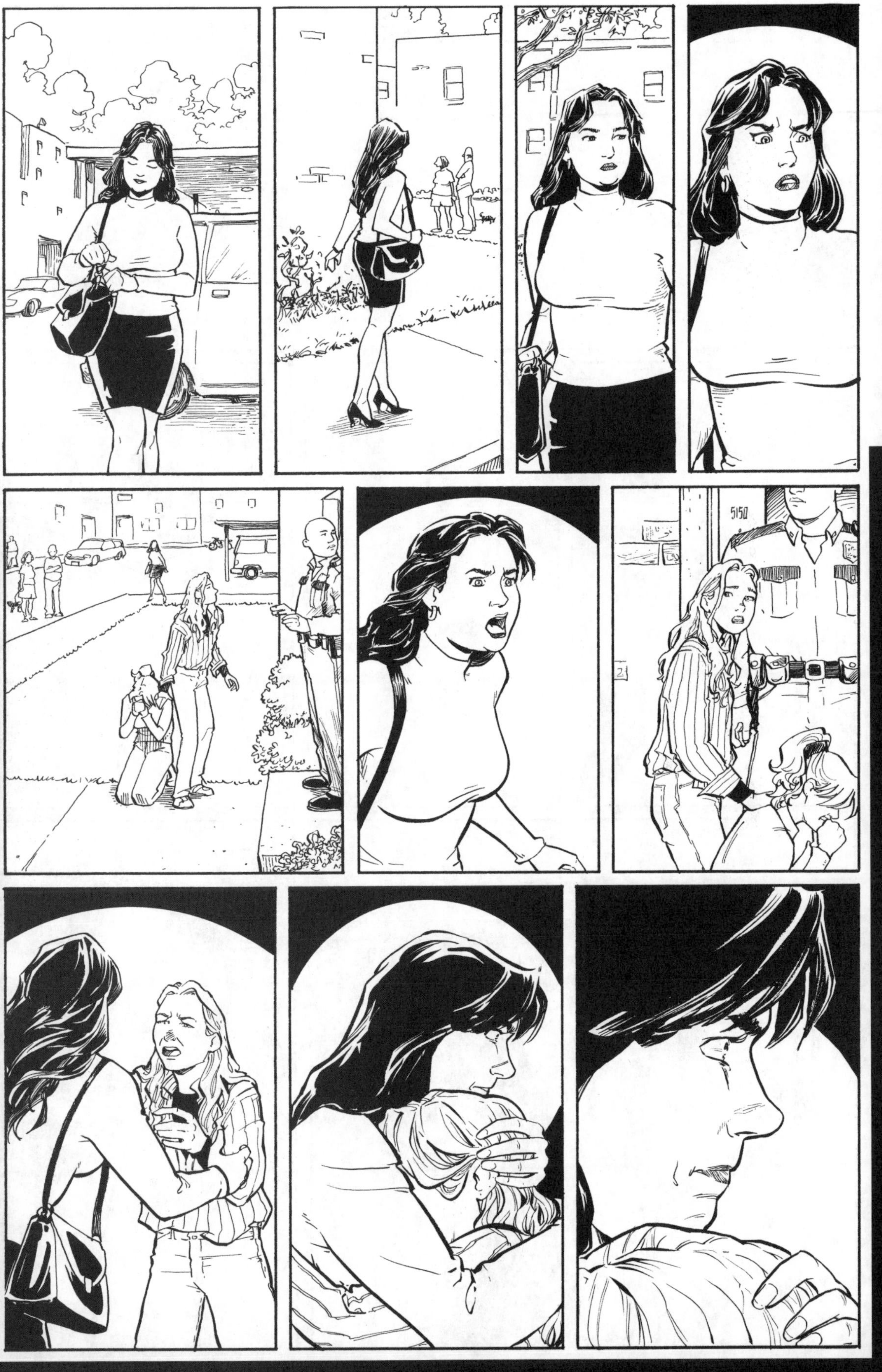
5150

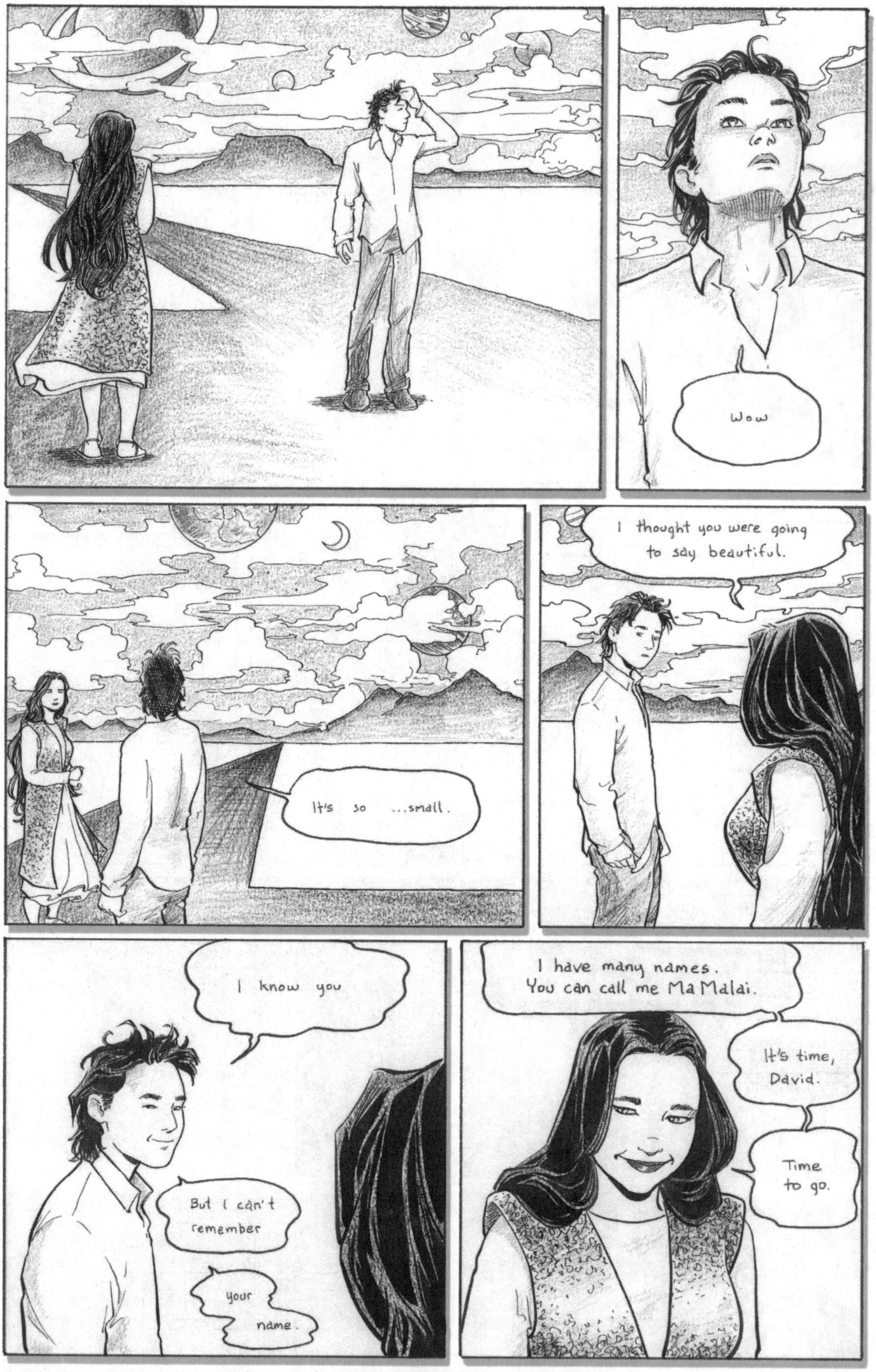
Wow
It's so ...small.
I thought you were going to say beautiful.
I know you
But I can't remember
your name.
I have many names. You can call me Ma Malai.
It's time, David.
Time to go.

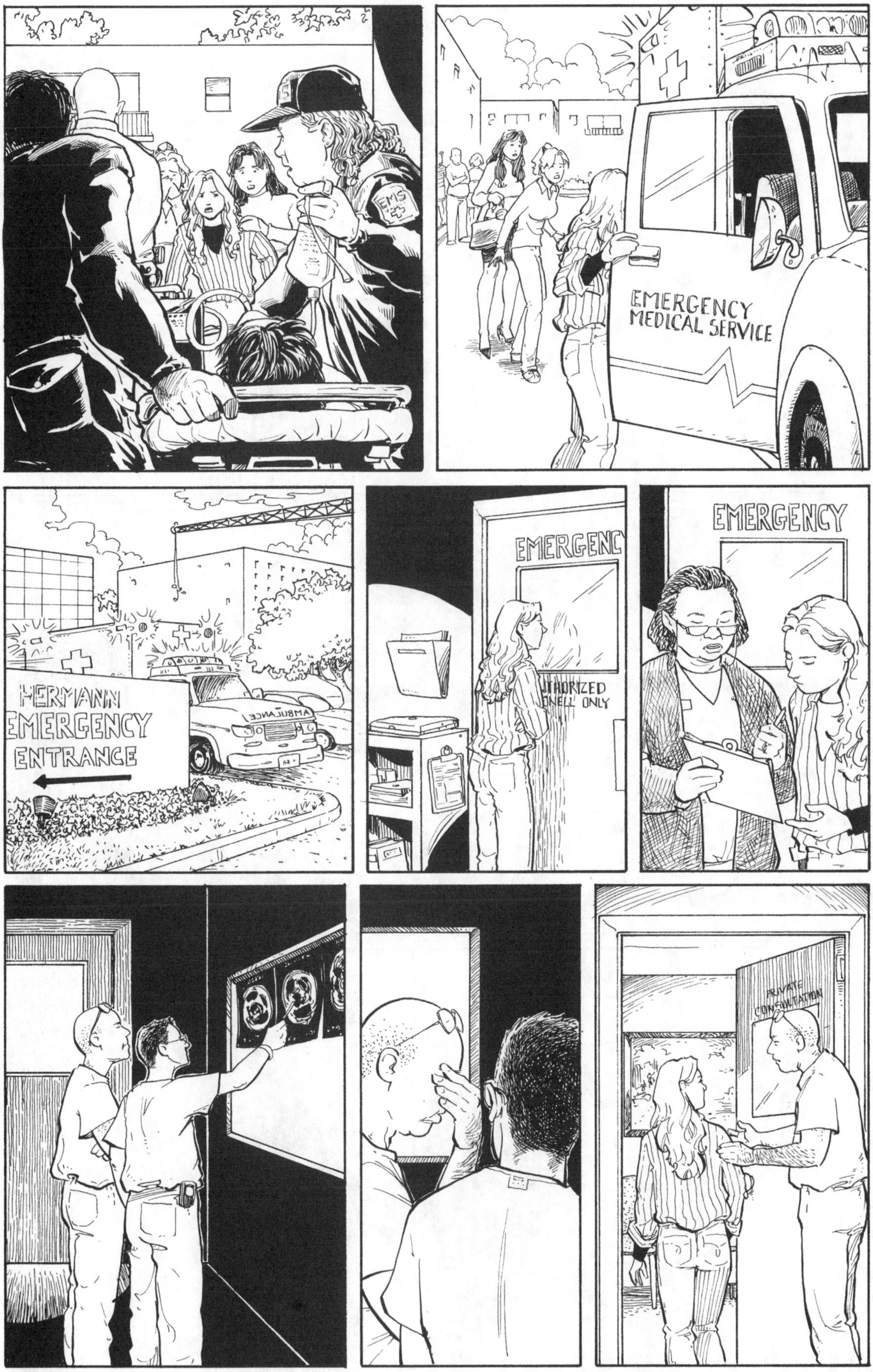
EMS
EMERGENCY
MEDICAL SERVICE
HERMANN
EMERGENCY
ENTRANCE
EMERGENCY
PRIVATE
CONSULTATION

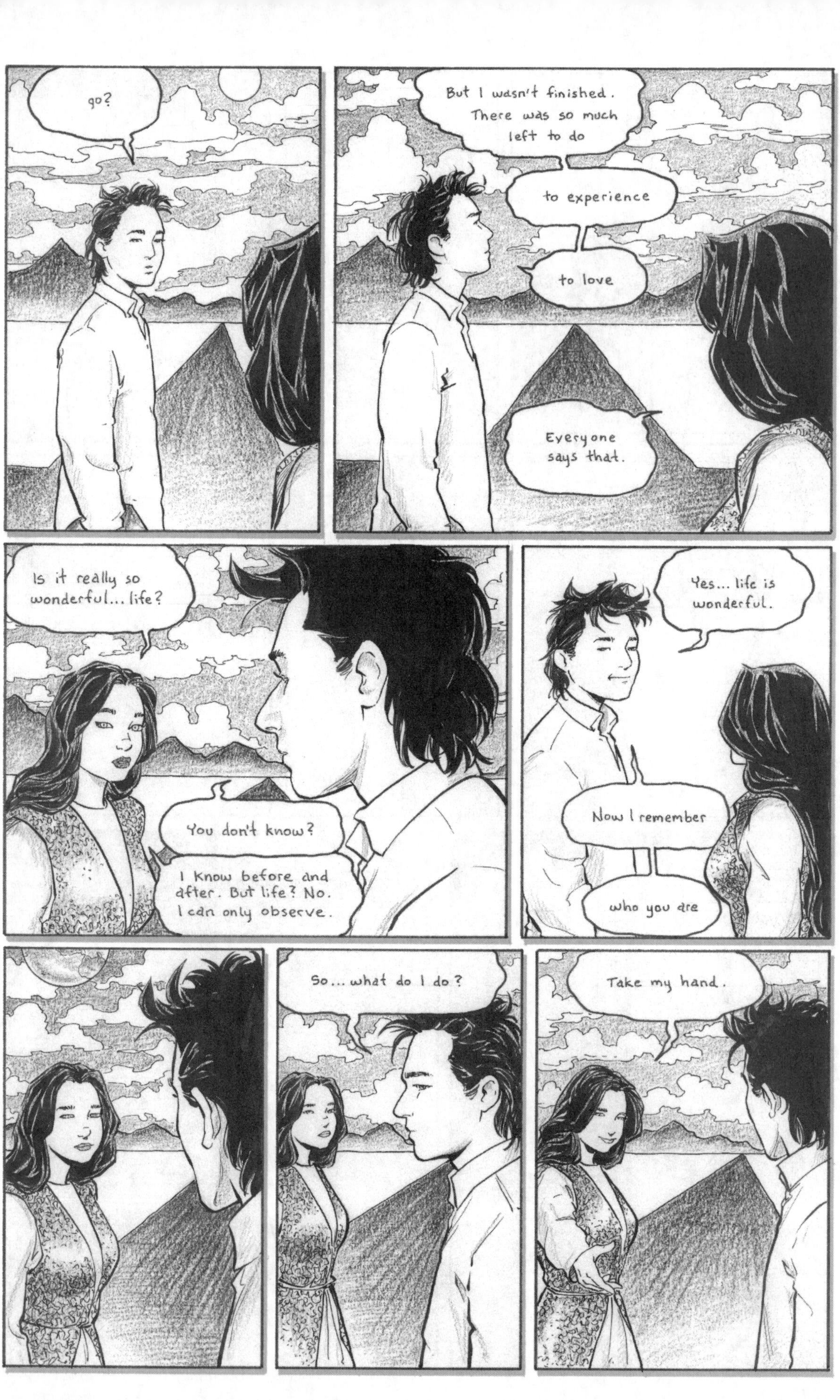
go?
But I wasn't finished. There was so much left to do
to experience
to love
Everyone says that.
Is it really so wonderful... life?
You don't know?
I know before and after. But life? No. I can only observe.
Yes... life is wonderful.
Now I remember
who you are
So... what do I do?
Take my hand.

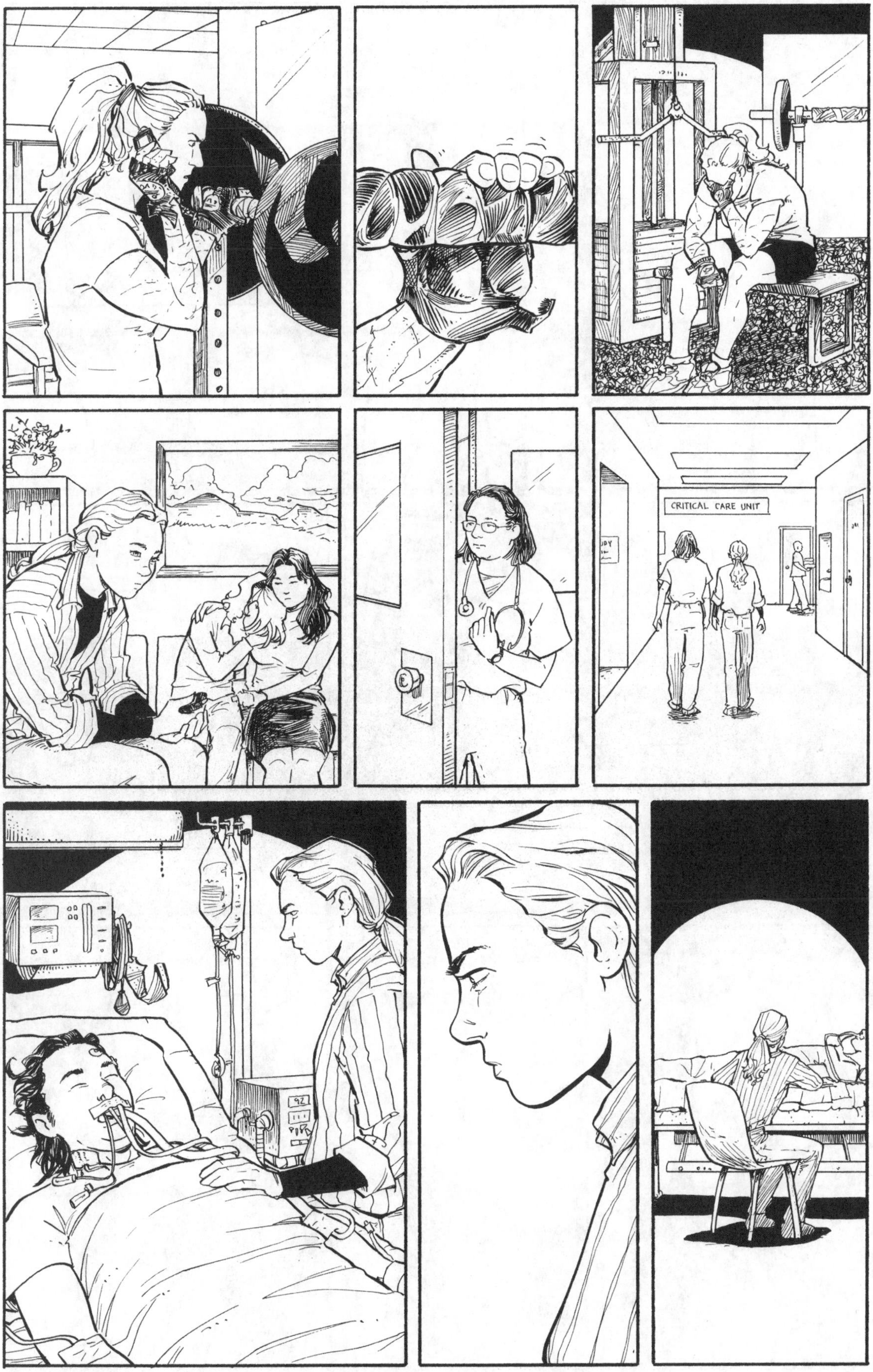
CRITICAL CARE UNIT

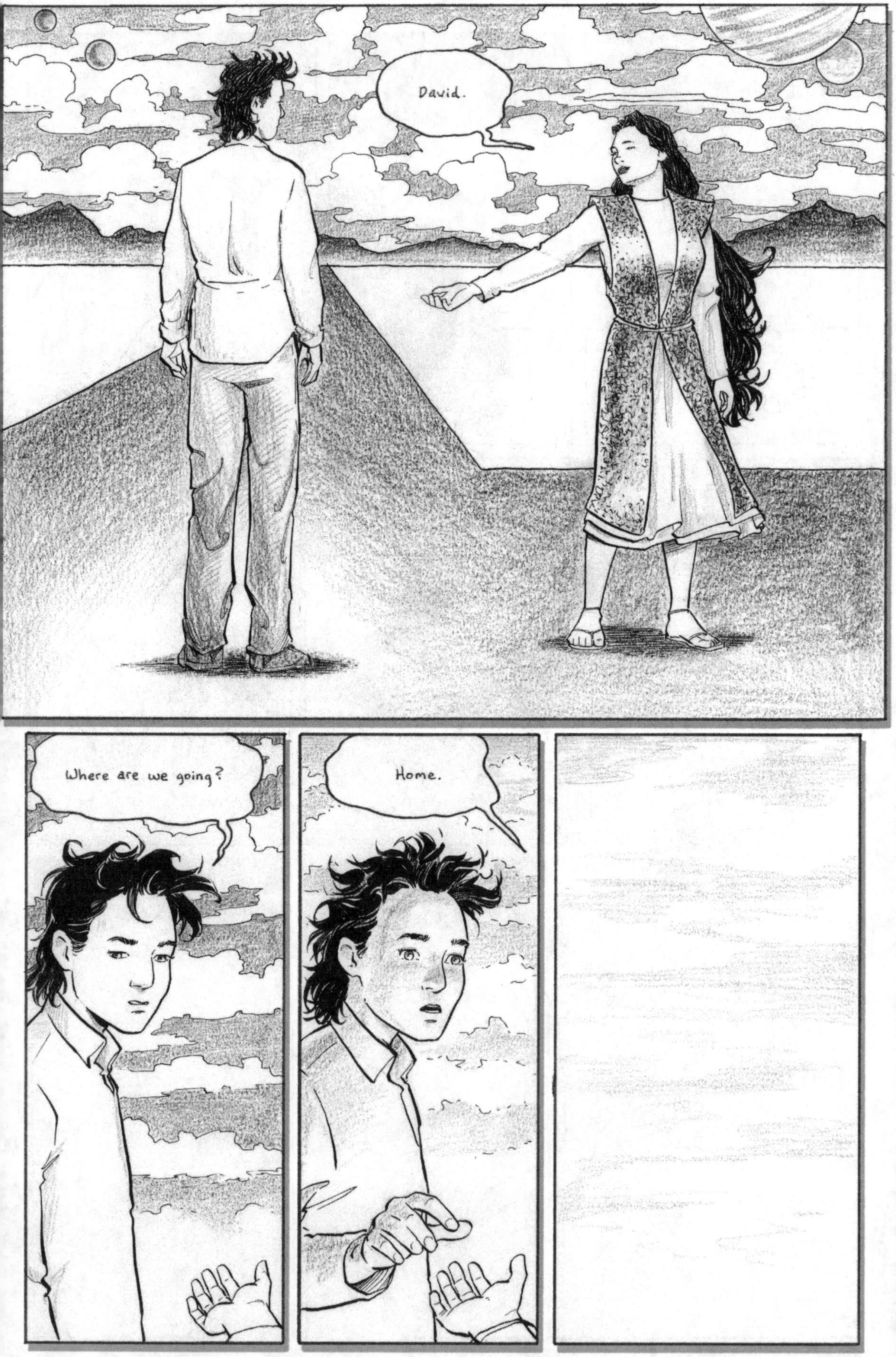
David.
Where are we going?
Home.

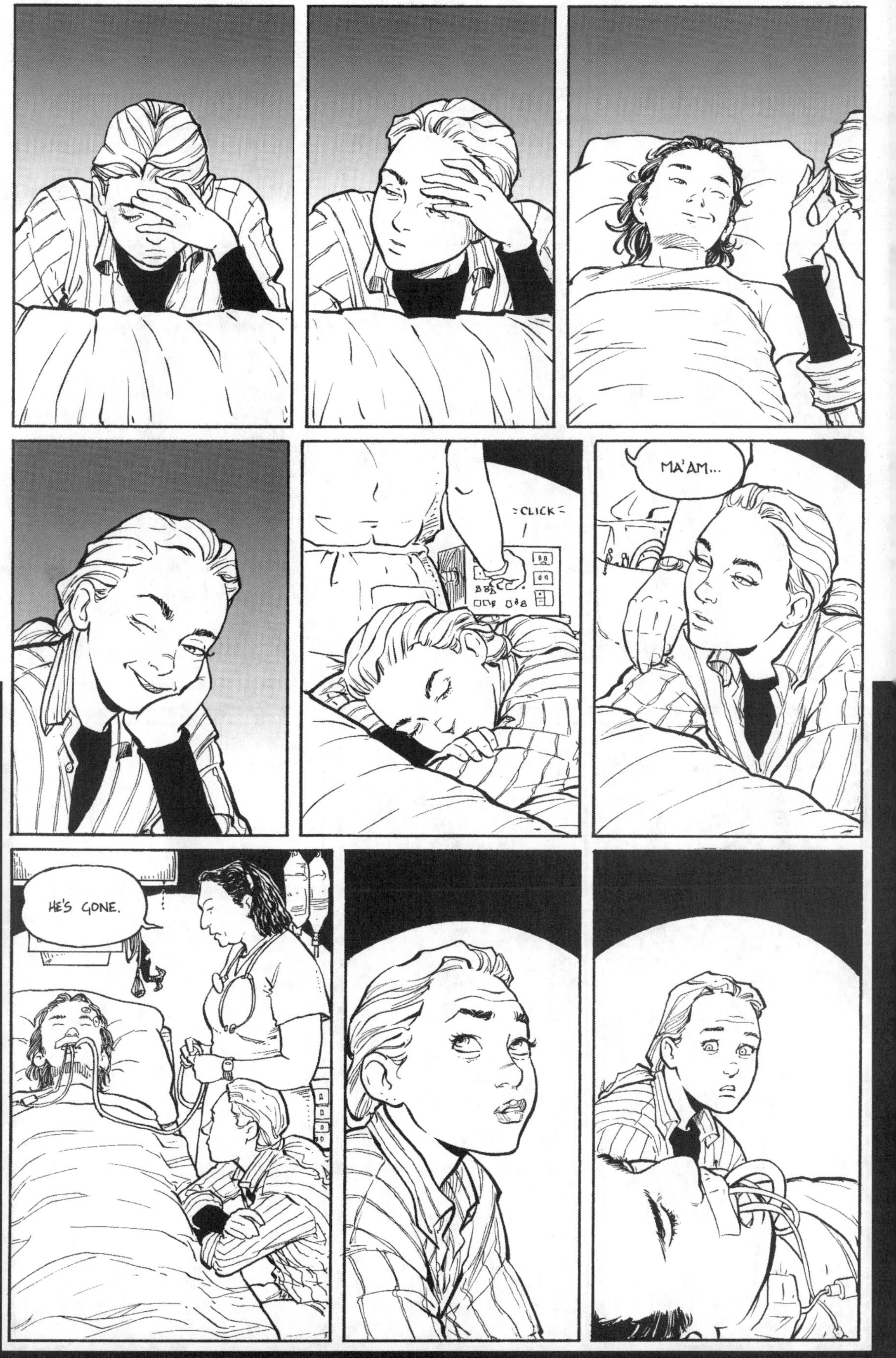
CLICK
MA'AM...
HE'S GONE.

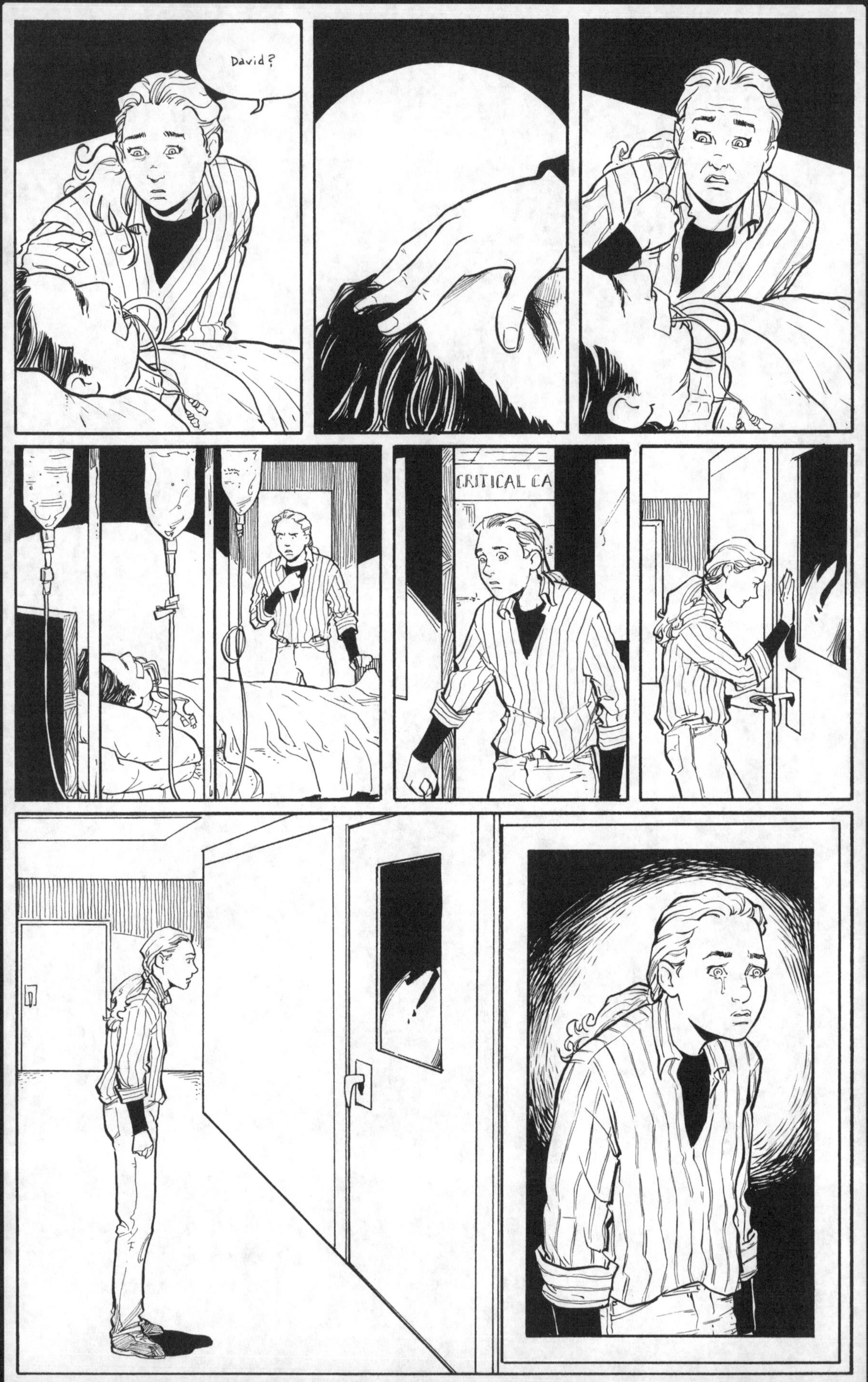
David?
CRITICAL CA

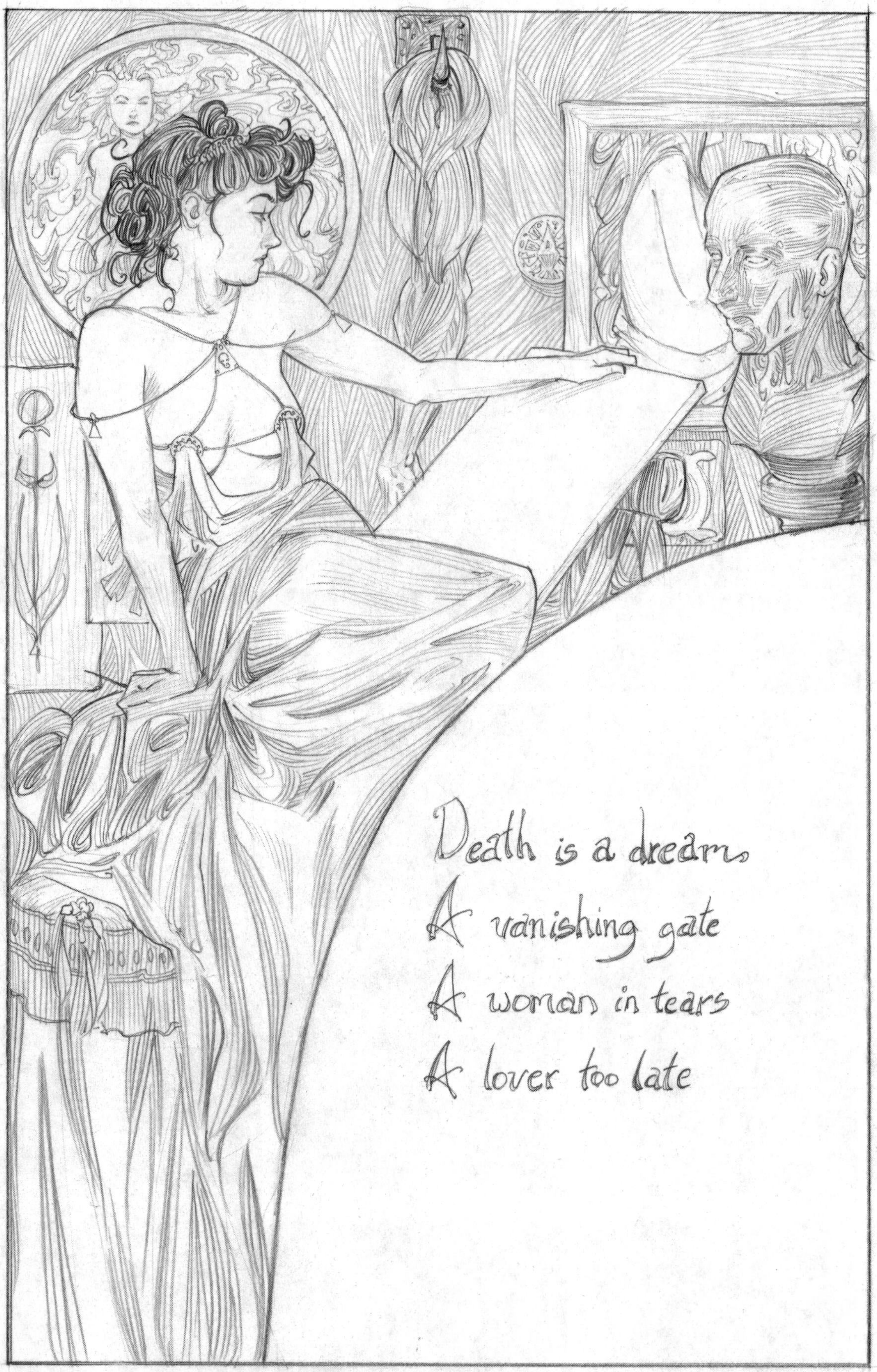
Death is a dream
A vanishing gate
A woman in tears
A lover too late

[redacted]

[redacted]

[redacted]

[redacted]

[redacted]

[redacted]

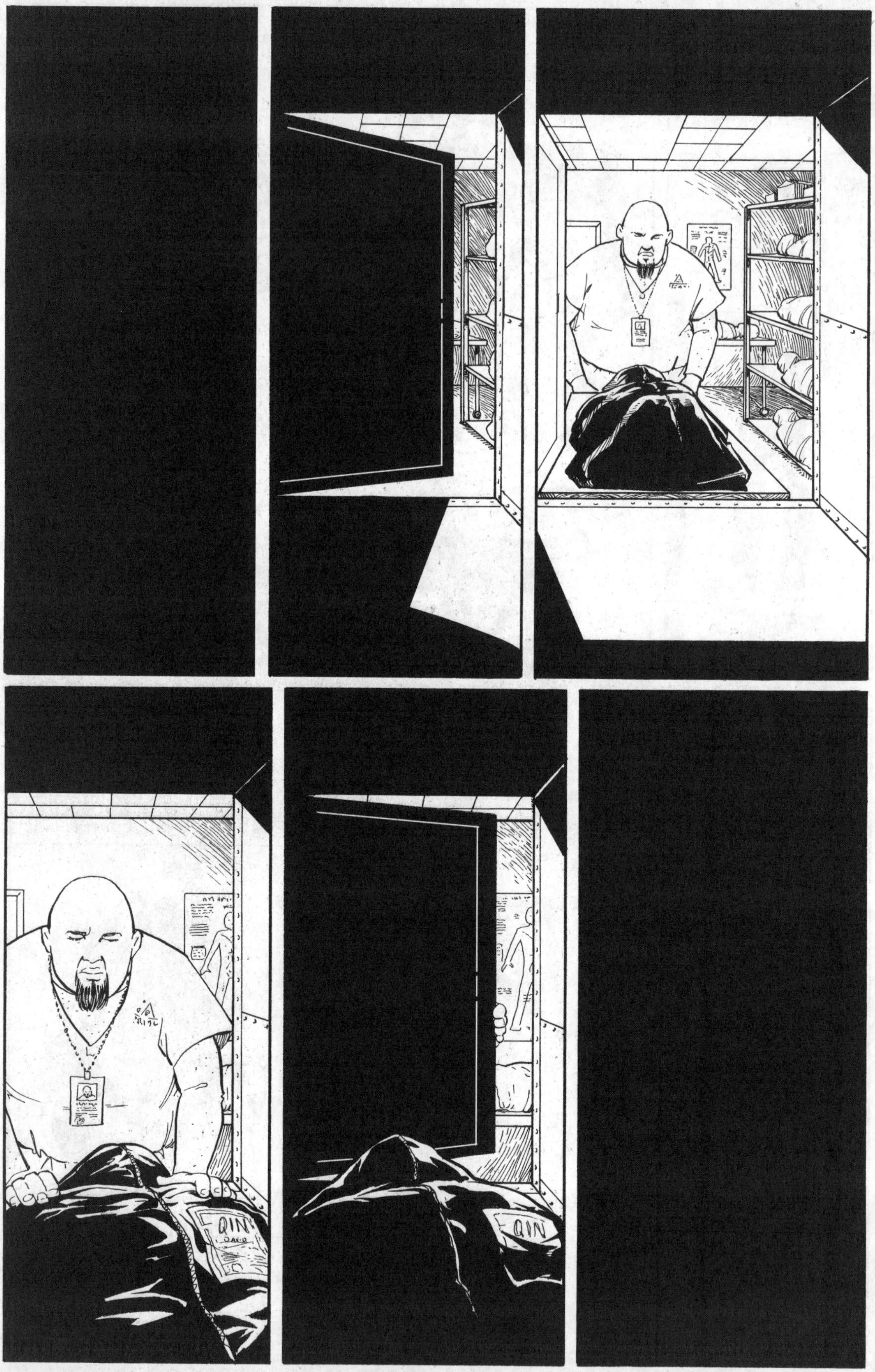
QIN
QIN

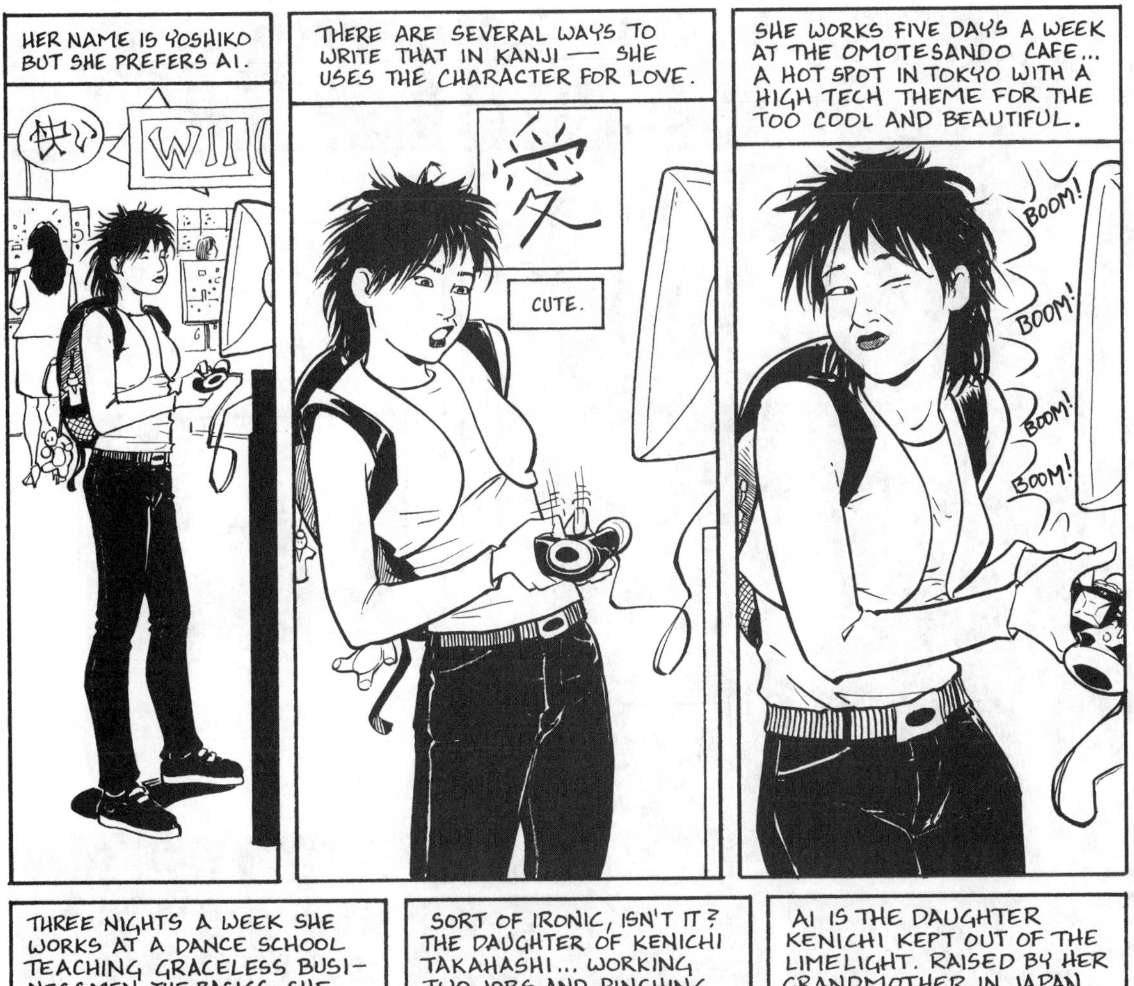

HER NAME IS YOSHIKO BUT SHE PREFERS AI.
快い
WII
THERE ARE SEVERAL WAYS TO WRITE THAT IN KANJI — SHE USES THE CHARACTER FOR LOVE.
愛
CUTE.
SHE WORKS FIVE DAYS A WEEK AT THE OMOTESANDO CAFE... A HOT SPOT IN TOKYO WITH A HIGH TECH THEME FOR THE TOO COOL AND BEAUTIFUL.
BOOM!
BOOM!
BOOM!
BOOM!
THREE NIGHTS A WEEK SHE WORKS AT A DANCE SCHOOL TEACHING GRACELESS BUSINESSMEN THE BASICS. SHE LIKES TO WINDOW SHOP BUT IS VERY FRUGAL WITH MONEY.
SuperStar!
SORT OF IRONIC, ISN'T IT? THE DAUGHTER OF KENICHI TAKAHASHI... WORKING TWO JOBS AND PINCHING PENNIES LIKE SHE WAS JUST ANY OTHER YOUNG WOMAN IN TOKYO.
SHE DOESN'T KNOW.
BEND SPACE TIME!
FUJI
AI IS THE DAUGHTER KENICHI KEPT OUT OF THE LIMELIGHT. RAISED BY HER GRANDMOTHER IN JAPAN, AI HAS NO IDEA HER FATHER WAS THE LEADER OF THE AMERICAN YAKUZA .... WORTH MILLIONS.
SHE DOESN'T KNOW HER STEP-SISTER WAS A BILLIONAIRE WITCH WHO DESERVED WHAT SHE GOT... OR THAT SHE HAS A BROTHER IN TEXAS WHO IS HER FRATERNAL TWIN.

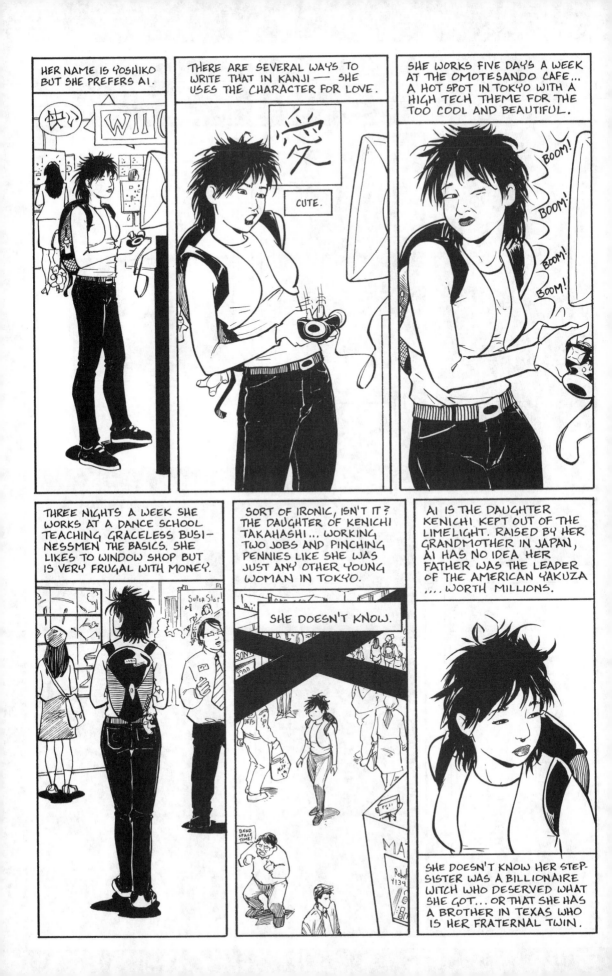

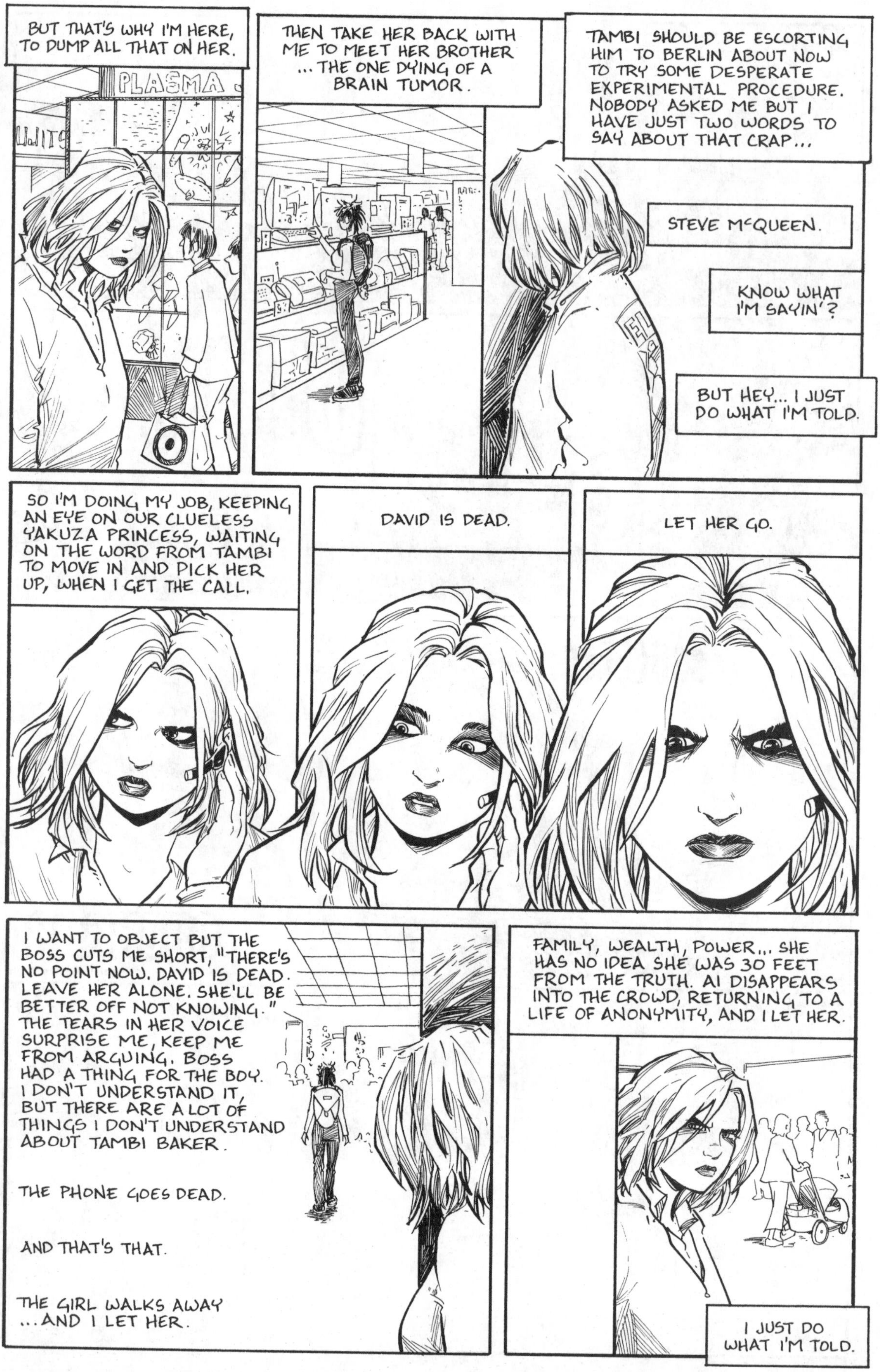
BUT THAT'S WHY I'M HERE, TO DUMP ALL THAT ON HER.
PLASMA
THEN TAKE HER BACK WITH ME TO MEET HER BROTHER ... THE ONE DYING OF A BRAIN TUMOR.
TAMBI SHOULD BE ESCORTING HIM TO BERLIN ABOUT NOW TO TRY SOME DESPERATE EXPERIMENTAL PROCEDURE. NOBODY ASKED ME BUT I HAVE JUST TWO WORDS TO SAY ABOUT THAT CRAP...
STEVE McQUEEN.
KNOW WHAT I'M SAYIN'?
BUT HEY... I JUST DO WHAT I'M TOLD.
SO I'M DOING MY JOB, KEEPING AN EYE ON OUR CLUELESS YAKUZA PRINCESS, WAITING ON THE WORD FROM TAMBI TO MOVE IN AND PICK HER UP, WHEN I GET THE CALL.
DAVID IS DEAD.
LET HER GO.
I WANT TO OBJECT BUT THE BOSS CUTS ME SHORT, "THERE'S NO POINT NOW. DAVID IS DEAD. LEAVE HER ALONE. SHE'LL BE BETTER OFF NOT KNOWING." THE TEARS IN HER VOICE SURPRISE ME, KEEP ME FROM ARGUING. BOSS HAD A THING FOR THE BOY. I DON'T UNDERSTAND IT, BUT THERE ARE A LOT OF THINGS I DON'T UNDERSTAND ABOUT TAMBI BAKER.
THE PHONE GOES DEAD.
AND THAT'S THAT.
THE GIRL WALKS AWAY ...AND I LET HER.
FAMILY, WEALTH, POWER... SHE HAS NO IDEA SHE WAS 30 FEET FROM THE TRUTH. AI DISAPPEARS INTO THE CROWD, RETURNING TO A LIFE OF ANONYMITY, AND I LET HER.
I JUST DO WHAT I'M TOLD.

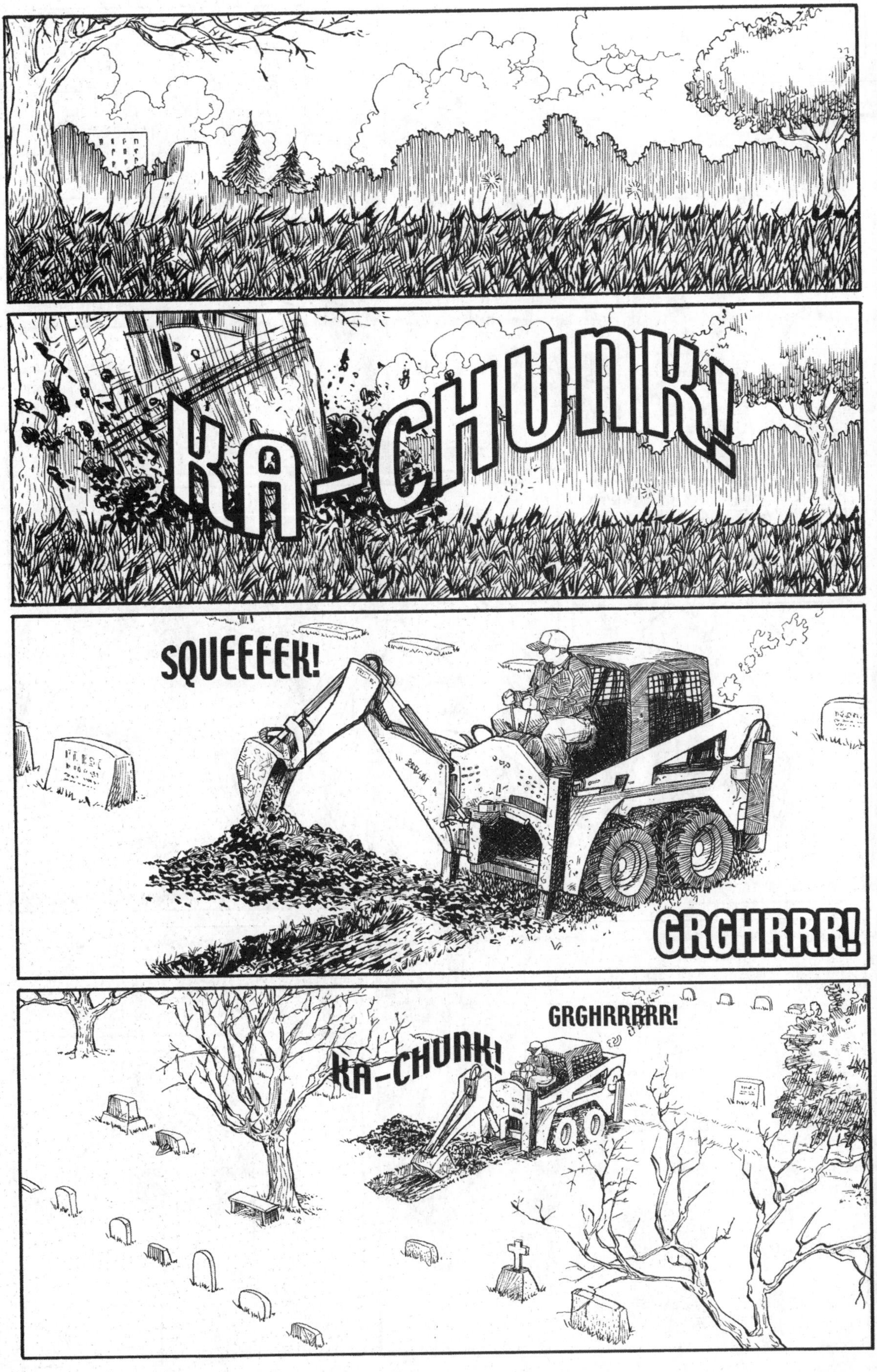
KA-CHUNK!
SQUEEEEK!
GRGHRRR!
GRGHRRRRR!
KA-CHUNK!

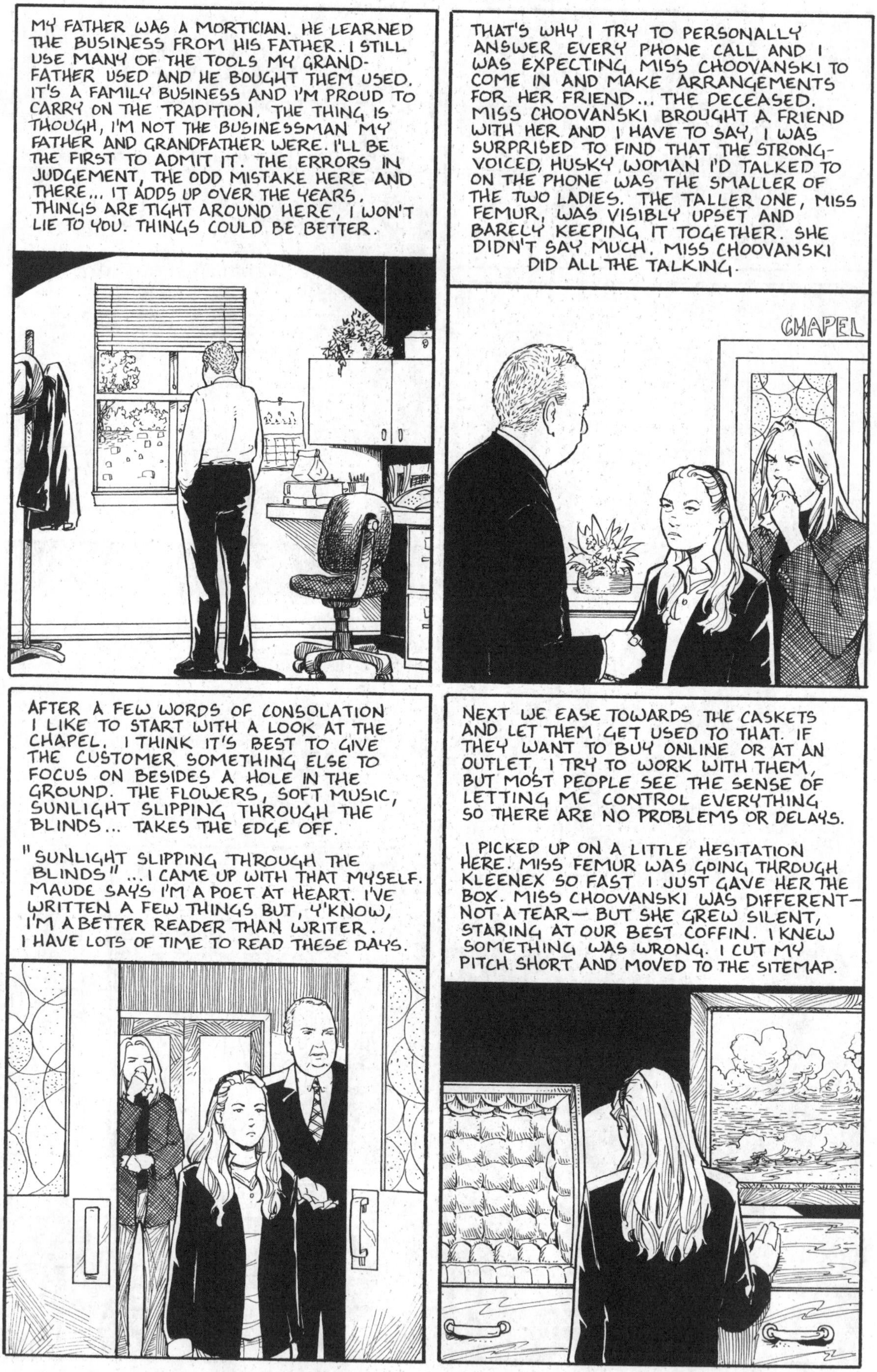
MY FATHER WAS A MORTICIAN. HE LEARNED THE BUSINESS FROM HIS FATHER. I STILL USE MANY OF THE TOOLS MY GRANDFATHER USED AND HE BOUGHT THEM USED. IT'S A FAMILY BUSINESS AND I'M PROUD TO CARRY ON THE TRADITION. THE THING IS THOUGH, I'M NOT THE BUSINESSMAN MY FATHER AND GRANDFATHER WERE. I'LL BE THE FIRST TO ADMIT IT. THE ERRORS IN JUDGEMENT, THE ODD MISTAKE HERE AND THERE... IT ADDS UP OVER THE YEARS. THINGS ARE TIGHT AROUND HERE, I WON'T LIE TO YOU. THINGS COULD BE BETTER.
THAT'S WHY I TRY TO PERSONALLY ANSWER EVERY PHONE CALL AND I WAS EXPECTING MISS CHOOVANSKI TO COME IN AND MAKE ARRANGEMENTS FOR HER FRIEND... THE DECEASED. MISS CHOOVANSKI BROUGHT A FRIEND WITH HER AND I HAVE TO SAY, I WAS SURPRISED TO FIND THAT THE STRONG-VOICED, HUSKY WOMAN I'D TALKED TO ON THE PHONE WAS THE SMALLER OF THE TWO LADIES. THE TALLER ONE, MISS FEMUR, WAS VISIBLY UPSET AND BARELY KEEPING IT TOGETHER. SHE DIDN'T SAY MUCH. MISS CHOOVANSKI DID ALL THE TALKING.
CHAPEL
AFTER A FEW WORDS OF CONSOLATION I LIKE TO START WITH A LOOK AT THE CHAPEL. I THINK IT'S BEST TO GIVE THE CUSTOMER SOMETHING ELSE TO FOCUS ON BESIDES A HOLE IN THE GROUND. THE FLOWERS, SOFT MUSIC, SUNLIGHT SLIPPING THROUGH THE BLINDS... TAKES THE EDGE OFF.
"SUNLIGHT SLIPPING THROUGH THE BLINDS"... I CAME UP WITH THAT MYSELF. MAUDE SAYS I'M A POET AT HEART. I'VE WRITTEN A FEW THINGS BUT, Y'KNOW, I'M A BETTER READER THAN WRITER. I HAVE LOTS OF TIME TO READ THESE DAYS.
NEXT WE EASE TOWARDS THE CASKETS AND LET THEM GET USED TO THAT. IF THEY WANT TO BUY ONLINE OR AT AN OUTLET, I TRY TO WORK WITH THEM, BUT MOST PEOPLE SEE THE SENSE OF LETTING ME CONTROL EVERYTHING SO THERE ARE NO PROBLEMS OR DELAYS.
I PICKED UP ON A LITTLE HESITATION HERE. MISS FEMUR WAS GOING THROUGH KLEENEX SO FAST I JUST GAVE HER THE BOX. MISS CHOOVANSKI WAS DIFFERENT— NOT A TEAR— BUT SHE GREW SILENT, STARING AT OUR BEST COFFIN. I KNEW SOMETHING WAS WRONG. I CUT MY PITCH SHORT AND MOVED TO THE SITEMAP.

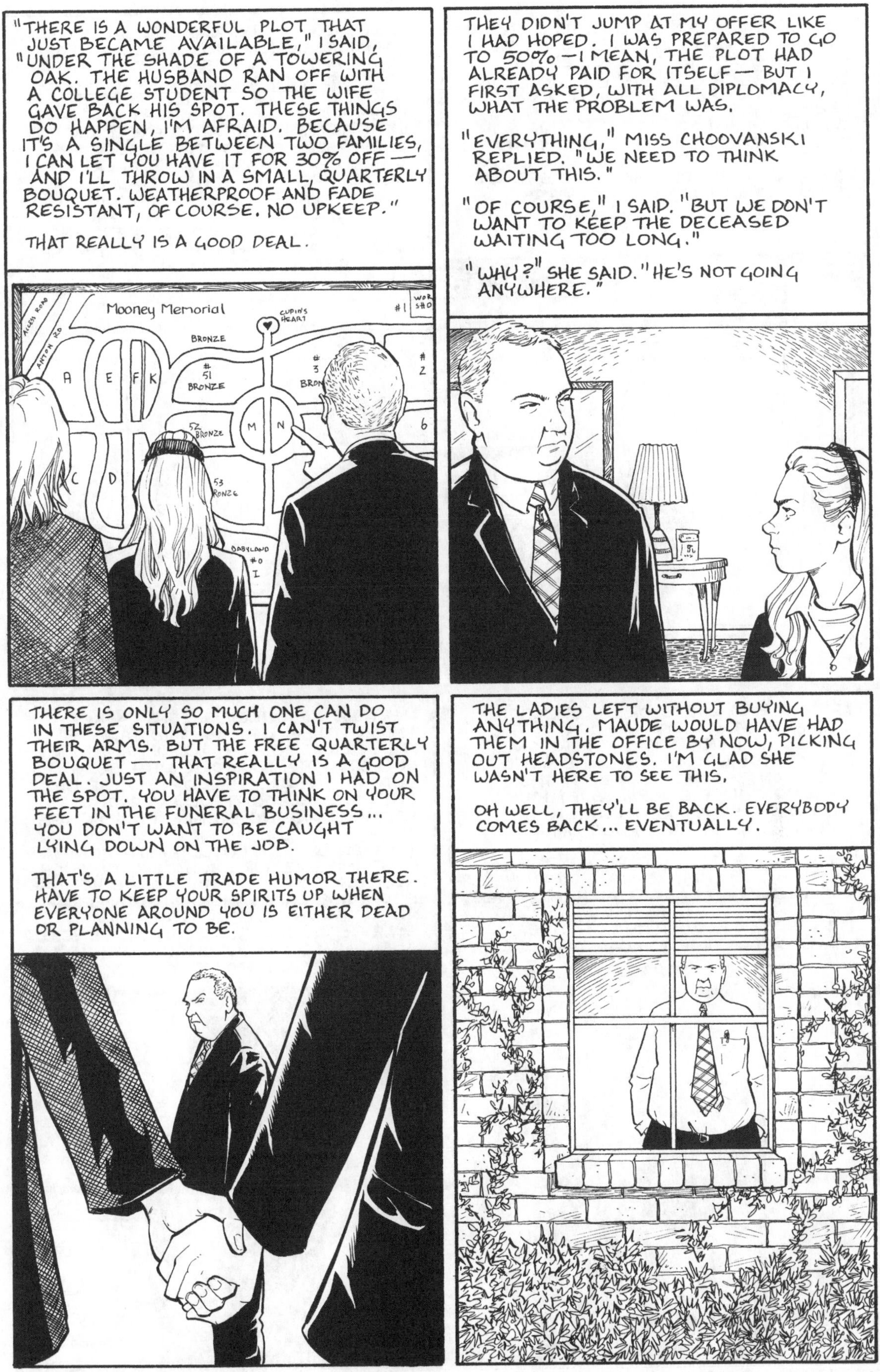
"THERE IS A WONDERFUL PLOT THAT JUST BECAME AVAILABLE," I SAID, "UNDER THE SHADE OF A TOWERING OAK. THE HUSBAND RAN OFF WITH A COLLEGE STUDENT SO THE WIFE GAVE BACK HIS SPOT. THESE THINGS DO HAPPEN, I'M AFRAID. BECAUSE IT'S A SINGLE BETWEEN TWO FAMILIES, I CAN LET YOU HAVE IT FOR 30% OFF — AND I'LL THROW IN A SMALL, QUARTERLY BOUQUET. WEATHERPROOF AND FADE RESISTANT, OF COURSE. NO UPKEEP."
THAT REALLY IS A GOOD DEAL.
Mooney Memorial
CUPID'S HEART
BRONZE
#51 BRONZE
52 BRONZE
BABYLAND #0
THEY DIDN'T JUMP AT MY OFFER LIKE I HAD HOPED. I WAS PREPARED TO GO TO 50% — I MEAN, THE PLOT HAD ALREADY PAID FOR ITSELF — BUT I FIRST ASKED, WITH ALL DIPLOMACY, WHAT THE PROBLEM WAS.
"EVERYTHING," MISS CHOOVANSKI REPLIED. "WE NEED TO THINK ABOUT THIS."
"OF COURSE," I SAID. "BUT WE DON'T WANT TO KEEP THE DECEASED WAITING TOO LONG."
"WHY?" SHE SAID. "HE'S NOT GOING ANYWHERE."
THERE IS ONLY SO MUCH ONE CAN DO IN THESE SITUATIONS. I CAN'T TWIST THEIR ARMS. BUT THE FREE QUARTERLY BOUQUET — THAT REALLY IS A GOOD DEAL. JUST AN INSPIRATION I HAD ON THE SPOT. YOU HAVE TO THINK ON YOUR FEET IN THE FUNERAL BUSINESS... YOU DON'T WANT TO BE CAUGHT LYING DOWN ON THE JOB.
THAT'S A LITTLE TRADE HUMOR THERE. HAVE TO KEEP YOUR SPIRITS UP WHEN EVERYONE AROUND YOU IS EITHER DEAD OR PLANNING TO BE.
THE LADIES LEFT WITHOUT BUYING ANYTHING. MAUDE WOULD HAVE HAD THEM IN THE OFFICE BY NOW, PICKING OUT HEADSTONES. I'M GLAD SHE WASN'T HERE TO SEE THIS.
OH WELL, THEY'LL BE BACK. EVERYBODY COMES BACK... EVENTUALLY.

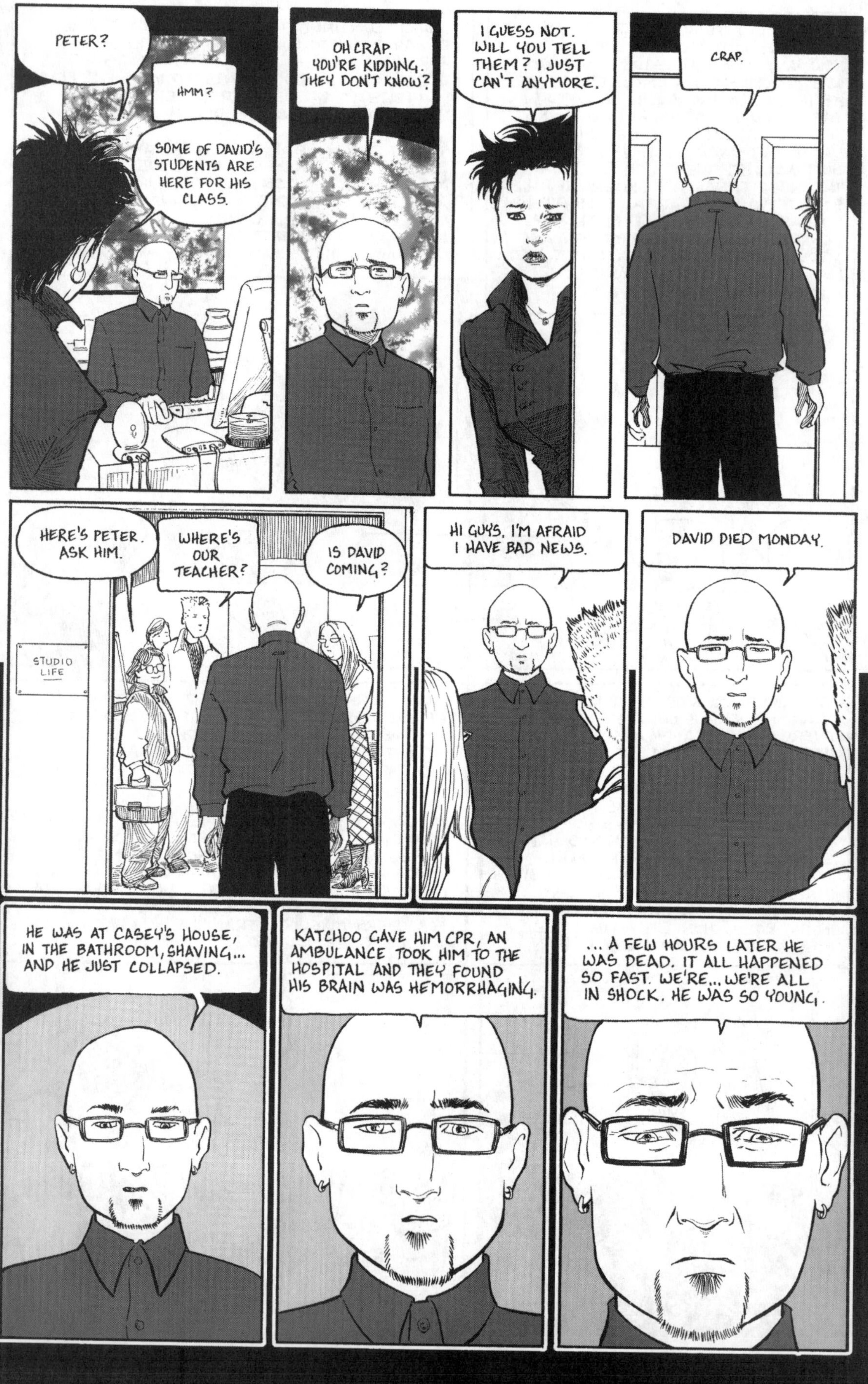
PETER?
HMM?
SOME OF DAVID'S STUDENTS ARE HERE FOR HIS CLASS.
OH CRAP. YOU'RE KIDDING. THEY DON'T KNOW?
I GUESS NOT. WILL YOU TELL THEM? I JUST CAN'T ANYMORE.
CRAP.
HERE'S PETER. ASK HIM.
WHERE'S OUR TEACHER?
IS DAVID COMING?
STUDIO LIFE
HI GUYS, I'M AFRAID I HAVE BAD NEWS.
DAVID DIED MONDAY.
HE WAS AT CASEY'S HOUSE, IN THE BATHROOM, SHAVING... AND HE JUST COLLAPSED.
KATCHOO GAVE HIM CPR, AN AMBULANCE TOOK HIM TO THE HOSPITAL AND THEY FOUND HIS BRAIN WAS HEMORRHAGING.
... A FEW HOURS LATER HE WAS DEAD. IT ALL HAPPENED SO FAST. WE'RE... WE'RE ALL IN SHOCK. HE WAS SO YOUNG.

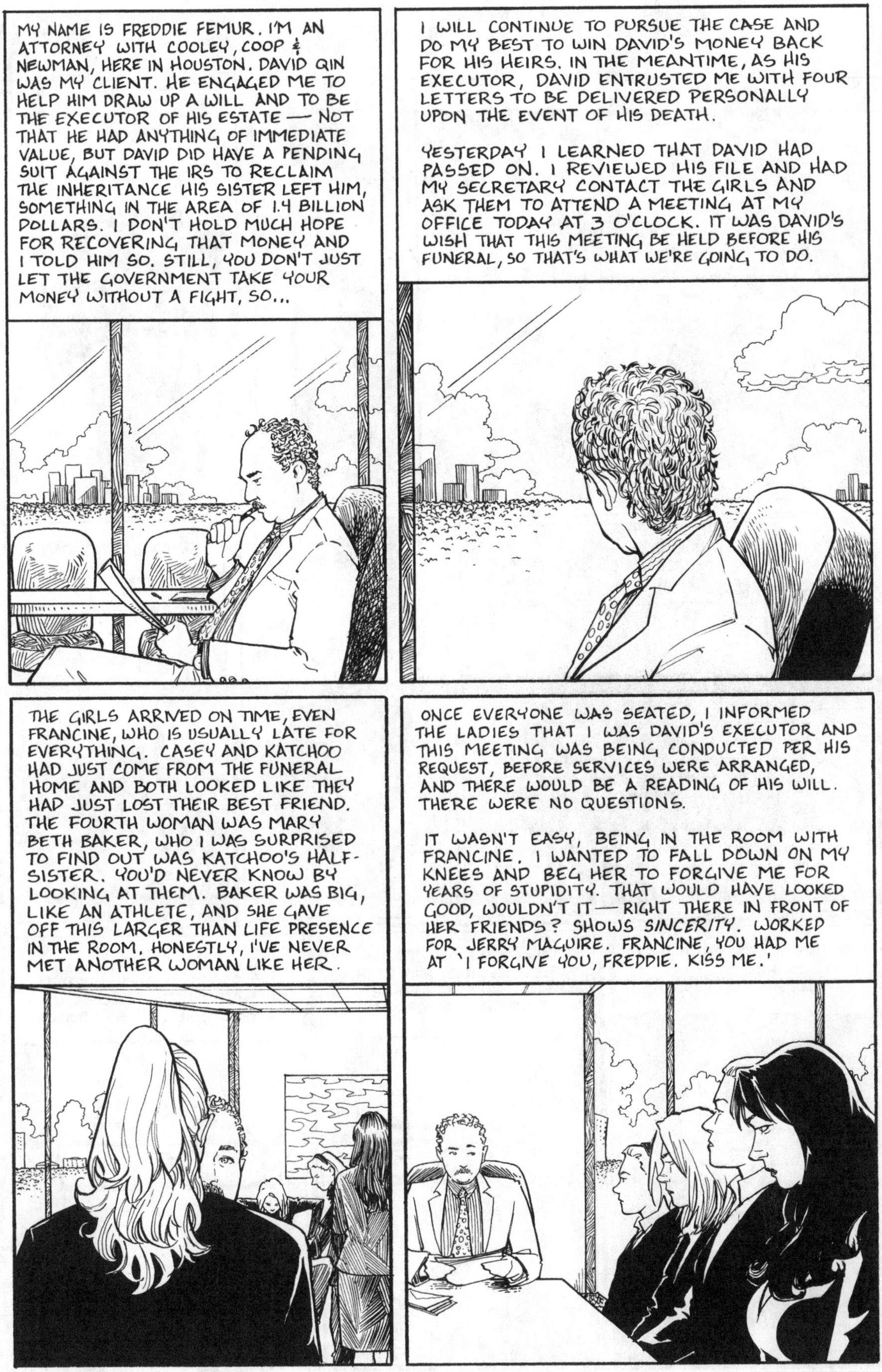
MY NAME IS FREDDIE FEMUR. I'M AN ATTORNEY WITH COOLEY, COOP & NEWMAN, HERE IN HOUSTON. DAVID QIN WAS MY CLIENT. HE ENGAGED ME TO HELP HIM DRAW UP A WILL AND TO BE THE EXECUTOR OF HIS ESTATE — NOT THAT HE HAD ANYTHING OF IMMEDIATE VALUE, BUT DAVID DID HAVE A PENDING SUIT AGAINST THE IRS TO RECLAIM THE INHERITANCE HIS SISTER LEFT HIM, SOMETHING IN THE AREA OF 1.4 BILLION DOLLARS. I DON'T HOLD MUCH HOPE FOR RECOVERING THAT MONEY AND I TOLD HIM SO. STILL, YOU DON'T JUST LET THE GOVERNMENT TAKE YOUR MONEY WITHOUT A FIGHT, SO...
I WILL CONTINUE TO PURSUE THE CASE AND DO MY BEST TO WIN DAVID'S MONEY BACK FOR HIS HEIRS. IN THE MEANTIME, AS HIS EXECUTOR, DAVID ENTRUSTED ME WITH FOUR LETTERS TO BE DELIVERED PERSONALLY UPON THE EVENT OF HIS DEATH.
YESTERDAY I LEARNED THAT DAVID HAD PASSED ON. I REVIEWED HIS FILE AND HAD MY SECRETARY CONTACT THE GIRLS AND ASK THEM TO ATTEND A MEETING AT MY OFFICE TODAY AT 3 O'CLOCK. IT WAS DAVID'S WISH THAT THIS MEETING BE HELD BEFORE HIS FUNERAL, SO THAT'S WHAT WE'RE GOING TO DO.
THE GIRLS ARRIVED ON TIME, EVEN FRANCINE, WHO IS USUALLY LATE FOR EVERYTHING. CASEY AND KATCHOO HAD JUST COME FROM THE FUNERAL HOME AND BOTH LOOKED LIKE THEY HAD JUST LOST THEIR BEST FRIEND. THE FOURTH WOMAN WAS MARY BETH BAKER, WHO I WAS SURPRISED TO FIND OUT WAS KATCHOO'S HALF-SISTER. YOU'D NEVER KNOW BY LOOKING AT THEM. BAKER WAS BIG, LIKE AN ATHLETE, AND SHE GAVE OFF THIS LARGER THAN LIFE PRESENCE IN THE ROOM. HONESTLY, I'VE NEVER MET ANOTHER WOMAN LIKE HER.
ONCE EVERYONE WAS SEATED, I INFORMED THE LADIES THAT I WAS DAVID'S EXECUTOR AND THIS MEETING WAS BEING CONDUCTED PER HIS REQUEST, BEFORE SERVICES WERE ARRANGED, AND THERE WOULD BE A READING OF HIS WILL. THERE WERE NO QUESTIONS.
IT WASN'T EASY, BEING IN THE ROOM WITH FRANCINE. I WANTED TO FALL DOWN ON MY KNEES AND BEG HER TO FORGIVE ME FOR YEARS OF STUPIDITY. THAT WOULD HAVE LOOKED GOOD, WOULDN'T IT — RIGHT THERE IN FRONT OF HER FRIENDS? SHOWS *SINCERITY*. WORKED FOR JERRY MAGUIRE. FRANCINE, YOU HAD ME AT `I FORGIVE YOU, FREDDIE. KISS ME.'

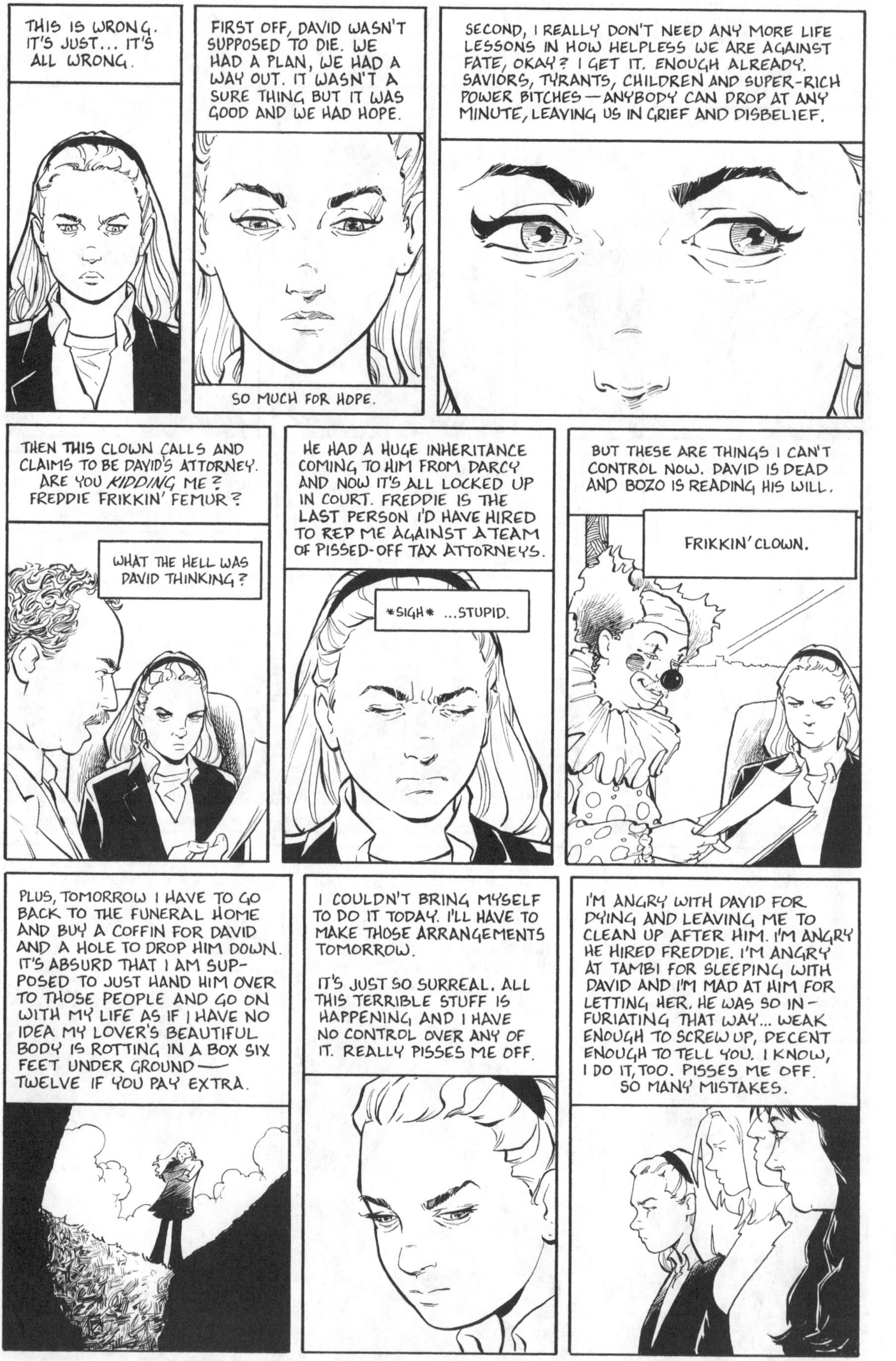

THIS IS WRONG. IT'S JUST... IT'S ALL WRONG.
FIRST OFF, DAVID WASN'T SUPPOSED TO DIE. WE HAD A PLAN, WE HAD A WAY OUT. IT WASN'T A SURE THING BUT IT WAS GOOD AND WE HAD HOPE.
SO MUCH FOR HOPE.
SECOND, I REALLY DON'T NEED ANY MORE LIFE LESSONS IN HOW HELPLESS WE ARE AGAINST FATE, OKAY? I GET IT. ENOUGH ALREADY. SAVIORS, TYRANTS, CHILDREN AND SUPER-RICH POWER BITCHES—ANYBODY CAN DROP AT ANY MINUTE, LEAVING US IN GRIEF AND DISBELIEF.
THEN THIS CLOWN CALLS AND CLAIMS TO BE DAVID'S ATTORNEY. ARE YOU KIDDING ME? FREDDIE FRIKKIN' FEMUR?
WHAT THE HELL WAS DAVID THINKING?
HE HAD A HUGE INHERITANCE COMING TO HIM FROM DARCY AND NOW IT'S ALL LOCKED UP IN COURT. FREDDIE IS THE LAST PERSON I'D HAVE HIRED TO REP ME AGAINST A TEAM OF PISSED-OFF TAX ATTORNEYS.
SIGH ...STUPID.
BUT THESE ARE THINGS I CAN'T CONTROL NOW. DAVID IS DEAD AND BOZO IS READING HIS WILL.
FRIKKIN' CLOWN.
PLUS, TOMORROW I HAVE TO GO BACK TO THE FUNERAL HOME AND BUY A COFFIN FOR DAVID AND A HOLE TO DROP HIM DOWN. IT'S ABSURD THAT I AM SUPPOSED TO JUST HAND HIM OVER TO THOSE PEOPLE AND GO ON WITH MY LIFE AS IF I HAVE NO IDEA MY LOVER'S BEAUTIFUL BODY IS ROTTING IN A BOX SIX FEET UNDER GROUND— TWELVE IF YOU PAY EXTRA.
I COULDN'T BRING MYSELF TO DO IT TODAY. I'LL HAVE TO MAKE THOSE ARRANGEMENTS TOMORROW.
IT'S JUST SO SURREAL. ALL THIS TERRIBLE STUFF IS HAPPENING, AND I HAVE NO CONTROL OVER ANY OF IT. REALLY PISSES ME OFF.
I'M ANGRY WITH DAVID FOR DYING AND LEAVING ME TO CLEAN UP AFTER HIM. I'M ANGRY HE HIRED FREDDIE. I'M ANGRY AT TAMBI FOR SLEEPING WITH DAVID AND I'M MAD AT HIM FOR LETTING HER. HE WAS SO INFURIATING THAT WAY... WEAK ENOUGH TO SCREW UP, DECENT ENOUGH TO TELL YOU. I KNOW, I DO IT, TOO. PISSES ME OFF. SO MANY MISTAKES.

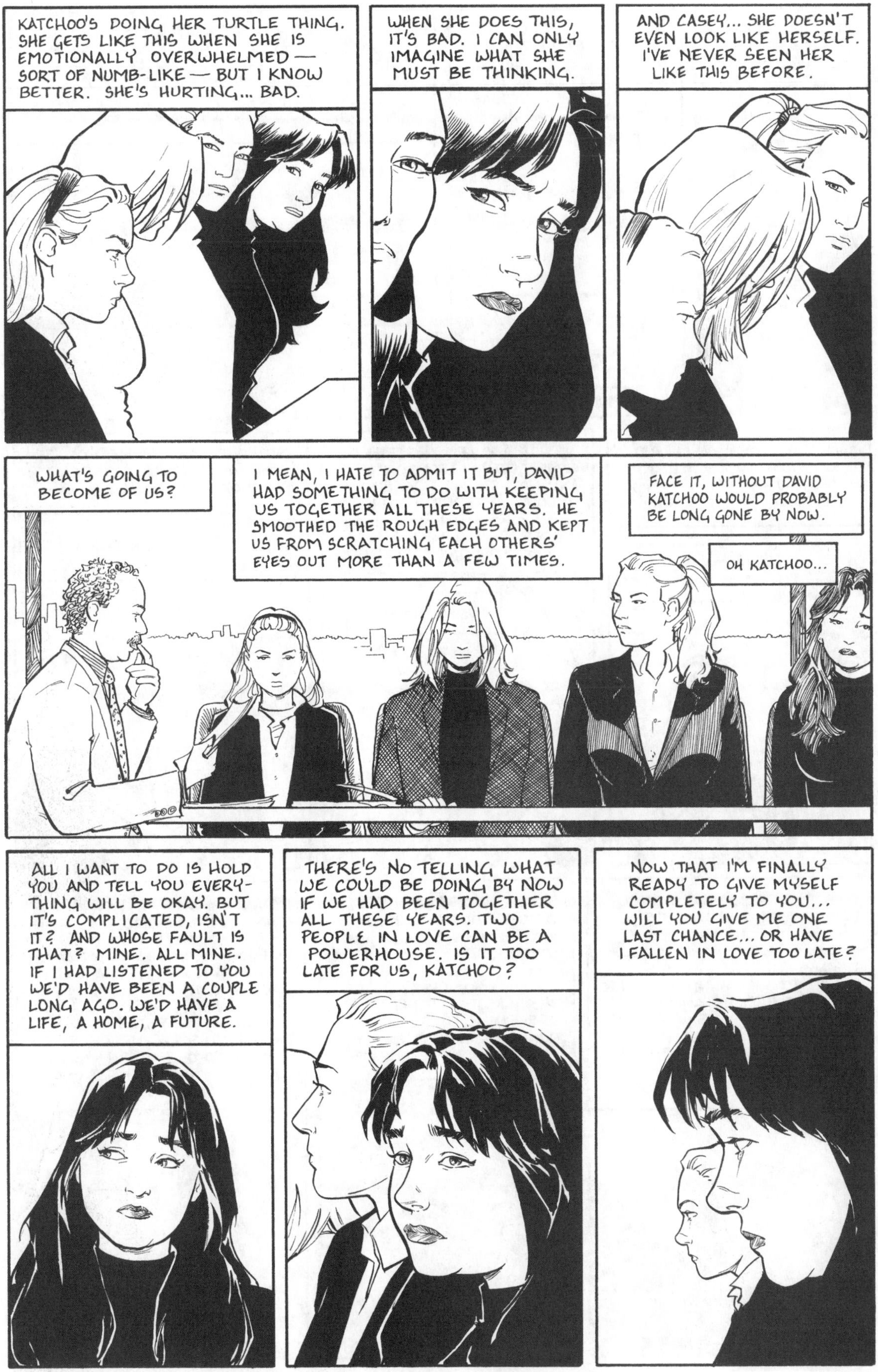
KATCHOO'S DOING HER TURTLE THING. SHE GETS LIKE THIS WHEN SHE IS EMOTIONALLY OVERWHELMED — SORT OF NUMB-LIKE — BUT I KNOW BETTER. SHE'S HURTING... BAD.
WHEN SHE DOES THIS, IT'S BAD. I CAN ONLY IMAGINE WHAT SHE MUST BE THINKING.
AND CASEY... SHE DOESN'T EVEN LOOK LIKE HERSELF. I'VE NEVER SEEN HER LIKE THIS BEFORE.
WHAT'S GOING TO BECOME OF US?
I MEAN, I HATE TO ADMIT IT BUT, DAVID HAD SOMETHING TO DO WITH KEEPING US TOGETHER ALL THESE YEARS. HE SMOOTHED THE ROUGH EDGES AND KEPT US FROM SCRATCHING EACH OTHERS' EYES OUT MORE THAN A FEW TIMES.
FACE IT, WITHOUT DAVID KATCHOO WOULD PROBABLY BE LONG GONE BY NOW.
OH KATCHOO...
ALL I WANT TO DO IS HOLD YOU AND TELL YOU EVERY-THING WILL BE OKAY. BUT IT'S COMPLICATED, ISN'T IT? AND WHOSE FAULT IS THAT? MINE. ALL MINE. IF I HAD LISTENED TO YOU WE'D HAVE BEEN A COUPLE LONG AGO. WE'D HAVE A LIFE, A HOME, A FUTURE.
THERE'S NO TELLING WHAT WE COULD BE DOING BY NOW IF WE HAD BEEN TOGETHER ALL THESE YEARS. TWO PEOPLE IN LOVE CAN BE A POWERHOUSE. IS IT TOO LATE FOR US, KATCHOO?
NOW THAT I'M FINALLY READY TO GIVE MYSELF COMPLETELY TO YOU... WILL YOU GIVE ME ONE LAST CHANCE... OR HAVE I FALLEN IN LOVE TOO LATE?

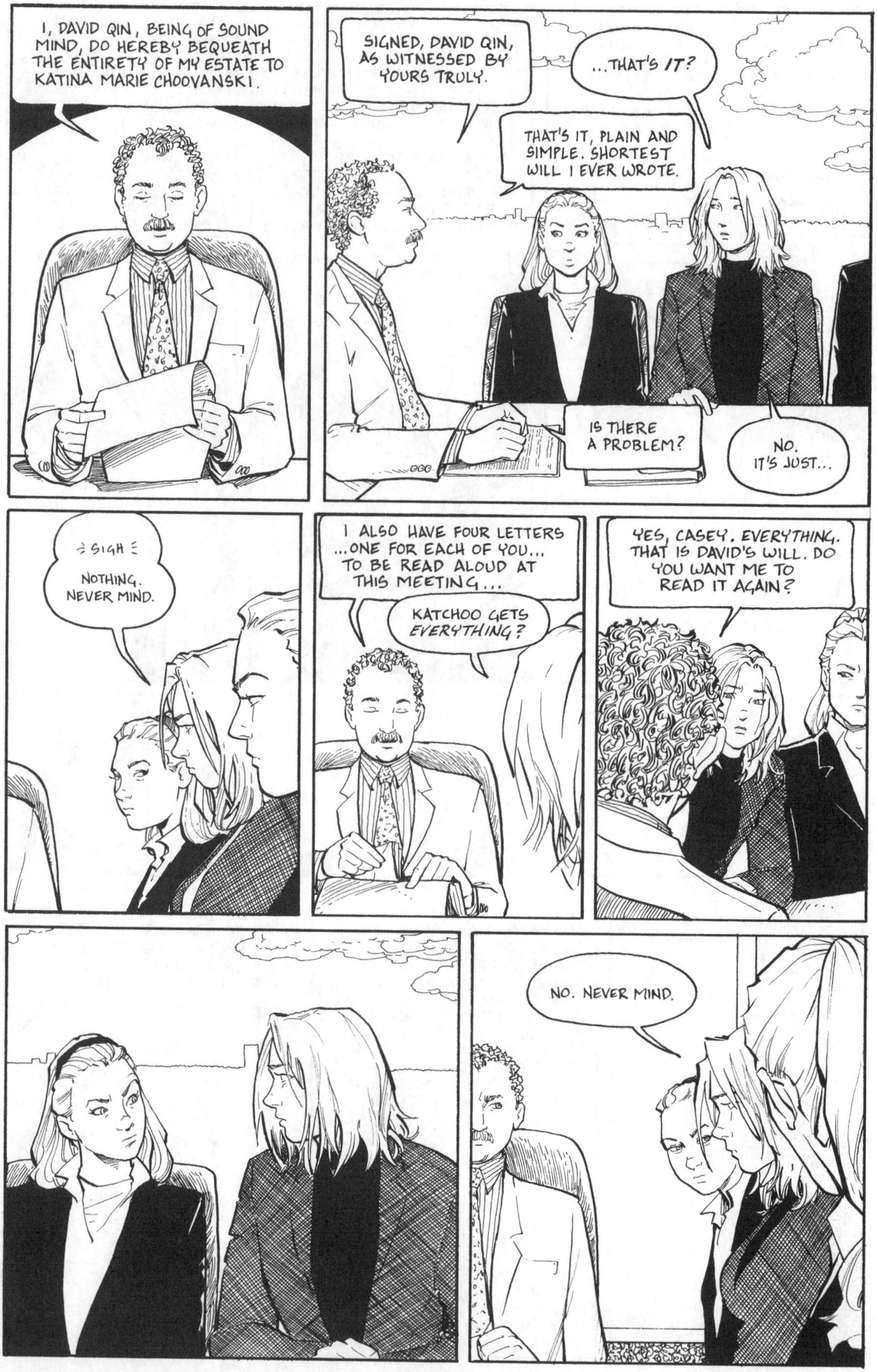
I, DAVID QIN, BEING OF SOUND MIND, DO HEREBY BEQUEATH THE ENTIRETY OF MY ESTATE TO KATINA MARIE CHOOVANSKI.
SIGNED, DAVID QIN, AS WITNESSED BY YOURS TRULY.
...THAT'S IT?
THAT'S IT, PLAIN AND SIMPLE. SHORTEST WILL I EVER WROTE.
IS THERE A PROBLEM?
NO. IT'S JUST...
SIGH
NOTHING. NEVER MIND.
I ALSO HAVE FOUR LETTERS ...ONE FOR EACH OF YOU... TO BE READ ALOUD AT THIS MEETING...
KATCHOO GETS EVERYTHING?
YES, CASEY. EVERYTHING. THAT IS DAVID'S WILL. DO YOU WANT ME TO READ IT AGAIN?
NO. NEVER MIND.

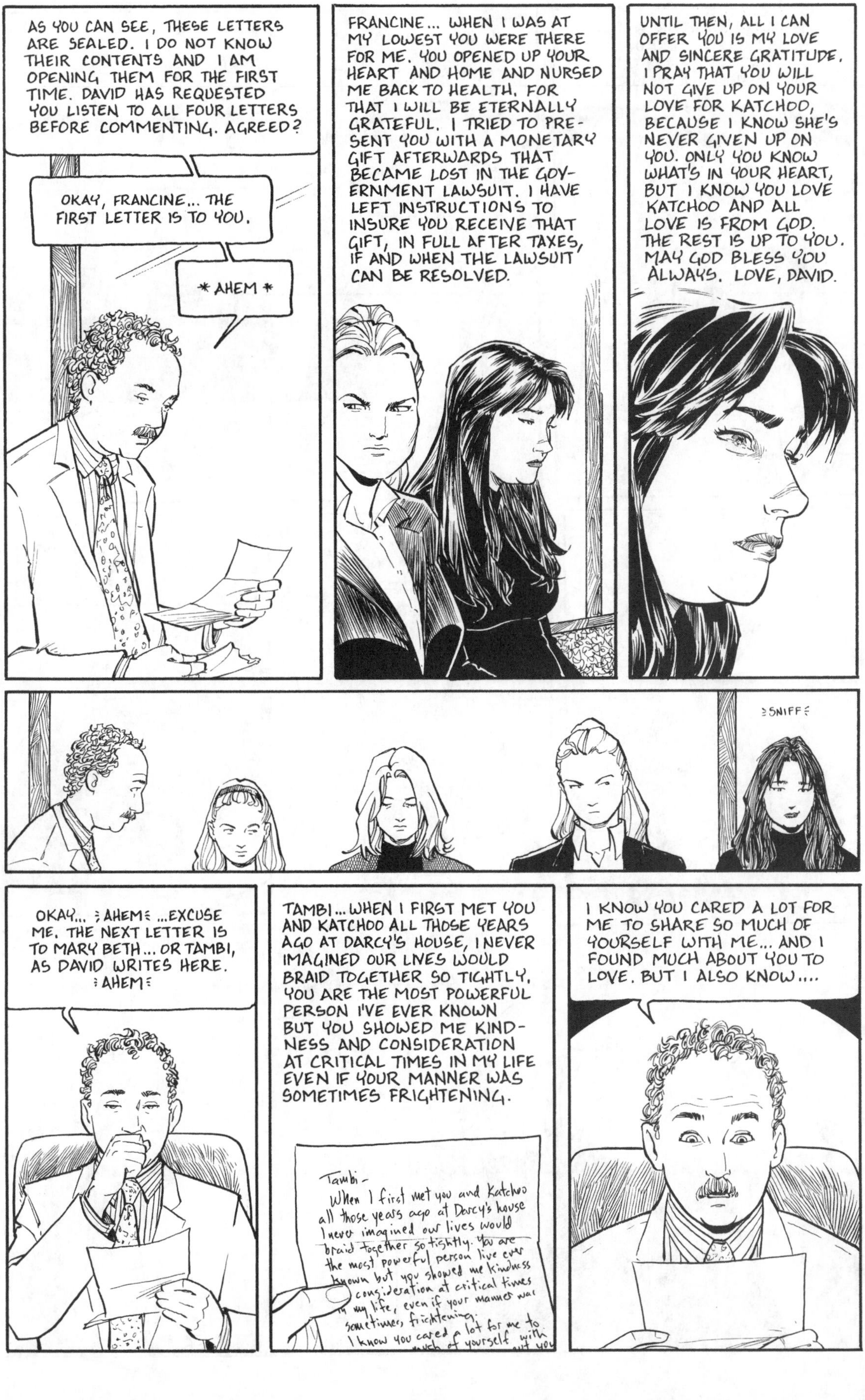

AS YOU CAN SEE, THESE LETTERS ARE SEALED. I DO NOT KNOW THEIR CONTENTS AND I AM OPENING THEM FOR THE FIRST TIME. DAVID HAS REQUESTED YOU LISTEN TO ALL FOUR LETTERS BEFORE COMMENTING. AGREED?
OKAY, FRANCINE... THE FIRST LETTER IS TO YOU.
* AHEM *
FRANCINE... WHEN I WAS AT MY LOWEST YOU WERE THERE FOR ME. YOU OPENED UP YOUR HEART AND HOME AND NURSED ME BACK TO HEALTH. FOR THAT I WILL BE ETERNALLY GRATEFUL. I TRIED TO PRESENT YOU WITH A MONETARY GIFT AFTERWARDS THAT BECAME LOST IN THE GOVERNMENT LAWSUIT. I HAVE LEFT INSTRUCTIONS TO INSURE YOU RECEIVE THAT GIFT, IN FULL AFTER TAXES, IF AND WHEN THE LAWSUIT CAN BE RESOLVED.
UNTIL THEN, ALL I CAN OFFER YOU IS MY LOVE AND SINCERE GRATITUDE. I PRAY THAT YOU WILL NOT GIVE UP ON YOUR LOVE FOR KATCHOO, BECAUSE I KNOW SHE'S NEVER GIVEN UP ON YOU. ONLY YOU KNOW WHAT'S IN YOUR HEART, BUT I KNOW YOU LOVE KATCHOO AND ALL LOVE IS FROM GOD. THE REST IS UP TO YOU. MAY GOD BLESS YOU ALWAYS. LOVE, DAVID.
SNIFF
OKAY... AHEM ...EXCUSE ME. THE NEXT LETTER IS TO MARY BETH... OR TAMBI, AS DAVID WRITES HERE. AHEM
TAMBI... WHEN I FIRST MET YOU AND KATCHOO ALL THOSE YEARS AGO AT DARCY'S HOUSE, I NEVER IMAGINED OUR LIVES WOULD BRAID TOGETHER SO TIGHTLY. YOU ARE THE MOST POWERFUL PERSON I'VE EVER KNOWN BUT YOU SHOWED ME KINDNESS AND CONSIDERATION AT CRITICAL TIMES IN MY LIFE EVEN IF YOUR MANNER WAS SOMETIMES FRIGHTENING.
Tambi -
When I first met you and Katchoo all those years ago at Darcy's house I never imagined our lives would braid together so tightly. You are the most powerful person I've ever known but you showed me kindness consideration at critical times in my life, even if your manner was sometimes frightening.
I know you cared a lot for me to
I KNOW YOU CARED A LOT FOR ME TO SHARE SO MUCH OF YOURSELF WITH ME... AND I FOUND MUCH ABOUT YOU TO LOVE. BUT I ALSO KNOW....

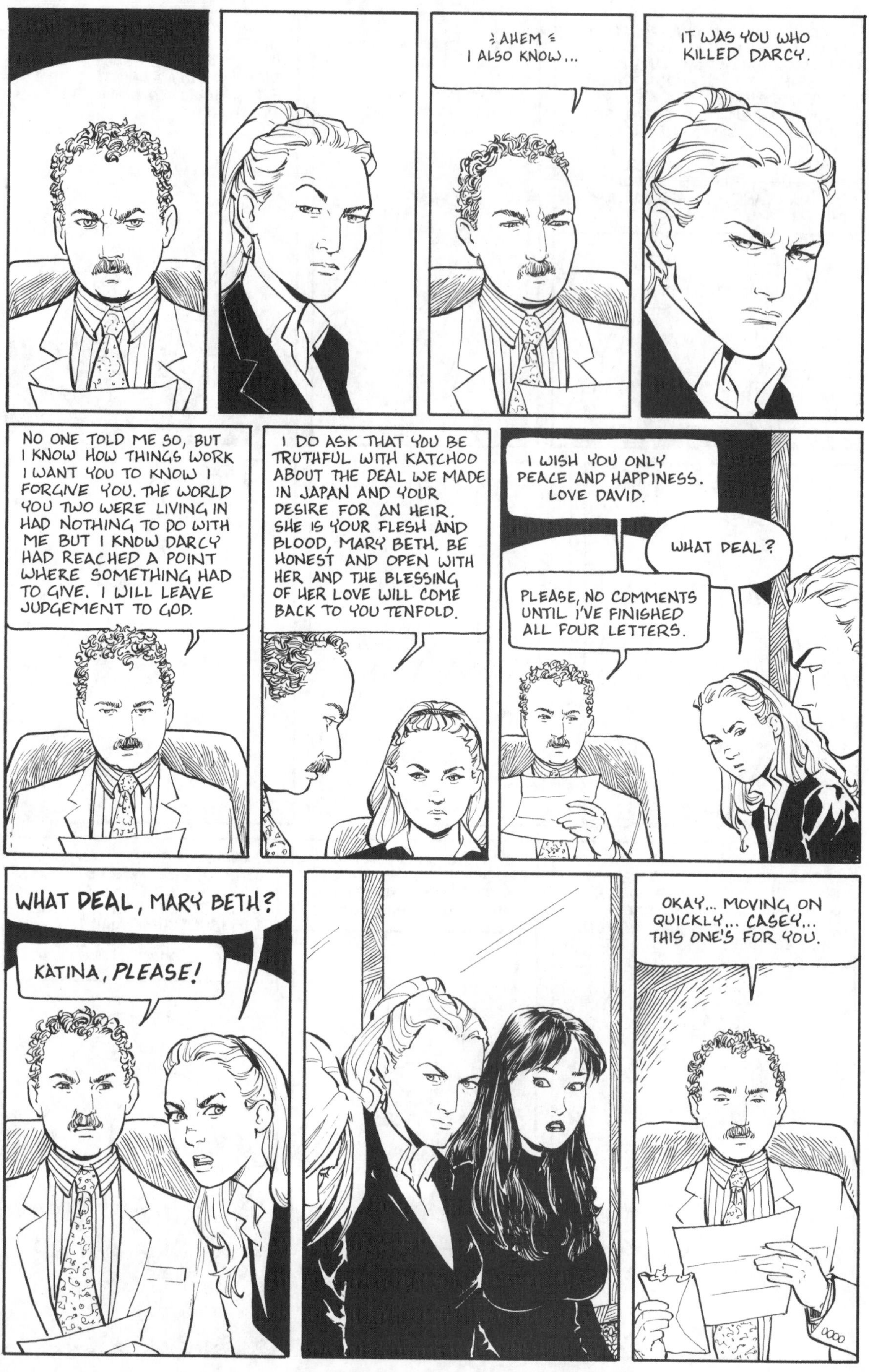

≈AHEM≈ I ALSO KNOW...
IT WAS YOU WHO KILLED DARCY.
NO ONE TOLD ME SO, BUT I KNOW HOW THINGS WORK I WANT YOU TO KNOW I FORGIVE YOU. THE WORLD YOU TWO WERE LIVING IN HAD NOTHING TO DO WITH ME BUT I KNOW DARCY HAD REACHED A POINT WHERE SOMETHING HAD TO GIVE. I WILL LEAVE JUDGEMENT TO GOD.
I DO ASK THAT YOU BE TRUTHFUL WITH KATCHOO ABOUT THE DEAL WE MADE IN JAPAN AND YOUR DESIRE FOR AN HEIR. SHE IS YOUR FLESH AND BLOOD, MARY BETH. BE HONEST AND OPEN WITH HER AND THE BLESSING OF HER LOVE WILL COME BACK TO YOU TENFOLD.
I WISH YOU ONLY PEACE AND HAPPINESS. LOVE DAVID.
WHAT DEAL?
PLEASE, NO COMMENTS UNTIL I'VE FINISHED ALL FOUR LETTERS.
WHAT DEAL, MARY BETH?
KATINA, *PLEASE!*
OKAY... MOVING ON QUICKLY... CASEY... THIS ONE'S FOR YOU.

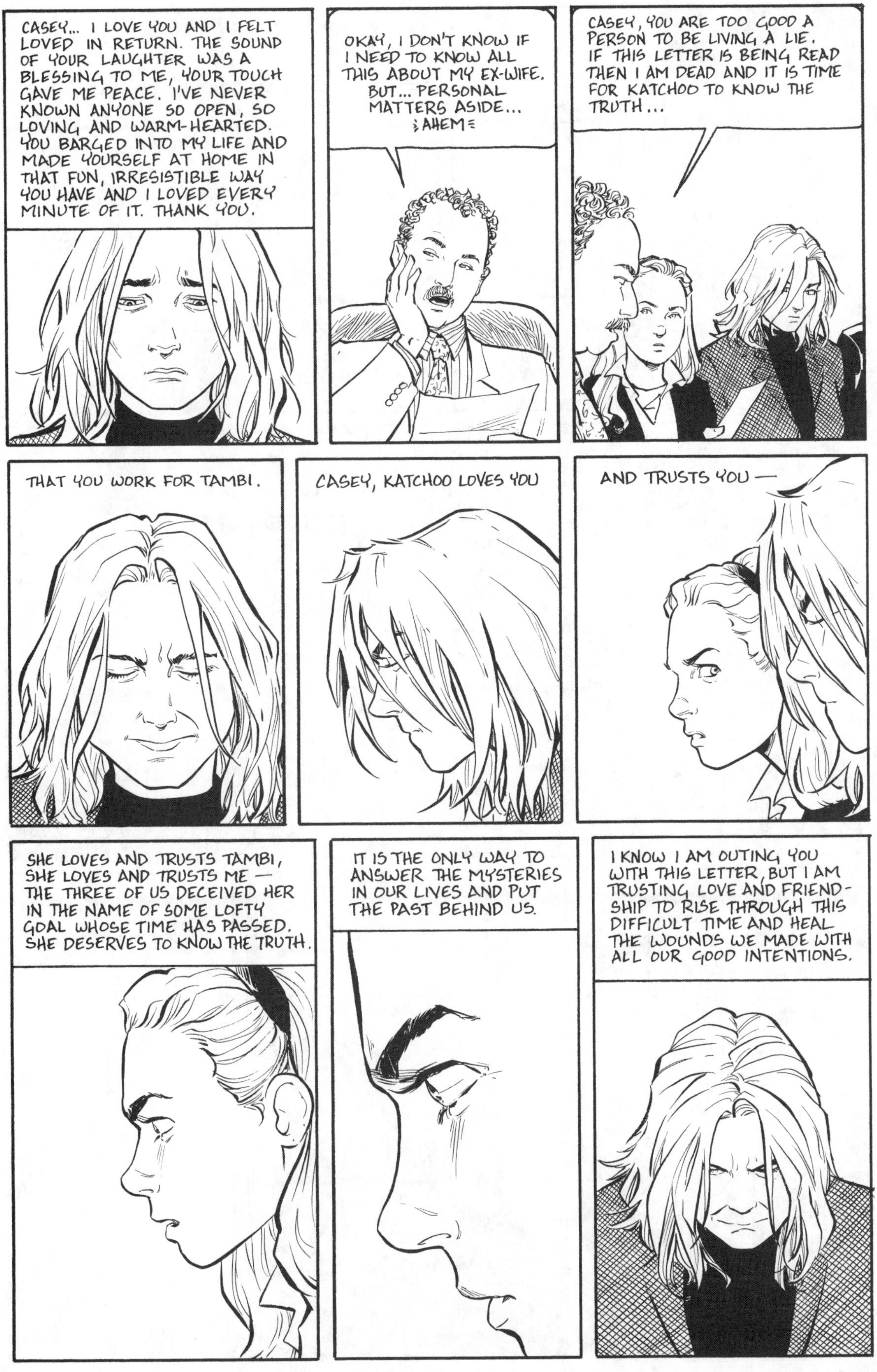
CASEY... I LOVE YOU AND I FELT LOVED IN RETURN. THE SOUND OF YOUR LAUGHTER WAS A BLESSING TO ME, YOUR TOUCH GAVE ME PEACE. I'VE NEVER KNOWN ANYONE SO OPEN, SO LOVING AND WARM-HEARTED. YOU BARGED INTO MY LIFE AND MADE YOURSELF AT HOME IN THAT FUN, IRRESISTIBLE WAY YOU HAVE AND I LOVED EVERY MINUTE OF IT. THANK YOU.
OKAY, I DON'T KNOW IF I NEED TO KNOW ALL THIS ABOUT MY EX-WIFE. BUT... PERSONAL MATTERS ASIDE... AHEM
CASEY, YOU ARE TOO GOOD A PERSON TO BE LIVING A LIE. IF THIS LETTER IS BEING READ THEN I AM DEAD AND IT IS TIME FOR KATCHOO TO KNOW THE TRUTH...
THAT YOU WORK FOR TAMBI.
CASEY, KATCHOO LOVES YOU
AND TRUSTS YOU —
SHE LOVES AND TRUSTS TAMBI, SHE LOVES AND TRUSTS ME — THE THREE OF US DECEIVED HER IN THE NAME OF SOME LOFTY GOAL WHOSE TIME HAS PASSED. SHE DESERVES TO KNOW THE TRUTH.
IT IS THE ONLY WAY TO ANSWER THE MYSTERIES IN OUR LIVES AND PUT THE PAST BEHIND US.
I KNOW I AM OUTING YOU WITH THIS LETTER, BUT I AM TRUSTING LOVE AND FRIENDSHIP TO RISE THROUGH THIS DIFFICULT TIME AND HEAL THE WOUNDS WE MADE WITH ALL OUR GOOD INTENTIONS.

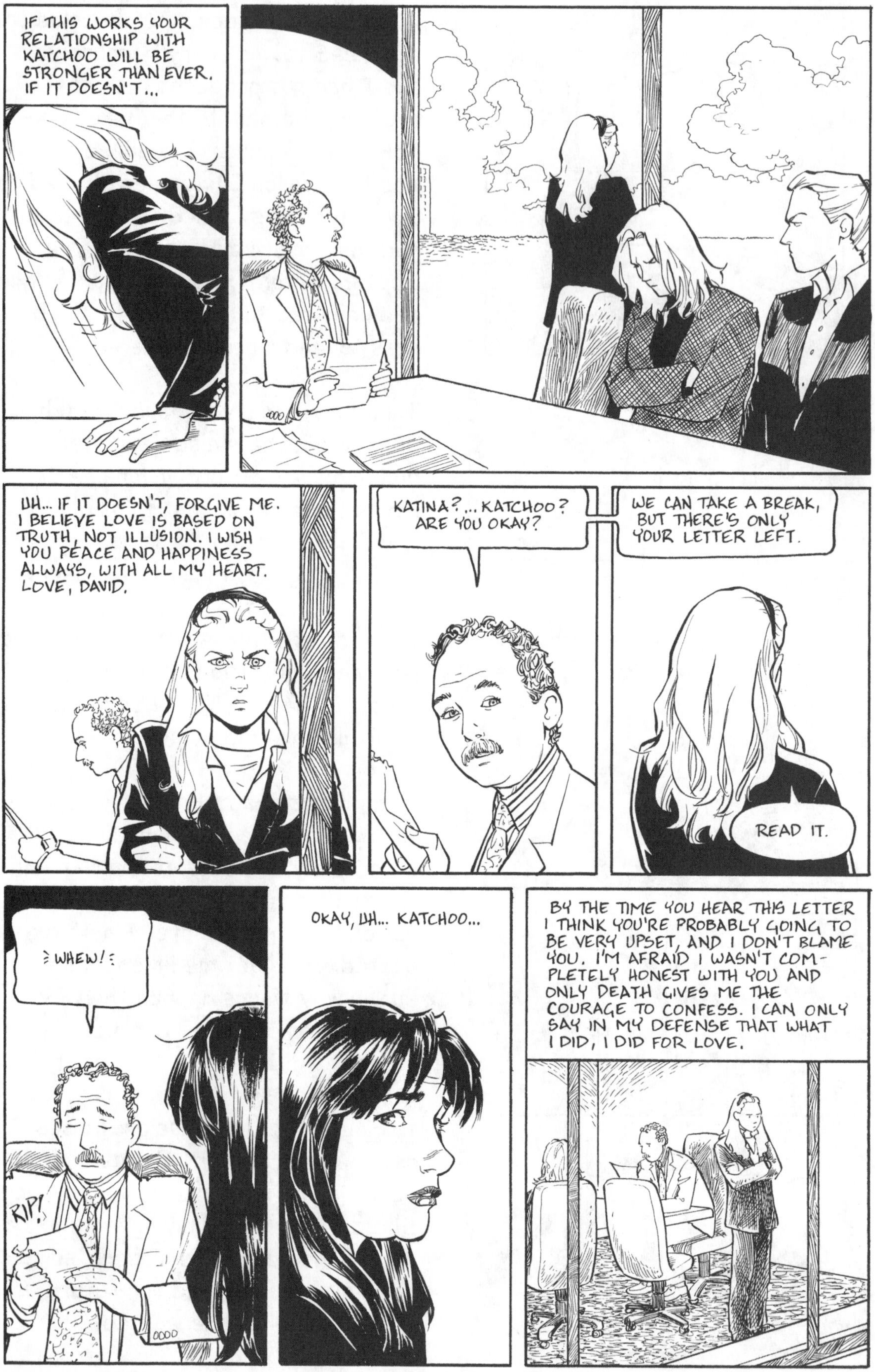

IF THIS WORKS YOUR RELATIONSHIP WITH KATCHOO WILL BE STRONGER THAN EVER. IF IT DOESN'T...
UH... IF IT DOESN'T, FORGIVE ME. I BELIEVE LOVE IS BASED ON TRUTH, NOT ILLUSION. I WISH YOU PEACE AND HAPPINESS ALWAYS, WITH ALL MY HEART. LOVE, DAVID.
KATINA?... KATCHOO? ARE YOU OKAY?
WE CAN TAKE A BREAK, BUT THERE'S ONLY YOUR LETTER LEFT.
READ IT.
WHEW!
RIP!
OKAY, UH... KATCHOO...
BY THE TIME YOU HEAR THIS LETTER I THINK YOU'RE PROBABLY GOING TO BE VERY UPSET, AND I DON'T BLAME YOU. I'M AFRAID I WASN'T COMPLETELY HONEST WITH YOU AND ONLY DEATH GIVES ME THE COURAGE TO CONFESS. I CAN ONLY SAY IN MY DEFENSE THAT WHAT I DID, I DID FOR LOVE.

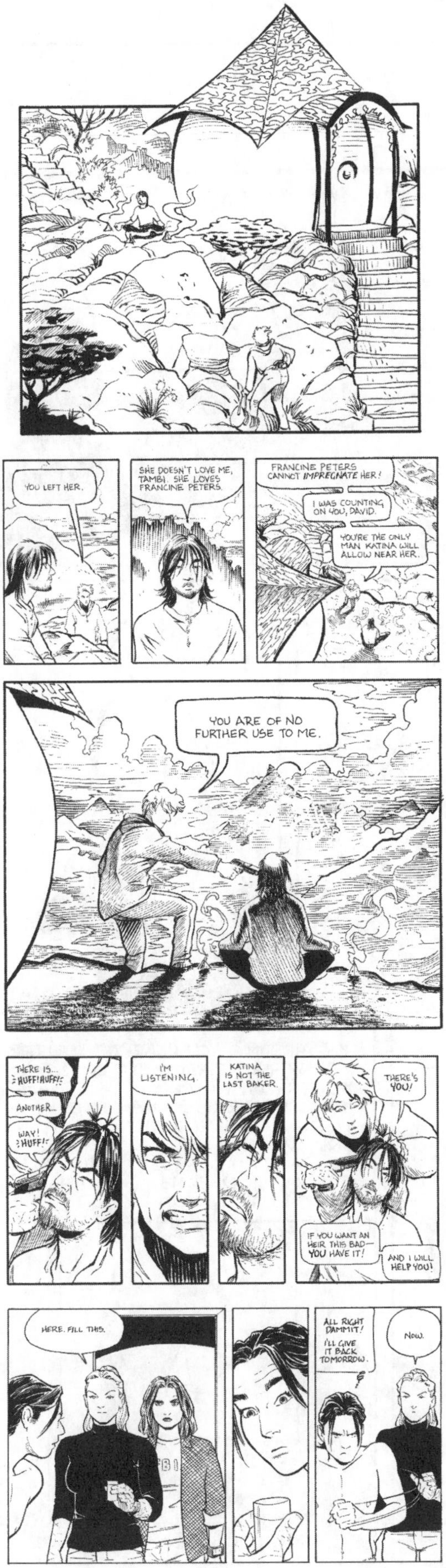
YOU LEFT HER.
SHE DOESN'T LOVE ME, TAMBI. SHE LOVES FRANCINE PETERS.
FRANCINE PETERS CANNOT *IMPREGNATE* HER!
I WAS COUNTING ON YOU, DAVID.
YOU'RE THE ONLY MAN KATINA WILL ALLOW NEAR HER.
YOU ARE OF NO FURTHER USE TO ME.
THERE IS... HUFF! HUFF!
ANOTHER...
WAY! HUFF!
I'M LISTENING.
KATINA IS NOT THE LAST BAKER.
THERE'S YOU!
IF YOU WANT AN HEIR THIS BAD— YOU HAVE IT!
AND I WILL HELP YOU!
HERE. FILL THIS.
ALL RIGHT DAMMIT!
I'LL GIVE IT BACK TOMORROW.
NOW.

When I was in Japan, Tambi came to see me. She was angry because you and I had not produced a child that could be the heir to the Baker and Takahashi families. I realized this was the reason I had been allowed to live after Darcy's death, the reason I had been allowed to get near you, and most importantly, the reason you had been allowed to leave the family business to lead a private life.

Tambi loves you very much, Katchoo, but I think she's also dedicated to building some future vision she believes to be paramount to us all. We had failed her and I was no longer useful. At gunpoint I made a deal with her: leave you to your private life and I would return to America to try and resume our relationship and hopefully produce the heir Tambi believed was so vitally important.

In all honesty Katchoo, I also offered to try and make this heir directly with Tambi, in hopes of sparing you any more drama. It was a desperate act on my part, an offer I half-expected would get me killed. Who knows why things happen the way they do sometimes. I don't understand it. All I know is, believe it or not, we did have sex and I returned to Houston under false pretenses. I assume my night with Tambi failed because she never mentioned it again. She did visit me at my apartment recently and demanded a sperm sample from me to be stored for future use. I gave her what she wanted.

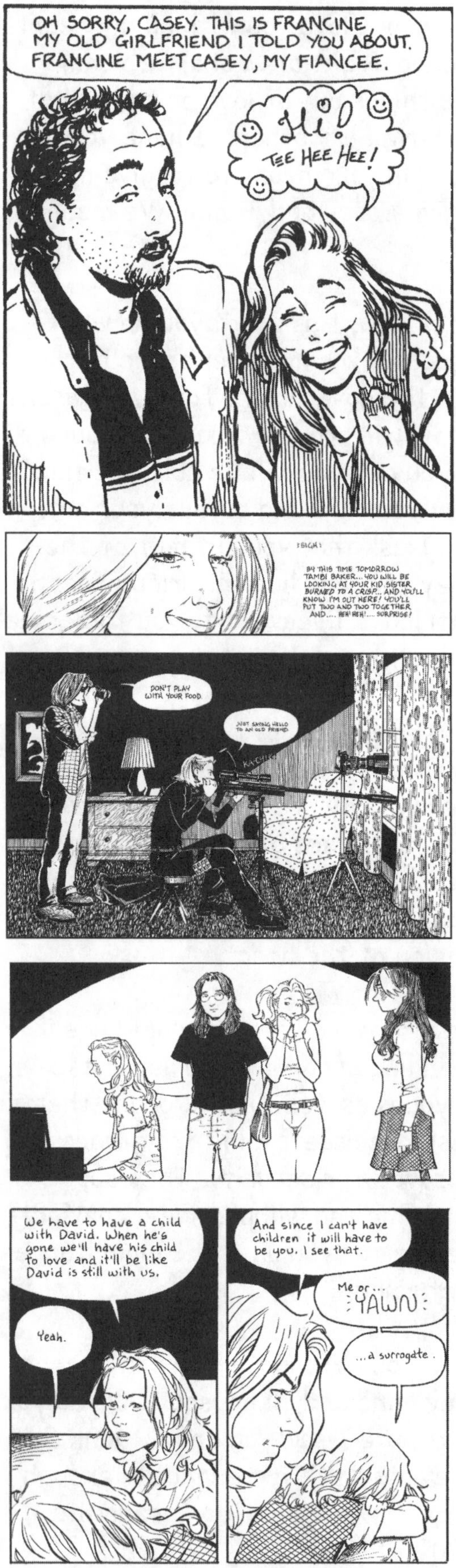
OH SORRY, CASEY. THIS IS FRANCINE, MY OLD GIRLFRIEND I TOLD YOU ABOUT. FRANCINE MEET CASEY, MY FIANCEE.
Hi! TEE HEE HEE!
:SIGH:
BY THIS TIME TOMORROW TAMBI BAKER... YOU WILL BE LOOKING AT YOUR KID SISTER BURNED TO A CRISP... AND YOU'LL KNOW I'M OUT HERE! YOU'LL PUT TWO AND TWO TOGETHER AND.... HEH! HEH!... SURPRISE!
DON'T PLAY WITH YOUR FOOD.
JUST SAYING HELLO TO AN OLD FRIEND.
We have to have a child with David. When he's gone we'll have his child to love and it'll be like David is still with us.
Yeah.
And since I can't have children it will have to be you. I see that.
Me or...
:YAWN:
...a surrogate.

Katchoo, in Japan Tambi told me Casey works for her. She's not a DUCk, she's a CPA who became bored as Tambi's accountant and asked for a field assignment. Tambi gave her us. This was back when Darcy was sending people after you, the Big Six were looking for you and everybody was worried about your safety. You might ask what good an accountant would be in a crisis, but Casey proved to be an incredibly brave person who kept your sister informed of anything suspicious that might be of danger to you. I'm sure Casey saved you from more trouble than you know. I know of one time when a former DUCk came after you and you never knew it. Casey alerted Tambi and the situation was handled by Cherry Hammer and Becky The Gun Girl. So don't be too hard on her, Katchoo. I think Casey was as honest with us as she could be and still do what she thought important, watch over you. I know she grew to love us and care for us and we felt the same for her. Don't forget that. You were never fully honest with Francine about your life, but you love her with all your heart, don't you? Remember that in the coming weeks as you guys talk and work things out. I would never have said anything if I didn't truly believe you would all be closer once the truth was known and put in the past. True peace and happiness can never come from a lie, and my only prayer for you now is peace and happiness.

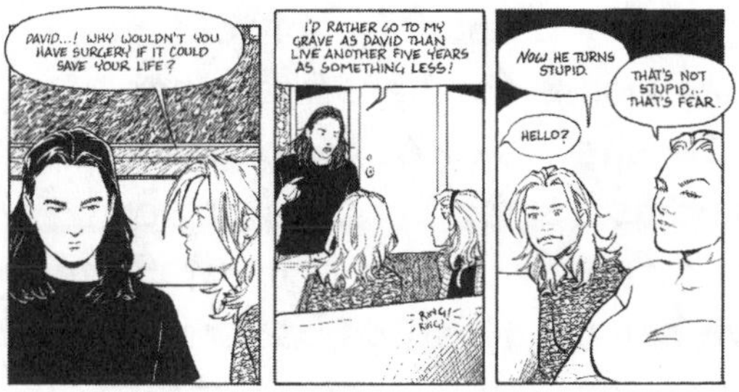
DAVID...! WHY WOULDN'T YOU HAVE SURGERY IF IT COULD SAVE YOUR LIFE?
I'D RATHER GO TO MY GRAVE AS DAVID THAN LIVE ANOTHER FIVE YEARS AS SOMETHING LESS!
RING! RING!
NOW HE TURNS STUPID.
HELLO?
THAT'S NOT STUPID... THAT'S FEAR.

You know I love you with all my heart, Katchoo. Right or wrong, we've all done things out of love or faith that may have hurt others. I hope you can find it in your heart to forgive me, forgive Casey and Tambi. We meant well.

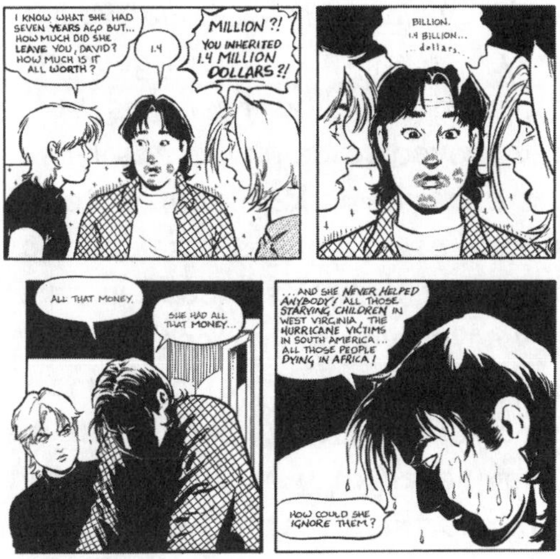
I KNOW WHAT SHE HAD SEVEN YEARS AGO BUT... HOW MUCH DID SHE LEAVE YOU, DAVID? HOW MUCH IS IT ALL WORTH?
1.4
MILLION?! YOU INHERITED 1.4 MILLION DOLLARS?!
BILLION. 1.4 BILLION... dollars.
ALL THAT MONEY.
SHE HAD ALL THAT MONEY...
...AND SHE NEVER HELPED ANYBODY! ALL THOSE STARVING CHILDREN IN WEST VIRGINIA, THE HURRICANE VICTIMS IN SOUTH AMERICA... ALL THOSE PEOPLE DYING IN AFRICA!
HOW COULD SHE IGNORE THEM?

As for now, I ask that you do what you can to win my inheritance back from the government for two reasons. One, it will provide financial security for you and you will be able to relax, enjoy your life and pursue your art. Two, I ask that you put half of the money towards humanitarian efforts in Africa. I'll leave it to you to decide the best route for that.

I've thought about it and decided I don't want a traditional burial. Please have my body cremated and take my ashes to a place of natural beauty and spread them there. Where this happens I leave to you. I think it will be a decision of the heart.

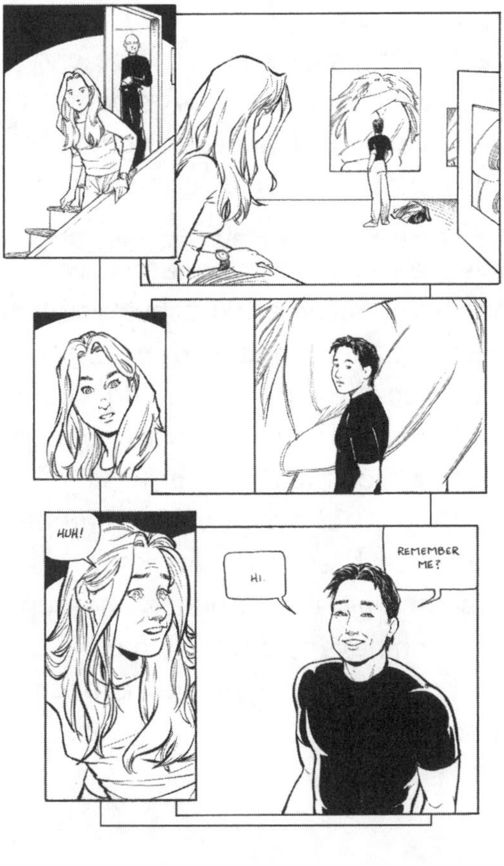
HUH!
HI.
REMEMBER ME?

I've left you a list of my holdings in Japan under my given name. These are yours as well. Don't forget them. These are assets I hid from Darcy and saved for security. They supported me and will provide a comfortable life for you until the inheritance is returned .

I love you Katchoo, with all my heart, all my mind and all my soul. I loved you the minute I saw you and I thank God for every day I've been lucky enough to spend with you. I don't regret a minute of it.

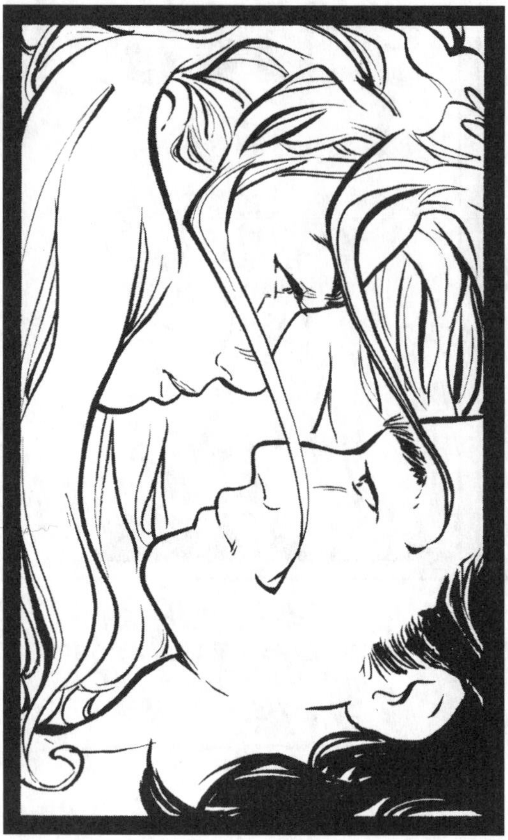

Thank you for sharing your life with me. Thank you for loving me. My faith compels me to believe there is a life beyond the grave, life with God, life with love, and we will be together again someday. Until then I hope you have a long life, peace, love and happiness. I love you.

Katchoo, you and Francine have something special. You know it, she knows it, we all know it. Francine is your future, Katchoo, because that's where the love is. Follow the love.

David

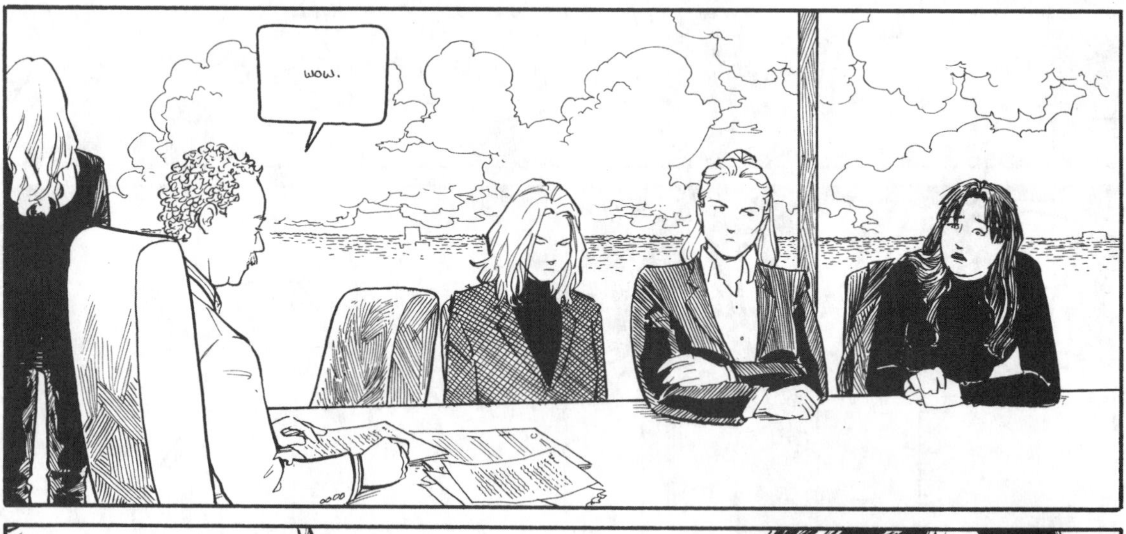
wow.

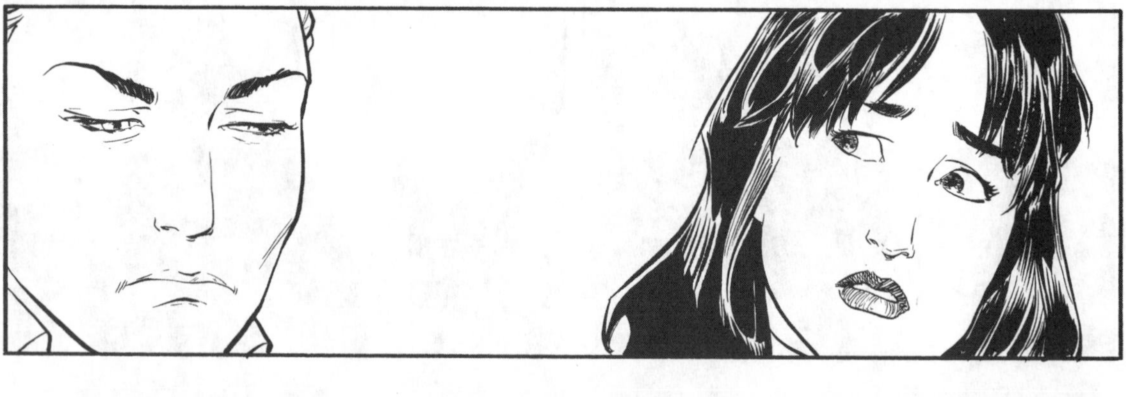

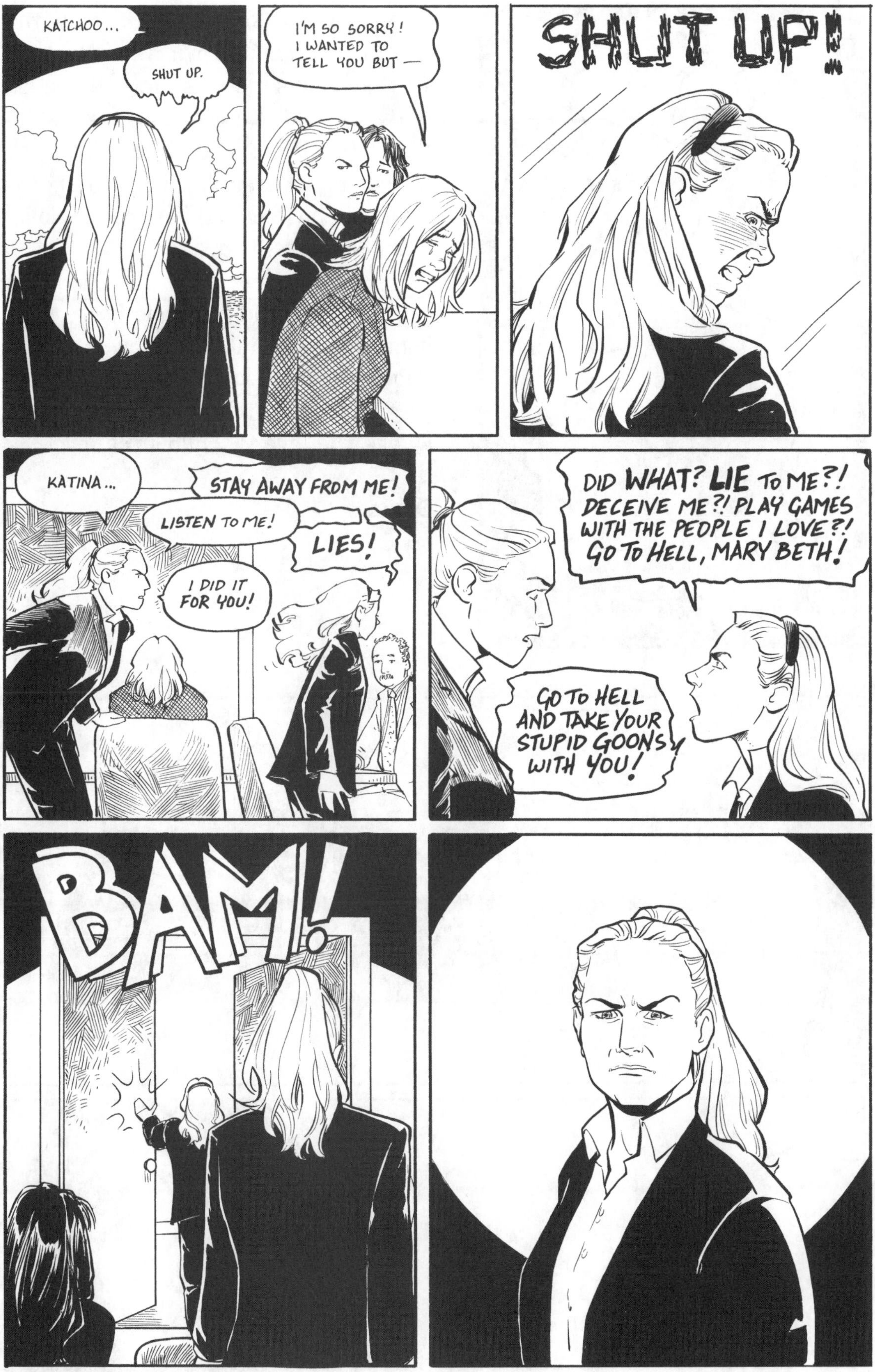
KATCHOO...
SHUT UP.
I'M SO SORRY! I WANTED TO TELL YOU BUT —
SHUT UP!
KATINA...
STAY AWAY FROM ME!
LISTEN TO ME!
LIES!
I DID IT FOR YOU!
DID WHAT? LIE TO ME?! DECEIVE ME?! PLAY GAMES WITH THE PEOPLE I LOVE?! GO TO HELL, MARY BETH!
GO TO HELL AND TAKE YOUR STUPID GOONS WITH YOU!
BAM!

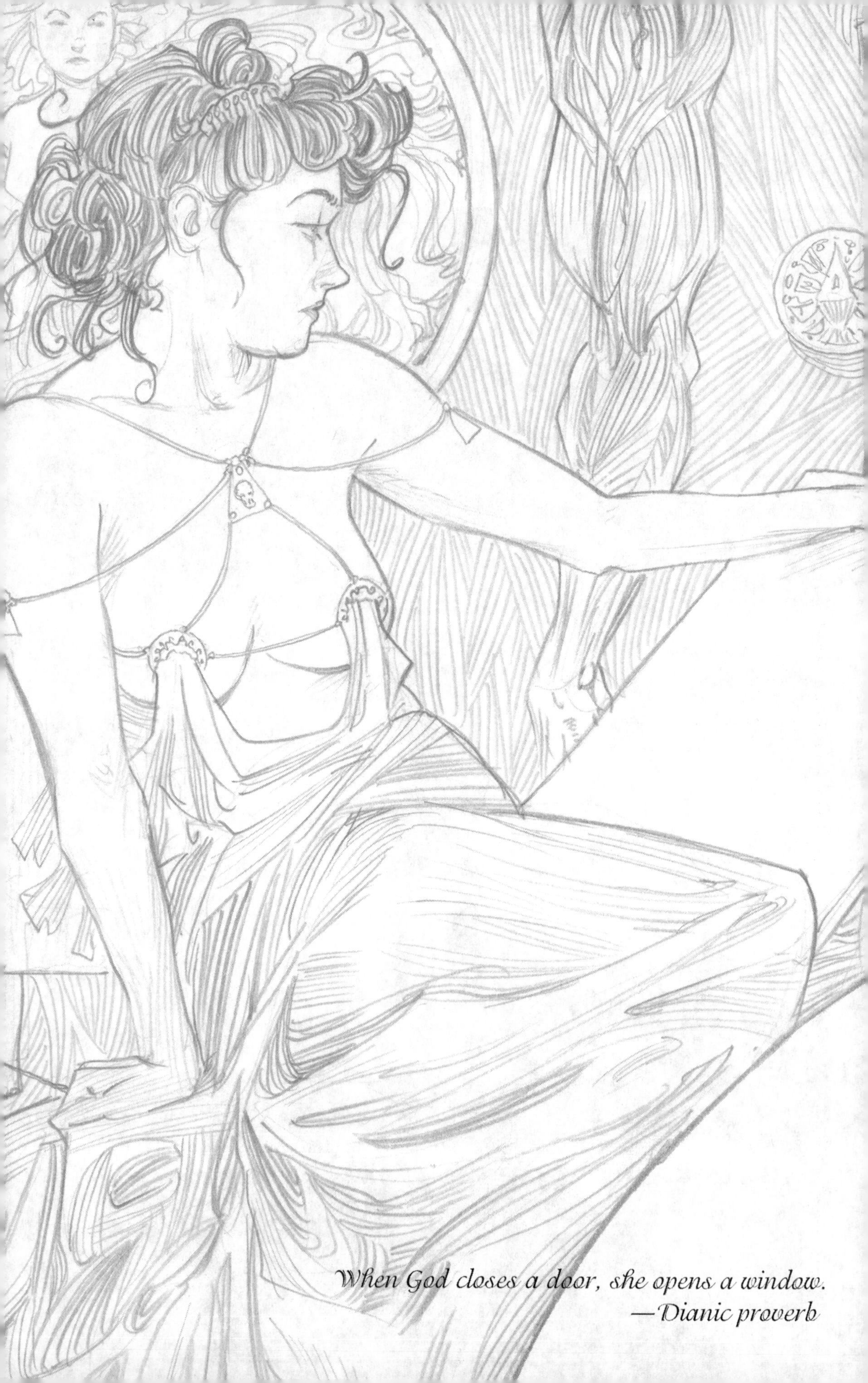

When God closes a door, she opens a window.
—Dianic proverb

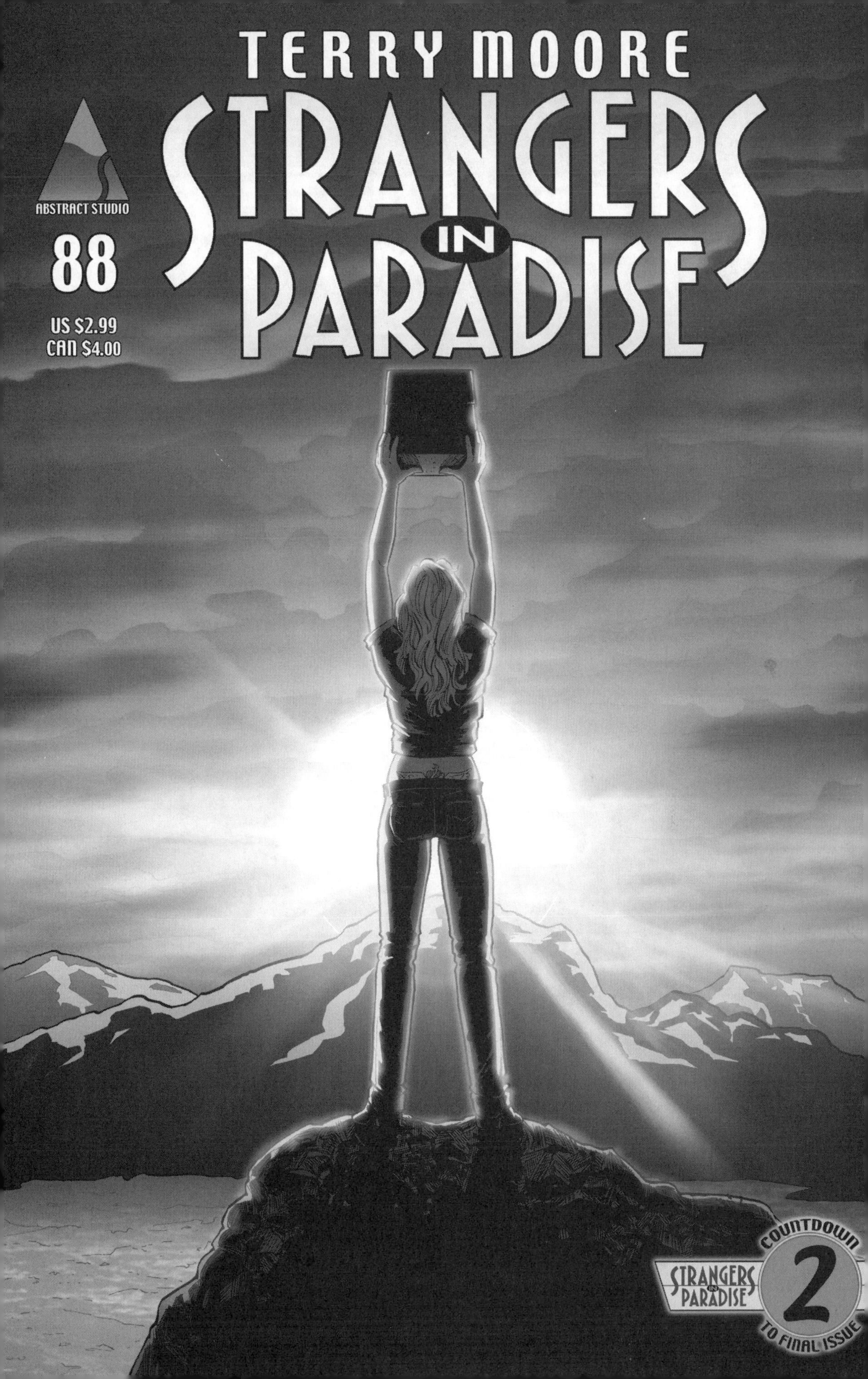
TERRY MOORE
STRANGERS IN PARADISE
ABSTRACT STUDIO
88
US $2.99
CAN $4.00
COUNTDOWN
STRANGERS IN PARADISE
2
TO FINAL ISSUE

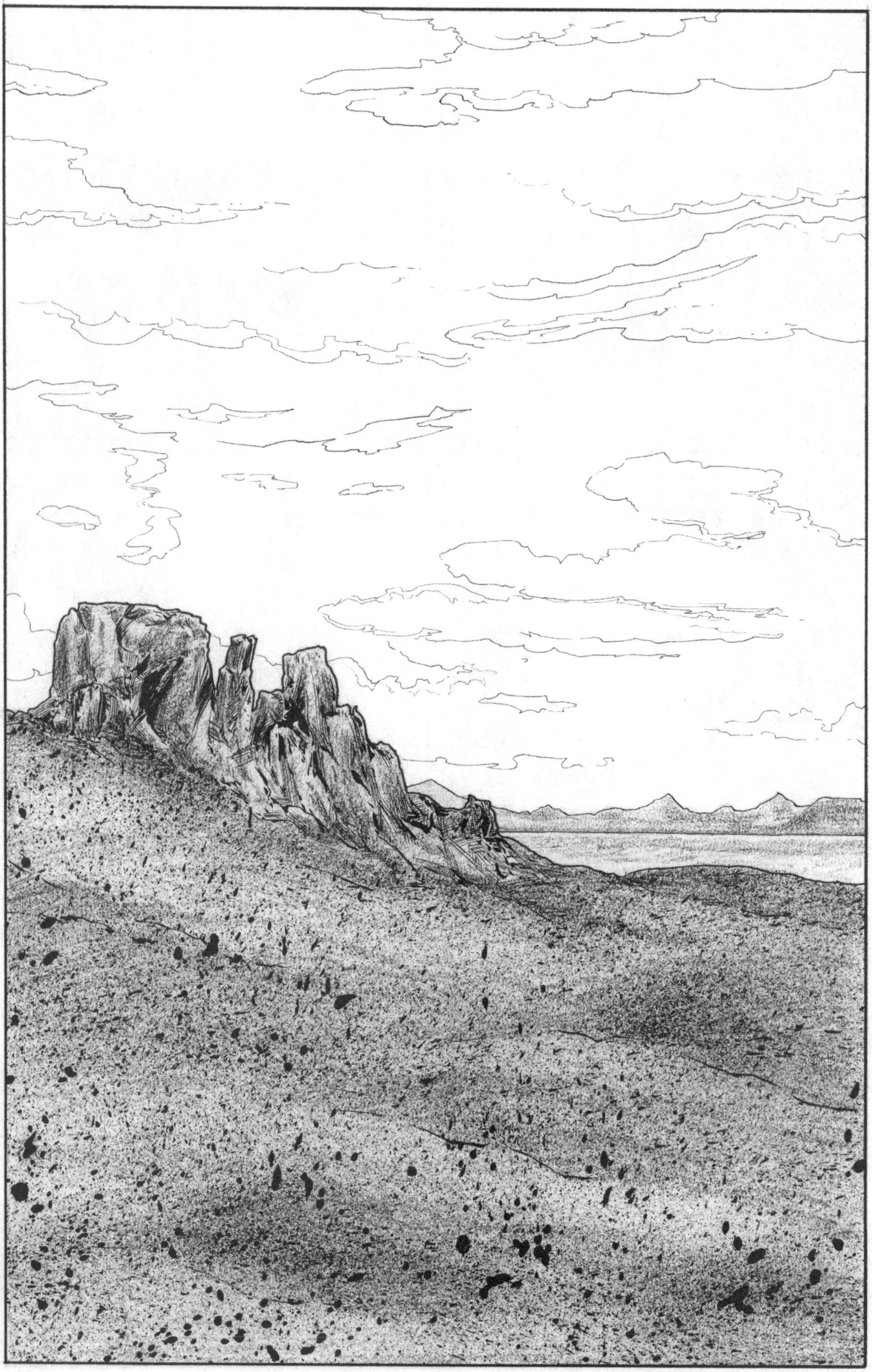

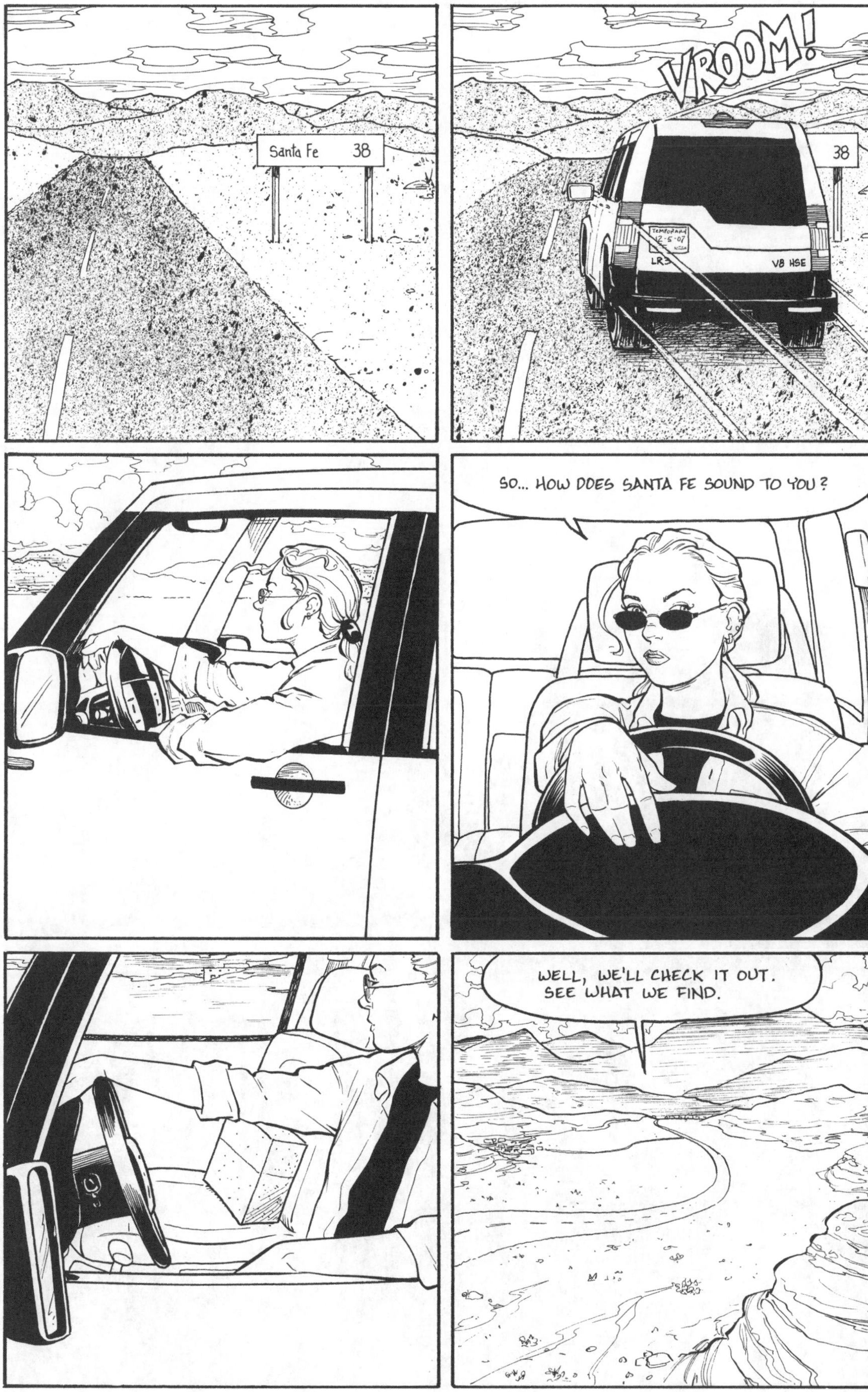
Santa Fe 38
VROOM!
38
TEMPORARY 12-5-07
LR3
V8 HSE
SO... HOW DOES SANTA FE SOUND TO YOU?
WELL, WE'LL CHECK IT OUT. SEE WHAT WE FIND.

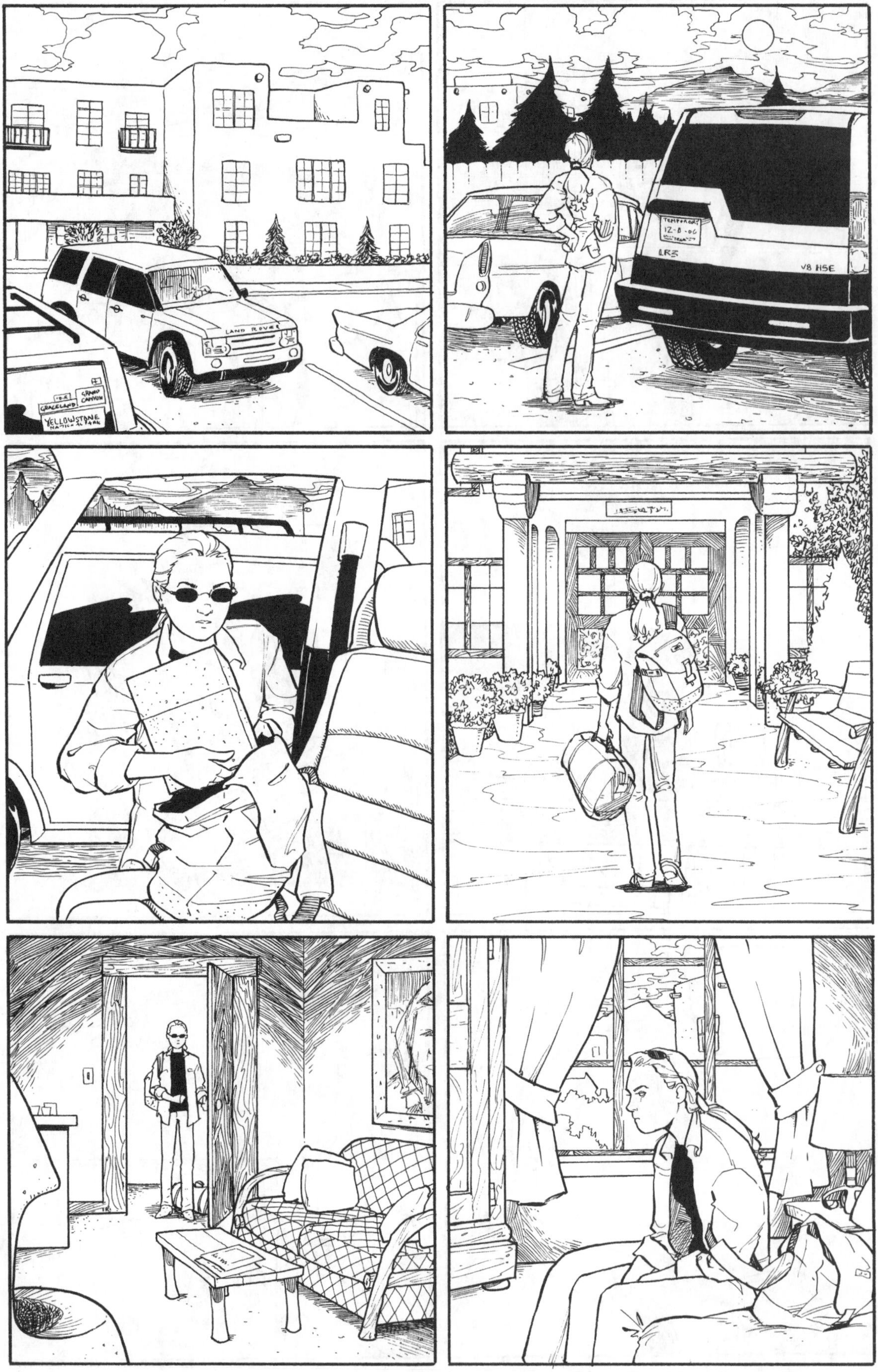
LAND ROVER
GRACELAND
GRAND CANYON
YELLOWSTONE NATIONAL PARK
V8 HSE

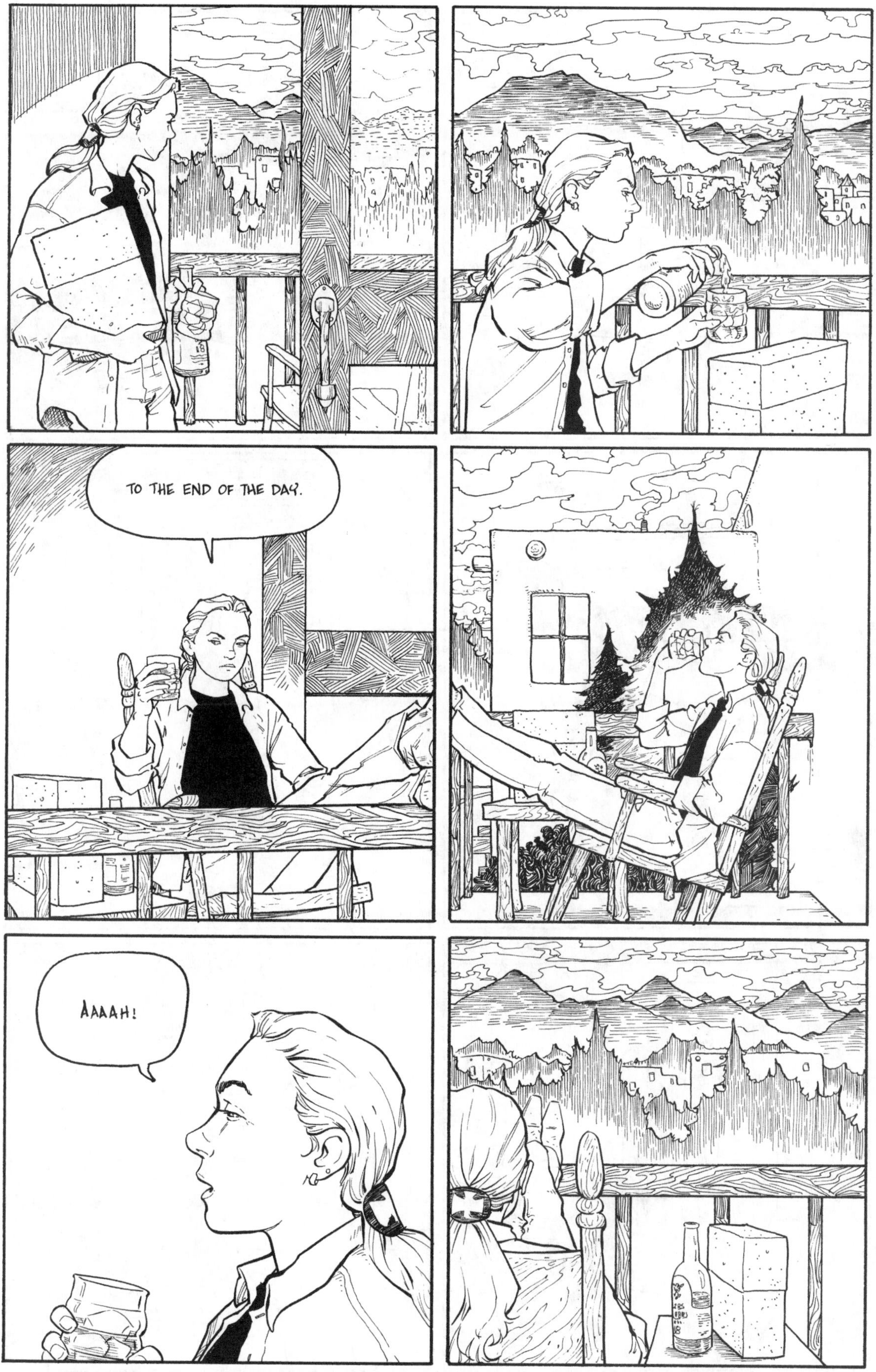
TO THE END OF THE DAY.
AAAAH!

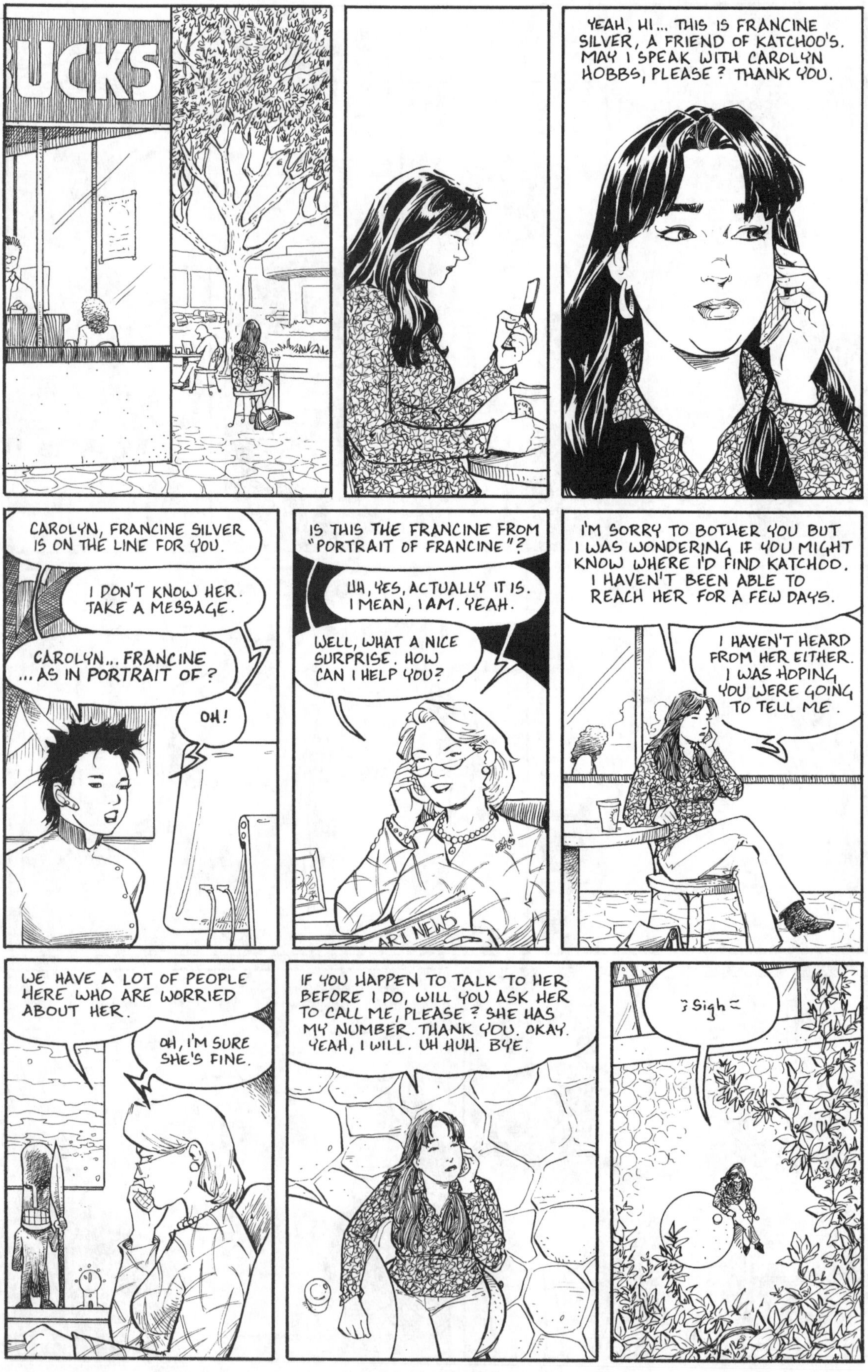
BUCKS
YEAH, HI... THIS IS FRANCINE SILVER, A FRIEND OF KATCHOO'S. MAY I SPEAK WITH CAROLYN HOBBS, PLEASE? THANK YOU.
CAROLYN, FRANCINE SILVER IS ON THE LINE FOR YOU.
I DON'T KNOW HER. TAKE A MESSAGE.
CAROLYN... FRANCINE ...AS IN PORTRAIT OF?
OH!
IS THIS THE FRANCINE FROM "PORTRAIT OF FRANCINE"?
UH, YES, ACTUALLY IT IS. I MEAN, I AM. YEAH.
WELL, WHAT A NICE SURPRISE. HOW CAN I HELP YOU?
ART NEWS
I'M SORRY TO BOTHER YOU BUT I WAS WONDERING IF YOU MIGHT KNOW WHERE I'D FIND KATCHOO. I HAVEN'T BEEN ABLE TO REACH HER FOR A FEW DAYS.
I HAVEN'T HEARD FROM HER EITHER. I WAS HOPING YOU WERE GOING TO TELL ME.
WE HAVE A LOT OF PEOPLE HERE WHO ARE WORRIED ABOUT HER.
OH, I'M SURE SHE'S FINE.
IF YOU HAPPEN TO TALK TO HER BEFORE I DO, WILL YOU ASK HER TO CALL ME, PLEASE? SHE HAS MY NUMBER. THANK YOU. OKAY. YEAH, I WILL. UH HUH. BYE.
Sigh

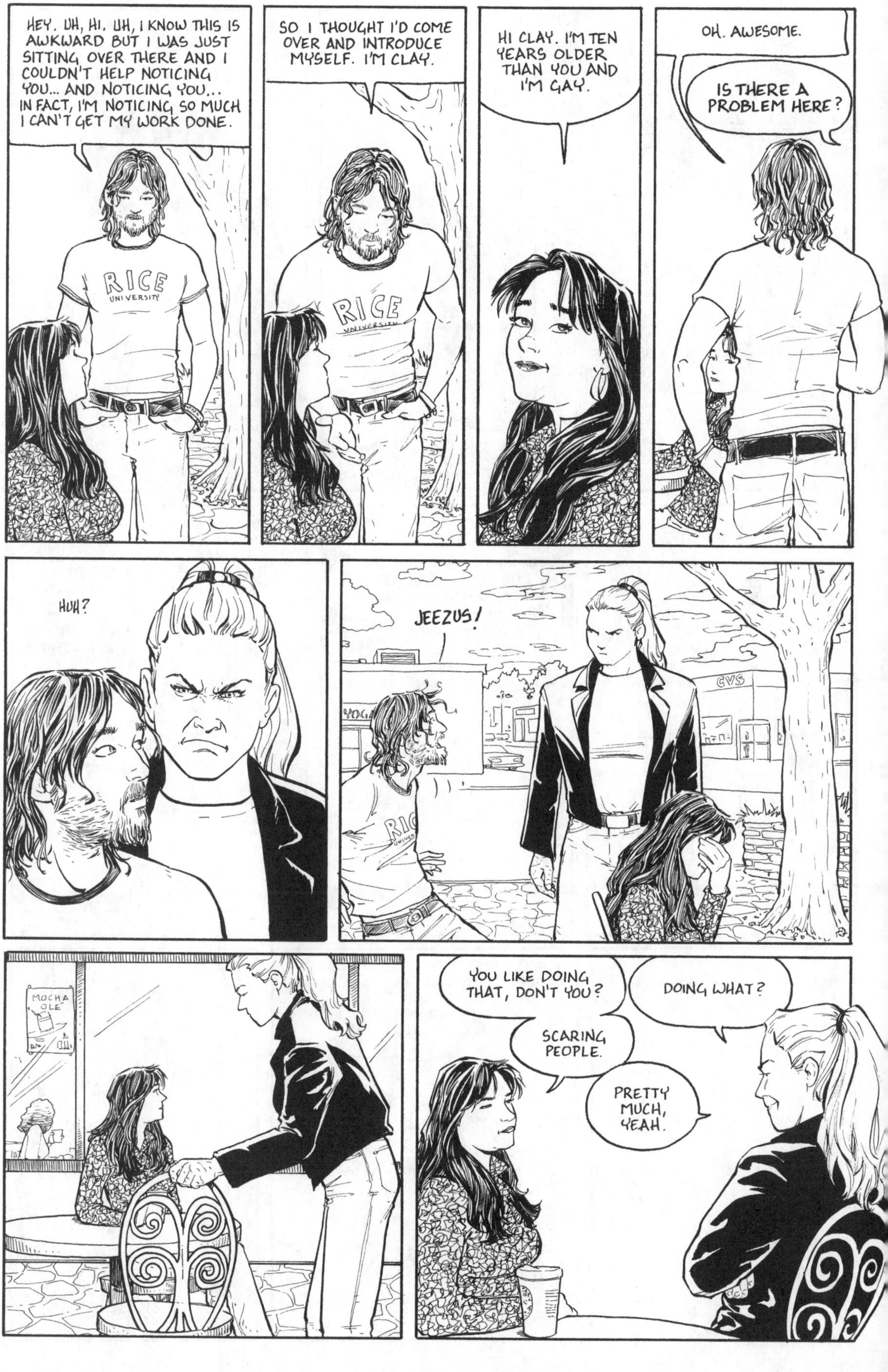
HEY. UH, HI. UH, I KNOW THIS IS AWKWARD BUT I WAS JUST SITTING OVER THERE AND I COULDN'T HELP NOTICING YOU... AND NOTICING YOU... IN FACT, I'M NOTICING SO MUCH I CAN'T GET MY WORK DONE.
RICE UNIVERSITY
SO I THOUGHT I'D COME OVER AND INTRODUCE MYSELF. I'M CLAY.
RICE UNIVERSITY
HI CLAY. I'M TEN YEARS OLDER THAN YOU AND I'M GAY.
OH. AWESOME.
IS THERE A PROBLEM HERE?
HUH?
JEEZUS!
CVS
MOCHA OLE
YOU LIKE DOING THAT, DON'T YOU?
DOING WHAT?
SCARING PEOPLE.
PRETTY MUCH, YEAH.

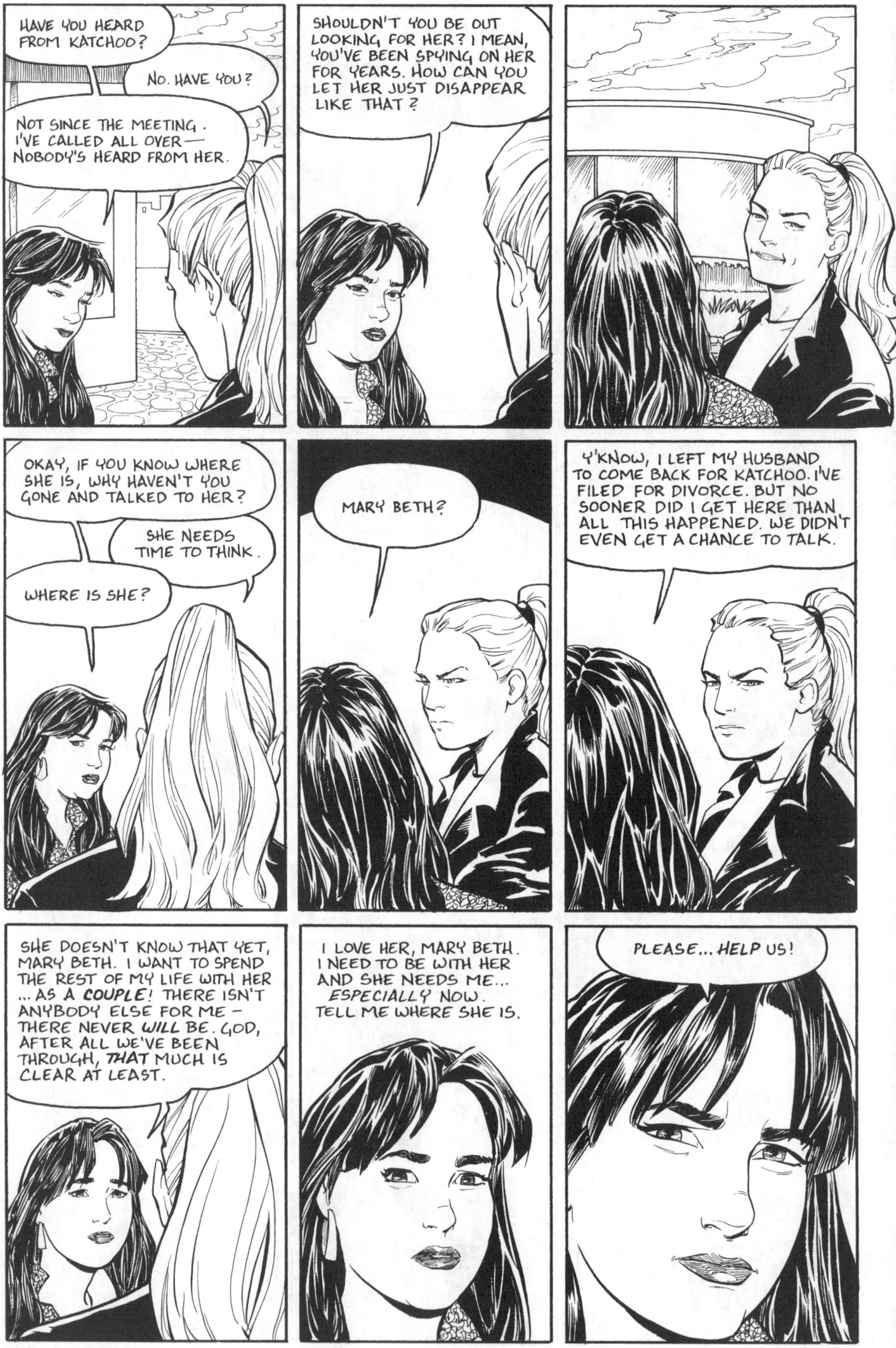
HAVE YOU HEARD FROM KATCHOO?
NO. HAVE YOU?
NOT SINCE THE MEETING. I'VE CALLED ALL OVER— NOBODY'S HEARD FROM HER.
SHOULDN'T YOU BE OUT LOOKING FOR HER? I MEAN, YOU'VE BEEN SPYING ON HER FOR YEARS. HOW CAN YOU LET HER JUST DISAPPEAR LIKE THAT?
OKAY, IF YOU KNOW WHERE SHE IS, WHY HAVEN'T YOU GONE AND TALKED TO HER?
SHE NEEDS TIME TO THINK.
WHERE IS SHE?
MARY BETH?
Y'KNOW, I LEFT MY HUSBAND TO COME BACK FOR KATCHOO. I'VE FILED FOR DIVORCE. BUT NO SOONER DID I GET HERE THAN ALL THIS HAPPENED. WE DIDN'T EVEN GET A CHANCE TO TALK.
SHE DOESN'T KNOW THAT YET, MARY BETH. I WANT TO SPEND THE REST OF MY LIFE WITH HER ...AS A *COUPLE*! THERE ISN'T ANYBODY ELSE FOR ME — THERE NEVER *WILL* BE. GOD, AFTER ALL WE'VE BEEN THROUGH, *THAT* MUCH IS CLEAR AT LEAST.
I LOVE HER, MARY BETH. I NEED TO BE WITH HER AND SHE NEEDS ME... *ESPECIALLY* NOW. TELL ME WHERE SHE IS.
PLEASE... *HELP* US!

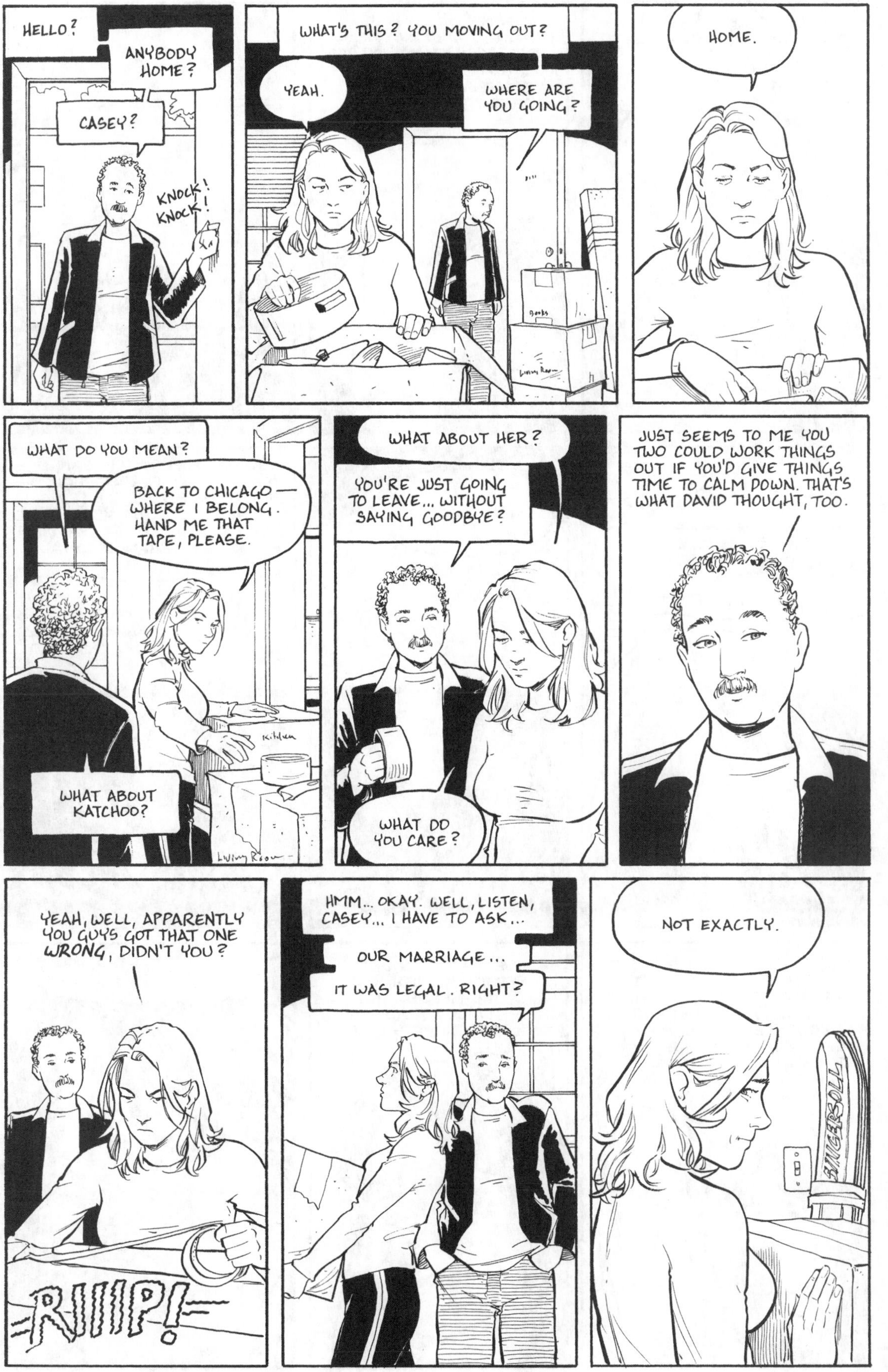
HELLO?
ANYBODY HOME?
CASEY?
KNOCK! KNOCK!
WHAT'S THIS? YOU MOVING OUT?
YEAH.
WHERE ARE YOU GOING?
HOME.
WHAT DO YOU MEAN?
BACK TO CHICAGO— WHERE I BELONG. HAND ME THAT TAPE, PLEASE.
WHAT ABOUT KATCHOO?
WHAT ABOUT HER?
YOU'RE JUST GOING TO LEAVE... WITHOUT SAYING GOODBYE?
WHAT DO YOU CARE?
JUST SEEMS TO ME YOU TWO COULD WORK THINGS OUT IF YOU'D GIVE THINGS TIME TO CALM DOWN. THAT'S WHAT DAVID THOUGHT, TOO.
YEAH, WELL, APPARENTLY YOU GUYS GOT THAT ONE WRONG, DIDN'T YOU?
RIIIP!
HMM... OKAY. WELL, LISTEN, CASEY... I HAVE TO ASK...
OUR MARRIAGE...
IT WAS LEGAL. RIGHT?
NOT EXACTLY.

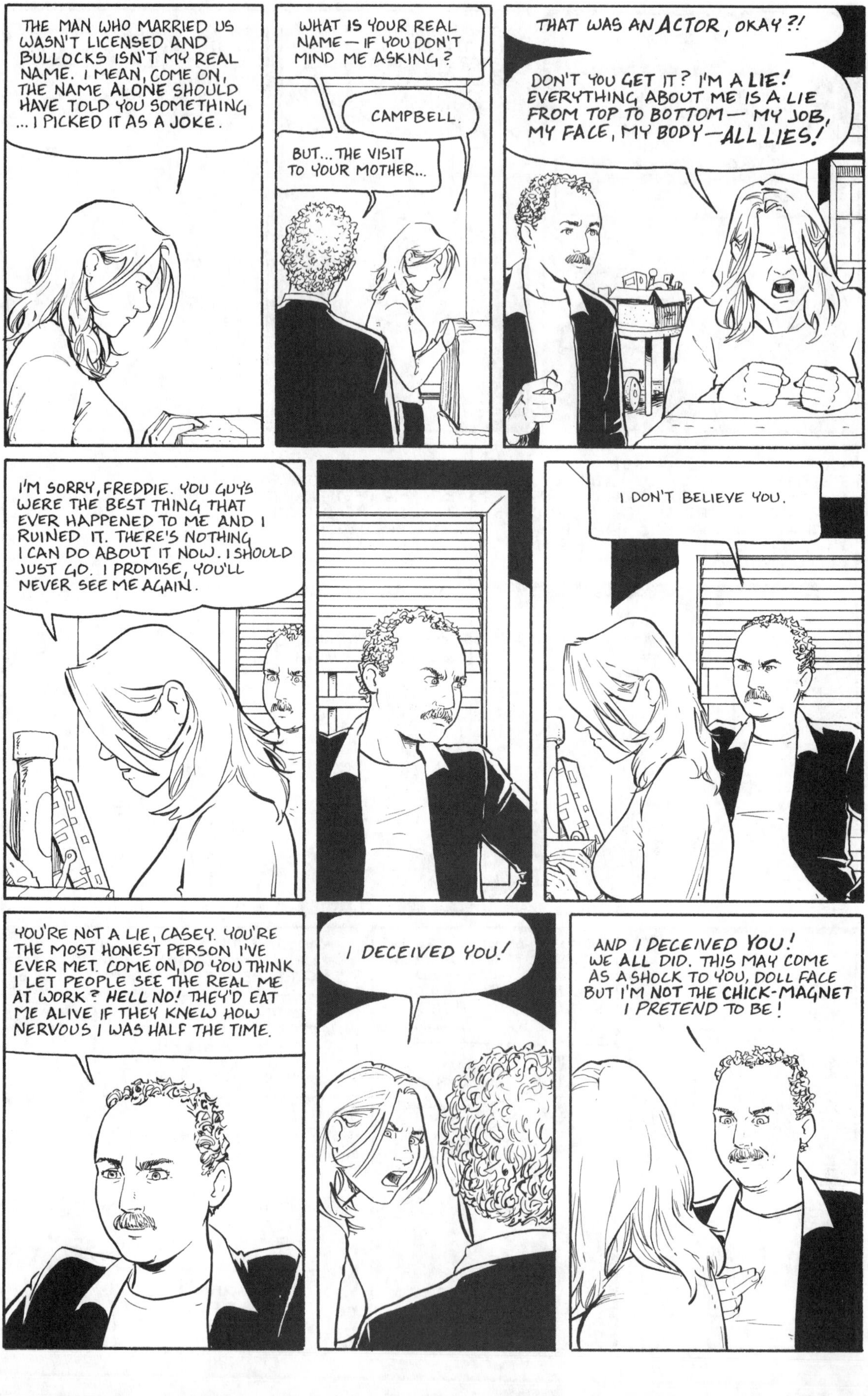
THE MAN WHO MARRIED US WASN'T LICENSED AND BULLOCKS ISN'T MY REAL NAME. I MEAN, COME ON, THE NAME ALONE SHOULD HAVE TOLD YOU SOMETHING ...I PICKED IT AS A JOKE.
WHAT IS YOUR REAL NAME — IF YOU DON'T MIND ME ASKING?
CAMPBELL.
BUT... THE VISIT TO YOUR MOTHER...
THAT WAS AN ACTOR, OKAY?!
DON'T YOU GET IT? I'M A LIE! EVERYTHING ABOUT ME IS A LIE FROM TOP TO BOTTOM — MY JOB, MY FACE, MY BODY — ALL LIES!
I'M SORRY, FREDDIE. YOU GUYS WERE THE BEST THING THAT EVER HAPPENED TO ME AND I RUINED IT. THERE'S NOTHING I CAN DO ABOUT IT NOW. I SHOULD JUST GO. I PROMISE, YOU'LL NEVER SEE ME AGAIN.
I DON'T BELIEVE YOU.
YOU'RE NOT A LIE, CASEY. YOU'RE THE MOST HONEST PERSON I'VE EVER MET. COME ON, DO YOU THINK I LET PEOPLE SEE THE REAL ME AT WORK? HELL NO! THEY'D EAT ME ALIVE IF THEY KNEW HOW NERVOUS I WAS HALF THE TIME.
I DECEIVED YOU!
AND I DECEIVED YOU! WE ALL DID. THIS MAY COME AS A SHOCK TO YOU, DOLL FACE BUT I'M NOT THE CHICK-MAGNET I PRETEND TO BE!

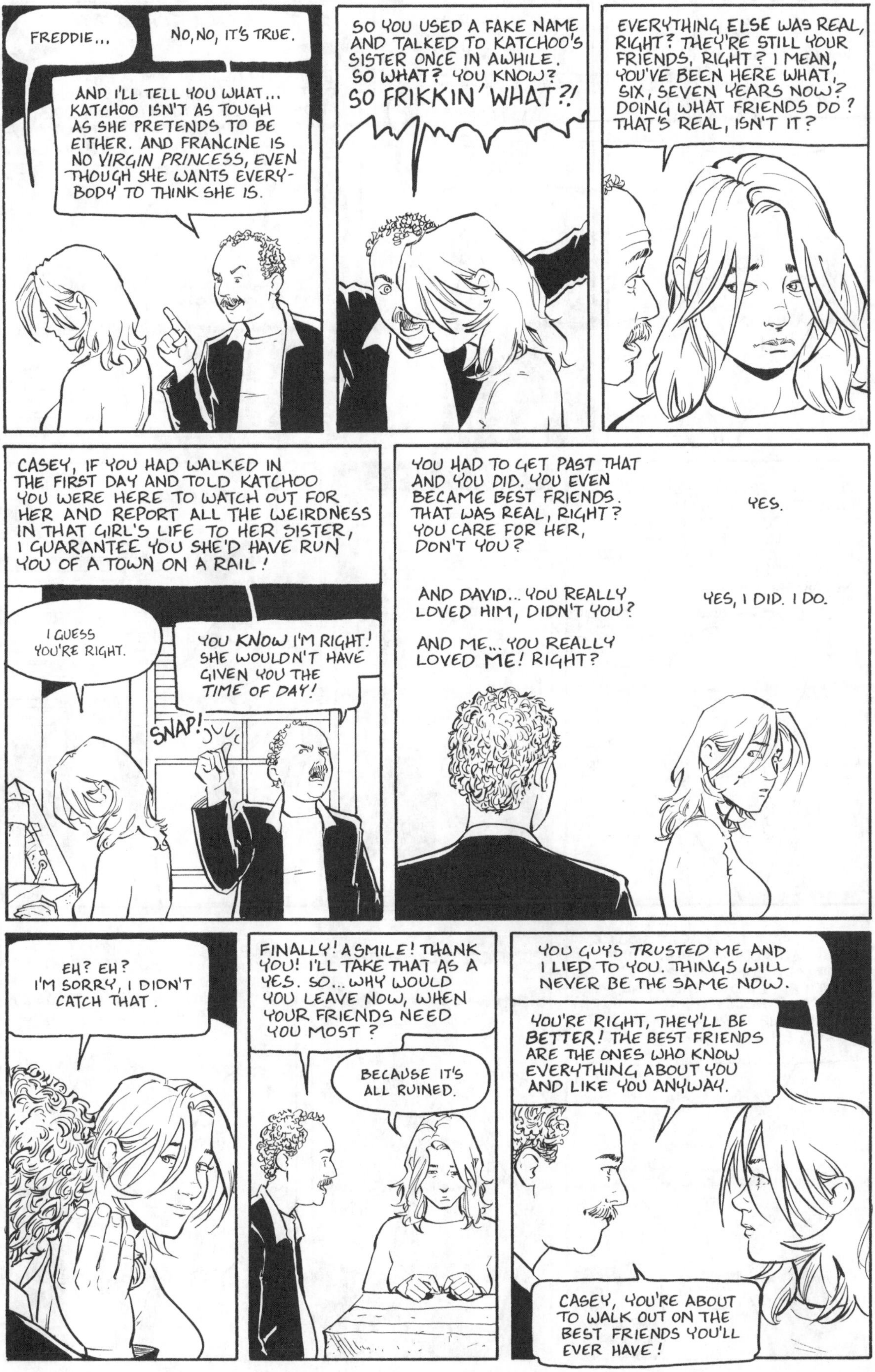
FREDDIE...
NO, NO, IT'S TRUE.
AND I'LL TELL YOU WHAT... KATCHOO ISN'T AS TOUGH AS SHE PRETENDS TO BE EITHER. AND FRANCINE IS NO VIRGIN PRINCESS, EVEN THOUGH SHE WANTS EVERYBODY TO THINK SHE IS.
SO YOU USED A FAKE NAME AND TALKED TO KATCHOO'S SISTER ONCE IN AWHILE. SO WHAT? YOU KNOW? SO FRIKKIN' WHAT?!
EVERYTHING ELSE WAS REAL, RIGHT? THEY'RE STILL YOUR FRIENDS, RIGHT? I MEAN, YOU'VE BEEN HERE WHAT, SIX, SEVEN YEARS NOW? DOING WHAT FRIENDS DO? THAT'S REAL, ISN'T IT?
CASEY, IF YOU HAD WALKED IN THE FIRST DAY AND TOLD KATCHOO YOU WERE HERE TO WATCH OUT FOR HER AND REPORT ALL THE WEIRDNESS IN THAT GIRL'S LIFE TO HER SISTER, I GUARANTEE YOU SHE'D HAVE RUN YOU OF A TOWN ON A RAIL!
I GUESS YOU'RE RIGHT.
YOU KNOW I'M RIGHT! SHE WOULDN'T HAVE GIVEN YOU THE TIME OF DAY!
SNAP!
YOU HAD TO GET PAST THAT AND YOU DID. YOU EVEN BECAME BEST FRIENDS. THAT WAS REAL, RIGHT? YOU CARE FOR HER, DON'T YOU?
YES.
AND DAVID... YOU REALLY LOVED HIM, DIDN'T YOU?
YES, I DID. I DO.
AND ME... YOU REALLY LOVED ME! RIGHT?
EH? EH? I'M SORRY, I DIDN'T CATCH THAT.
FINALLY! A SMILE! THANK YOU! I'LL TAKE THAT AS A YES. SO... WHY WOULD YOU LEAVE NOW, WHEN YOUR FRIENDS NEED YOU MOST?
BECAUSE IT'S ALL RUINED.
YOU GUYS TRUSTED ME AND I LIED TO YOU. THINGS WILL NEVER BE THE SAME NOW.
YOU'RE RIGHT, THEY'LL BE BETTER! THE BEST FRIENDS ARE THE ONES WHO KNOW EVERYTHING ABOUT YOU AND LIKE YOU ANYWAY.
CASEY, YOU'RE ABOUT TO WALK OUT ON THE BEST FRIENDS YOU'LL EVER HAVE!

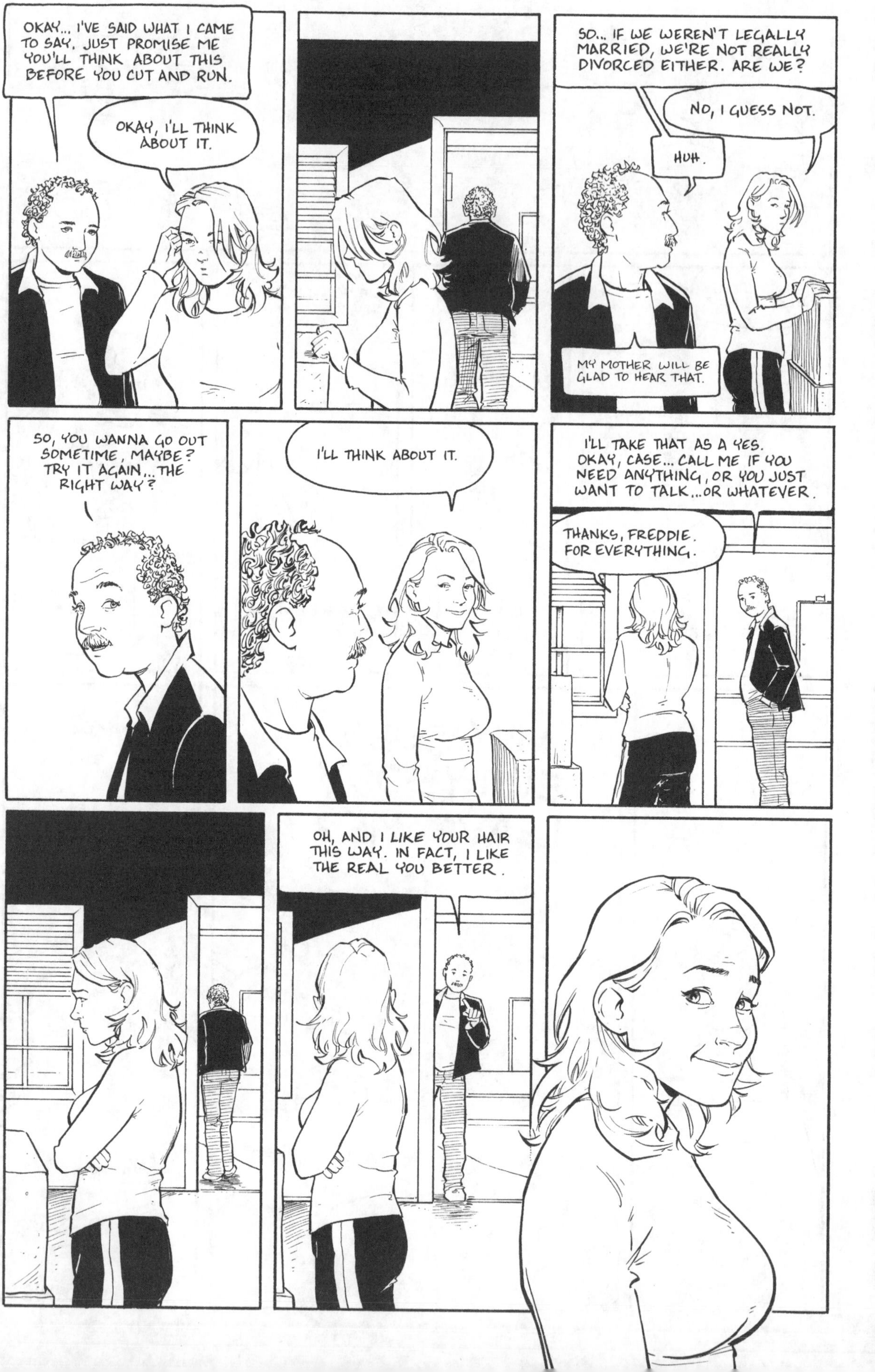
OKAY... I'VE SAID WHAT I CAME TO SAY. JUST PROMISE ME YOU'LL THINK ABOUT THIS BEFORE YOU CUT AND RUN.
OKAY, I'LL THINK ABOUT IT.
SO... IF WE WEREN'T LEGALLY MARRIED, WE'RE NOT REALLY DIVORCED EITHER. ARE WE?
NO, I GUESS NOT.
HUH.
MY MOTHER WILL BE GLAD TO HEAR THAT.
SO, YOU WANNA GO OUT SOMETIME, MAYBE? TRY IT AGAIN... THE RIGHT WAY?
I'LL THINK ABOUT IT.
I'LL TAKE THAT AS A YES. OKAY, CASE... CALL ME IF YOU NEED ANYTHING, OR YOU JUST WANT TO TALK... OR WHATEVER.
THANKS, FREDDIE. FOR EVERYTHING.
OH, AND I LIKE YOUR HAIR THIS WAY. IN FACT, I LIKE THE REAL YOU BETTER.

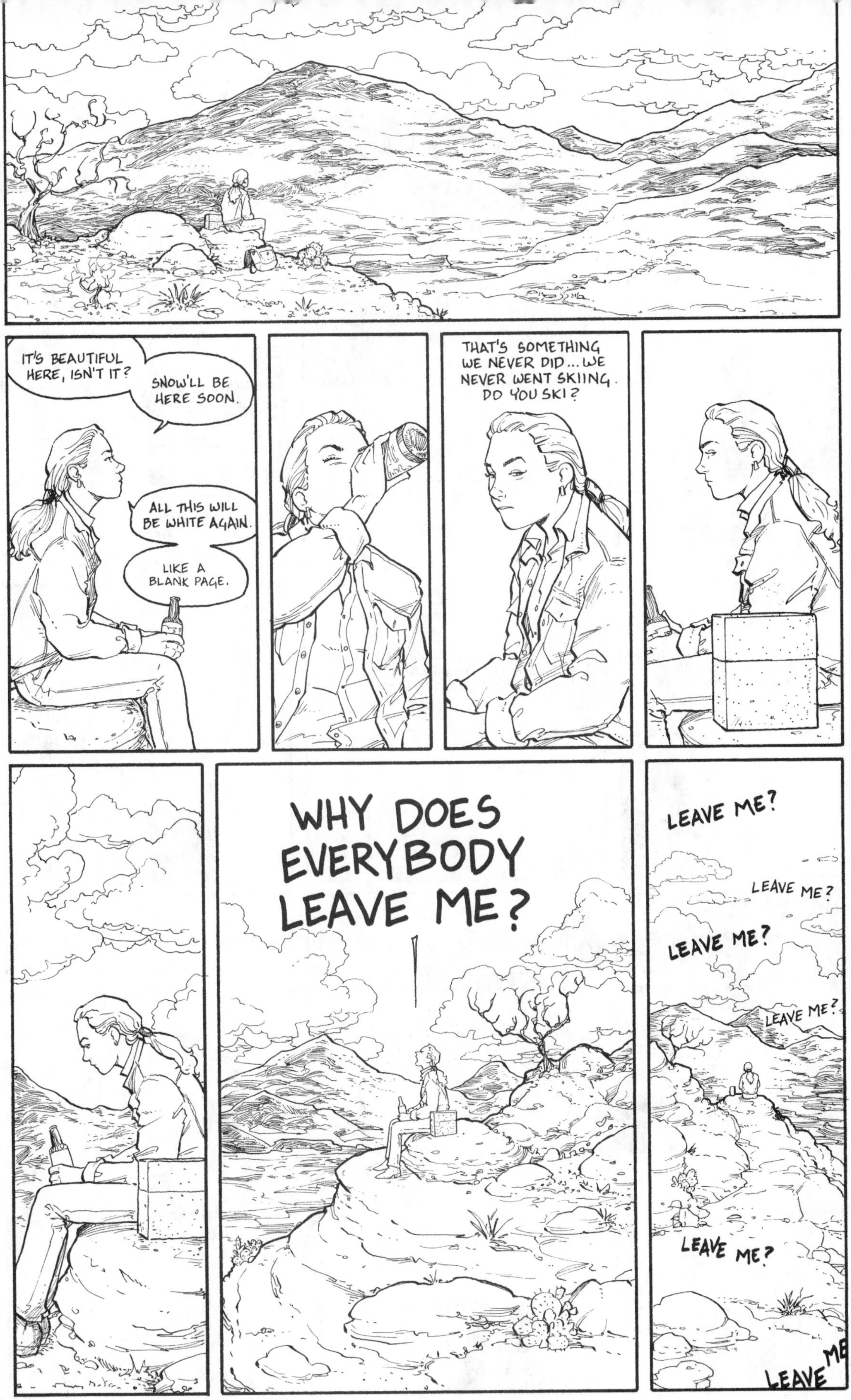
IT'S BEAUTIFUL HERE, ISN'T IT?
SNOW'LL BE HERE SOON.
ALL THIS WILL BE WHITE AGAIN.
LIKE A BLANK PAGE.
THAT'S SOMETHING WE NEVER DID... WE NEVER WENT SKIING. DO YOU SKI?
WHY DOES EVERYBODY LEAVE ME?
LEAVE ME?
LEAVE ME?
LEAVE ME?
LEAVE ME?
LEAVE ME?
LEAVE ME

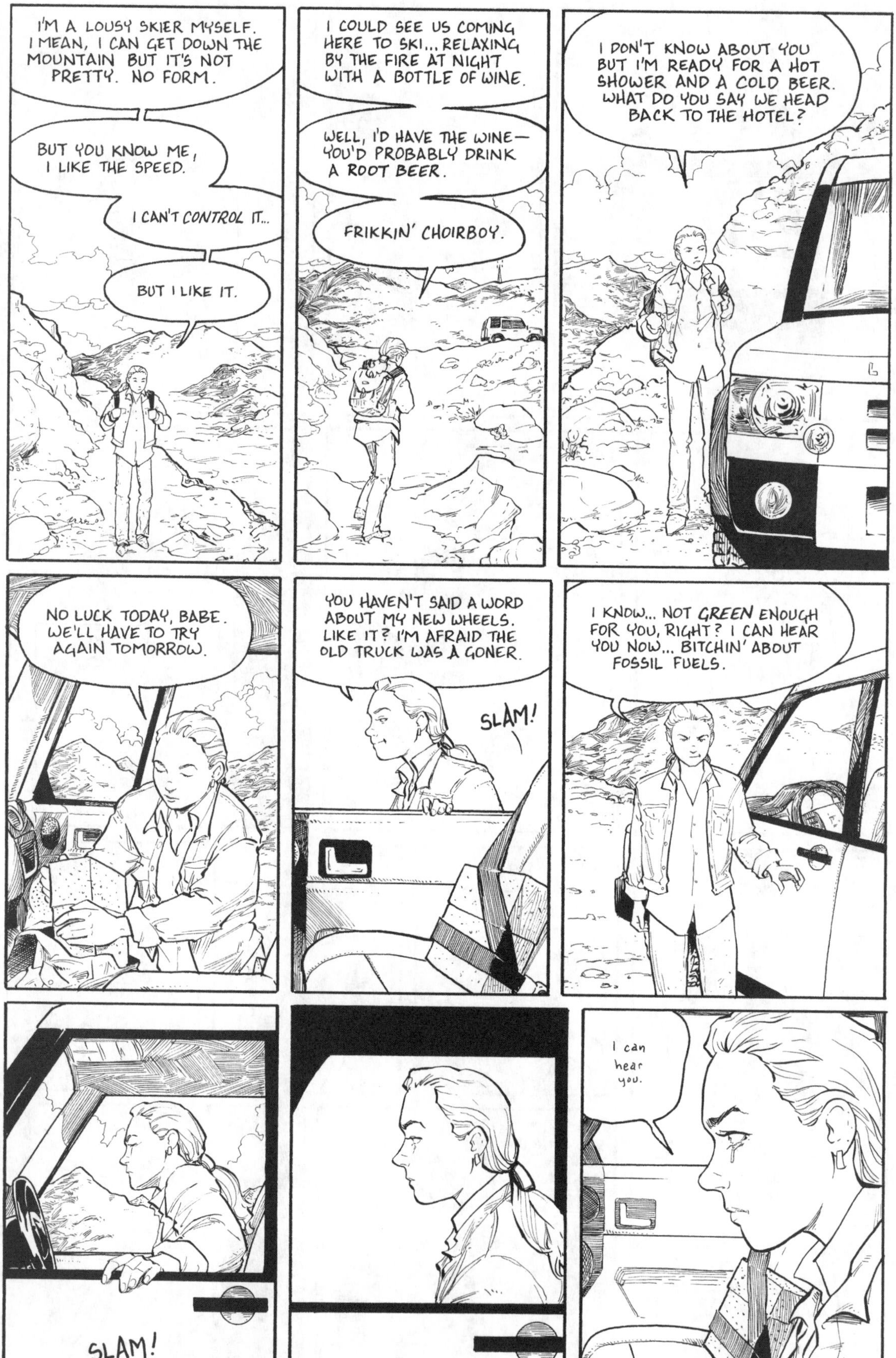
I'M A LOUSY SKIER MYSELF. I MEAN, I CAN GET DOWN THE MOUNTAIN BUT IT'S NOT PRETTY. NO FORM.
BUT YOU KNOW ME, I LIKE THE SPEED.
I CAN'T CONTROL IT...
BUT I LIKE IT.
I COULD SEE US COMING HERE TO SKI... RELAXING BY THE FIRE AT NIGHT WITH A BOTTLE OF WINE.
WELL, I'D HAVE THE WINE— YOU'D PROBABLY DRINK A ROOT BEER.
FRIKKIN' CHOIRBOY.
I DON'T KNOW ABOUT YOU BUT I'M READY FOR A HOT SHOWER AND A COLD BEER. WHAT DO YOU SAY WE HEAD BACK TO THE HOTEL?
NO LUCK TODAY, BABE. WE'LL HAVE TO TRY AGAIN TOMORROW.
YOU HAVEN'T SAID A WORD ABOUT MY NEW WHEELS. LIKE IT? I'M AFRAID THE OLD TRUCK WAS A GONER.
SLAM!
I KNOW... NOT GREEN ENOUGH FOR YOU, RIGHT? I CAN HEAR YOU NOW... BITCHIN' ABOUT FOSSIL FUELS.
SLAM!
I can hear you.

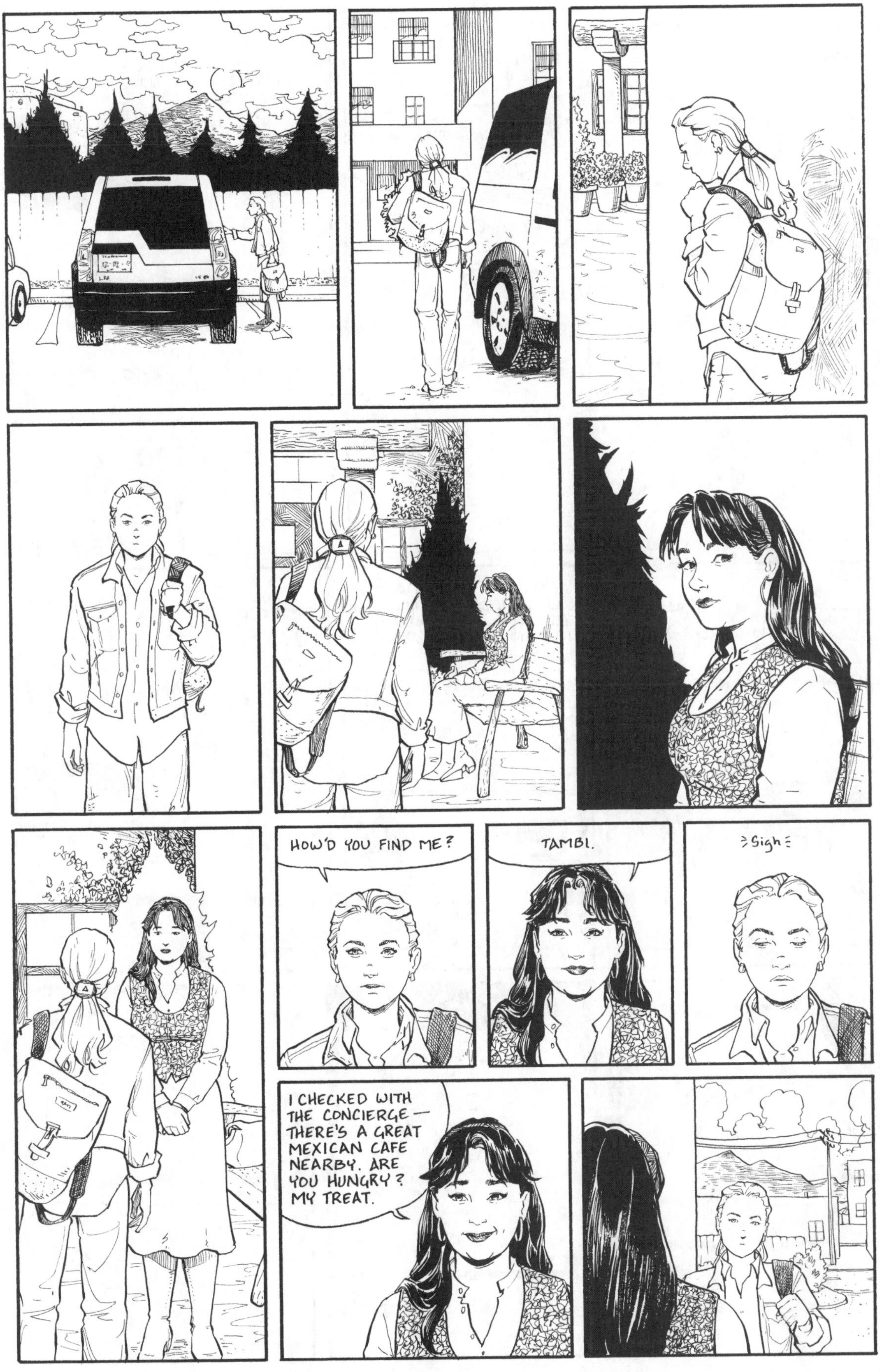
HOW'D YOU FIND ME?
TAMBI.
≈Sigh≈
I CHECKED WITH THE CONCIERGE— THERE'S A GREAT MEXICAN CAFE NEARBY. ARE YOU HUNGRY? MY TREAT.

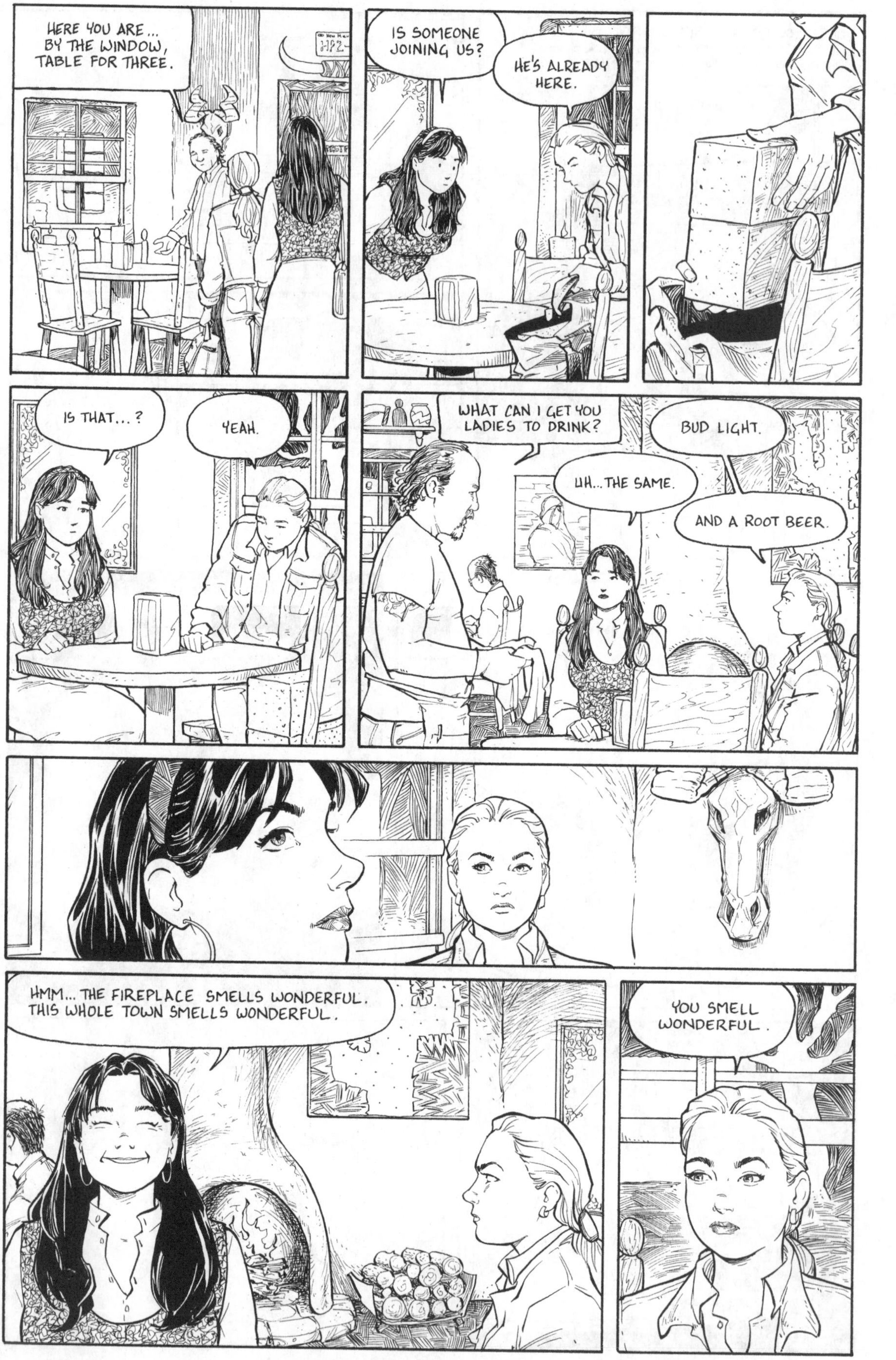
HERE YOU ARE... BY THE WINDOW, TABLE FOR THREE.
IS SOMEONE JOINING US?
HE'S ALREADY HERE.
IS THAT...?
YEAH.
WHAT CAN I GET YOU LADIES TO DRINK?
BUD LIGHT.
UH... THE SAME.
AND A ROOT BEER.
HMM... THE FIREPLACE SMELLS WONDERFUL. THIS WHOLE TOWN SMELLS WONDERFUL.
YOU SMELL WONDERFUL.

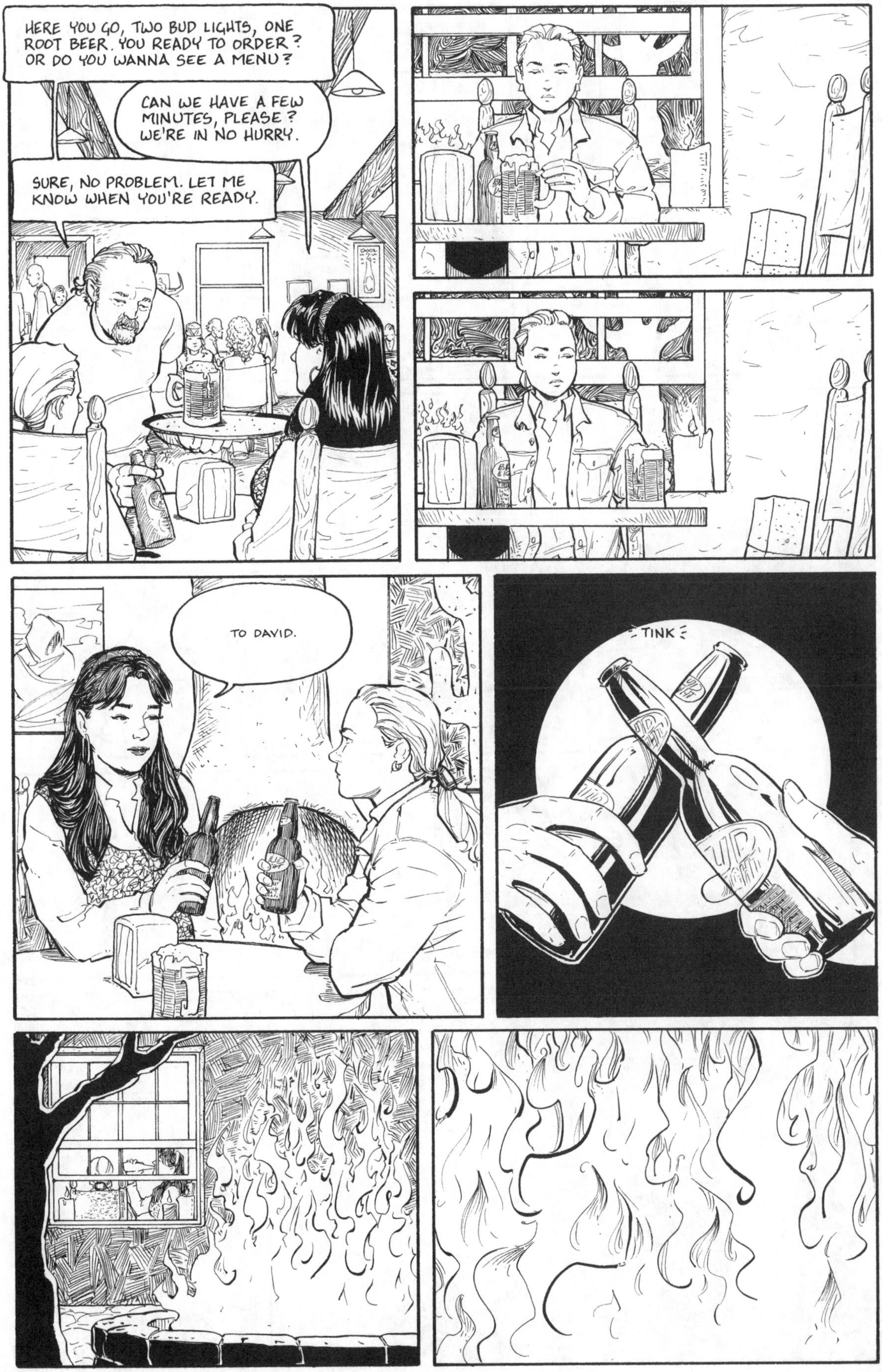
HERE YOU GO, TWO BUD LIGHTS, ONE ROOT BEER. YOU READY TO ORDER? OR DO YOU WANNA SEE A MENU?
CAN WE HAVE A FEW MINUTES, PLEASE? WE'RE IN NO HURRY.
SURE, NO PROBLEM. LET ME KNOW WHEN YOU'RE READY.
TO DAVID.
TINK

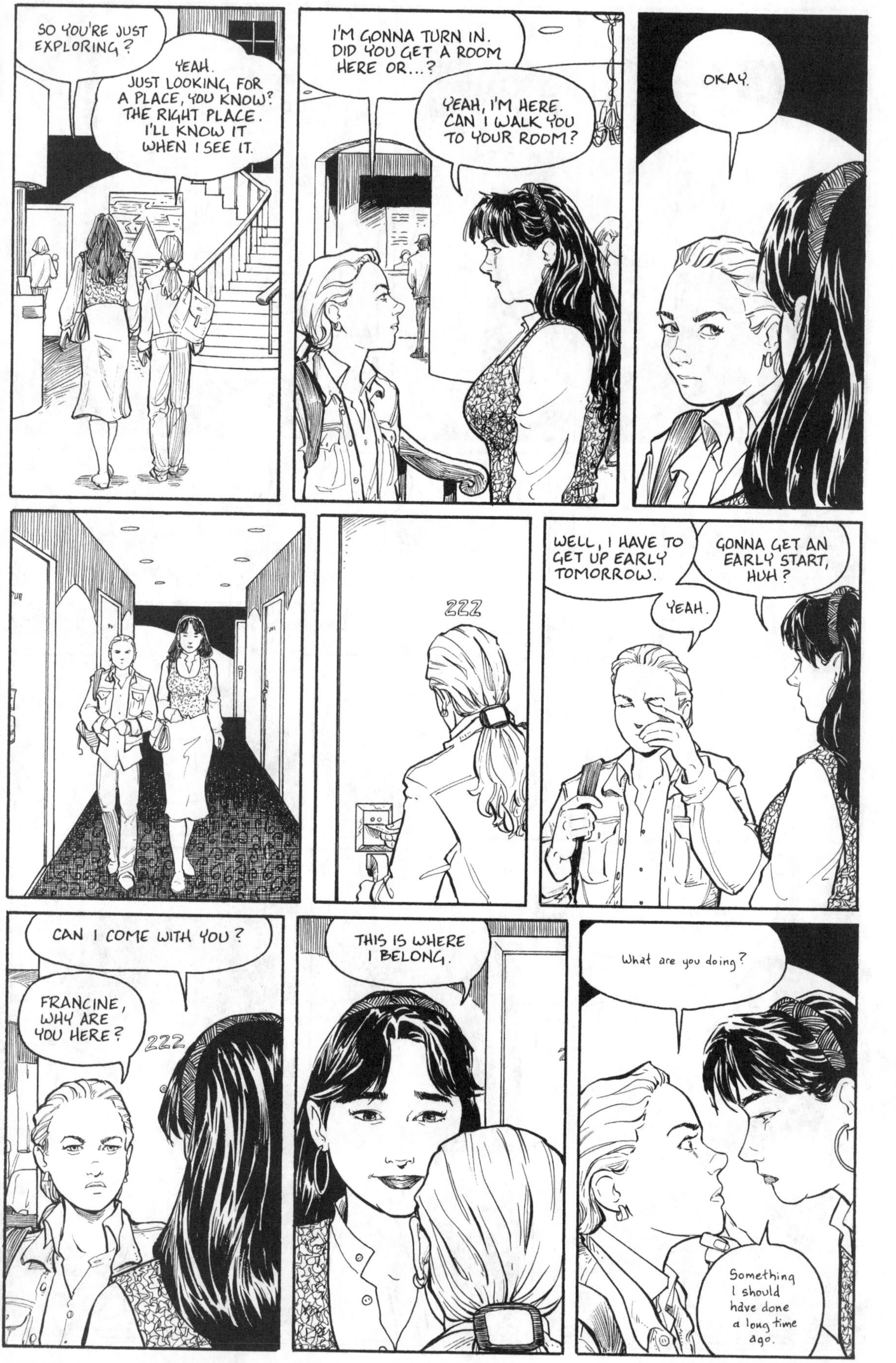
SO YOU'RE JUST EXPLORING?
YEAH. JUST LOOKING FOR A PLACE, YOU KNOW? THE RIGHT PLACE. I'LL KNOW IT WHEN I SEE IT.
I'M GONNA TURN IN. DID YOU GET A ROOM HERE OR...?
YEAH, I'M HERE. CAN I WALK YOU TO YOUR ROOM?
OKAY.
222
WELL, I HAVE TO GET UP EARLY TOMORROW.
GONNA GET AN EARLY START, HUH?
YEAH.
CAN I COME WITH YOU?
FRANCINE, WHY ARE YOU HERE?
222
THIS IS WHERE I BELONG.
What are you doing?
Something I should have done a long time ago.

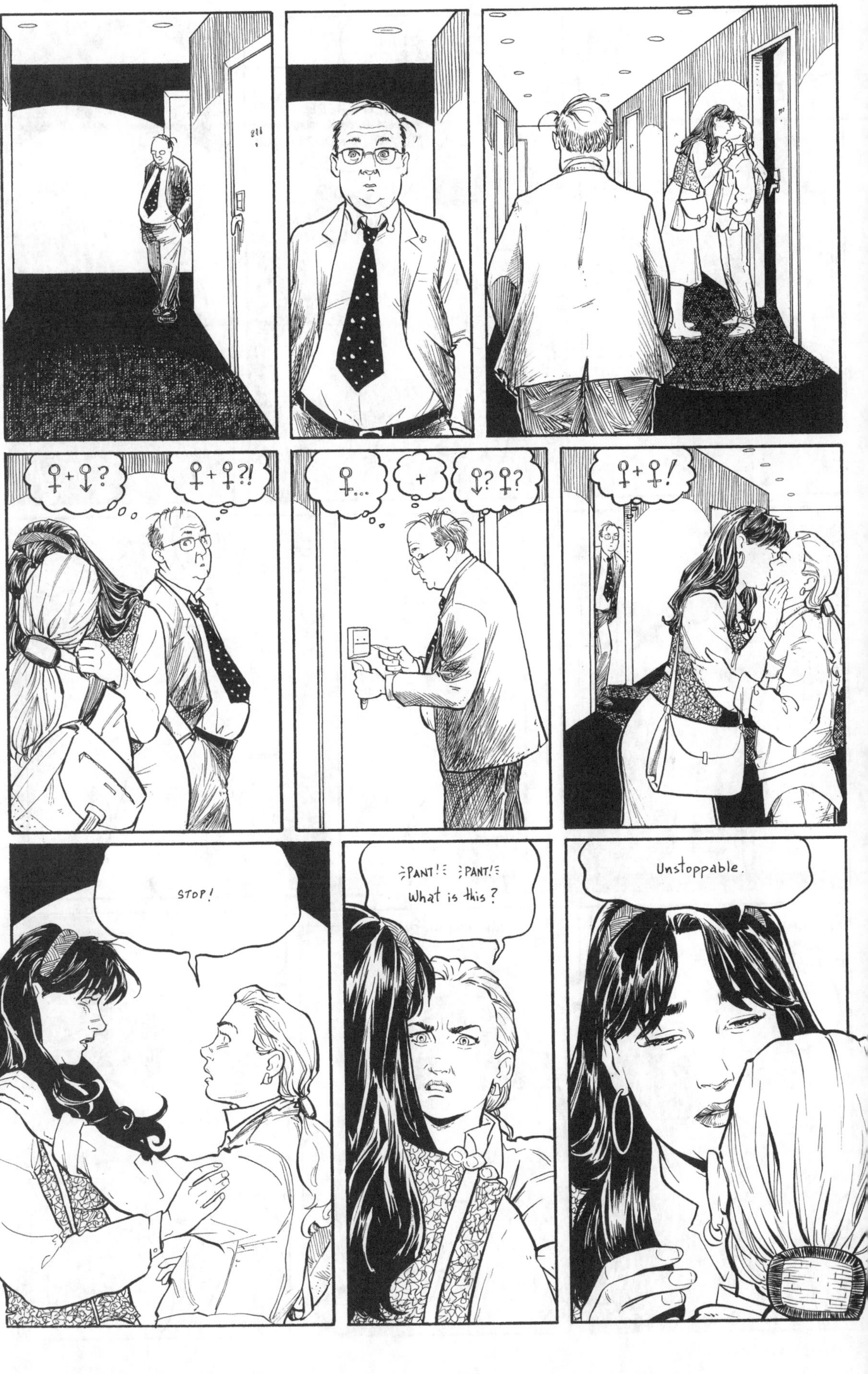
STOP!
PANT! PANT! What is this?
Unstoppable.

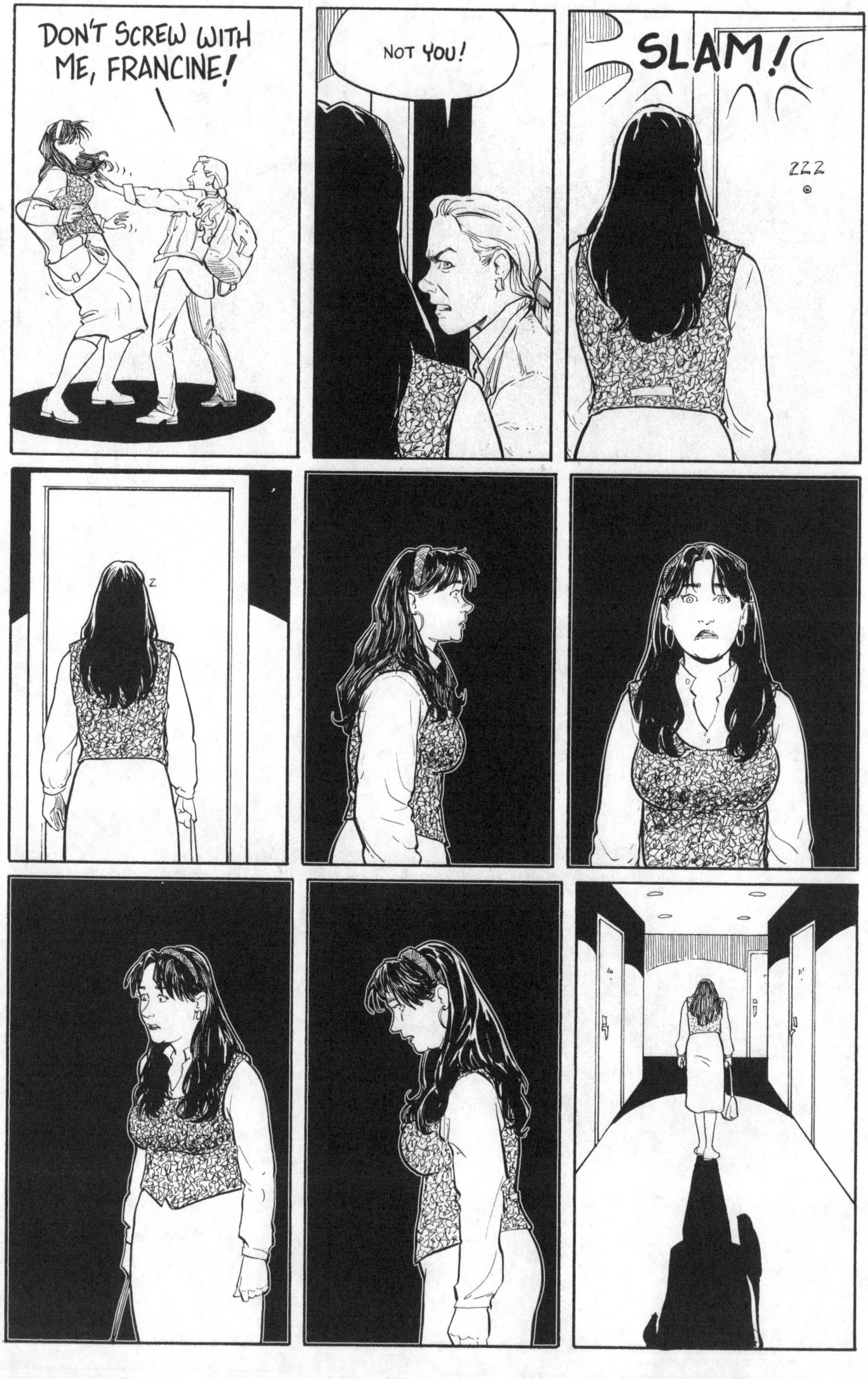
DON'T SCREW WITH ME, FRANCINE!
NOT YOU!
SLAM!
ZZZ
Z

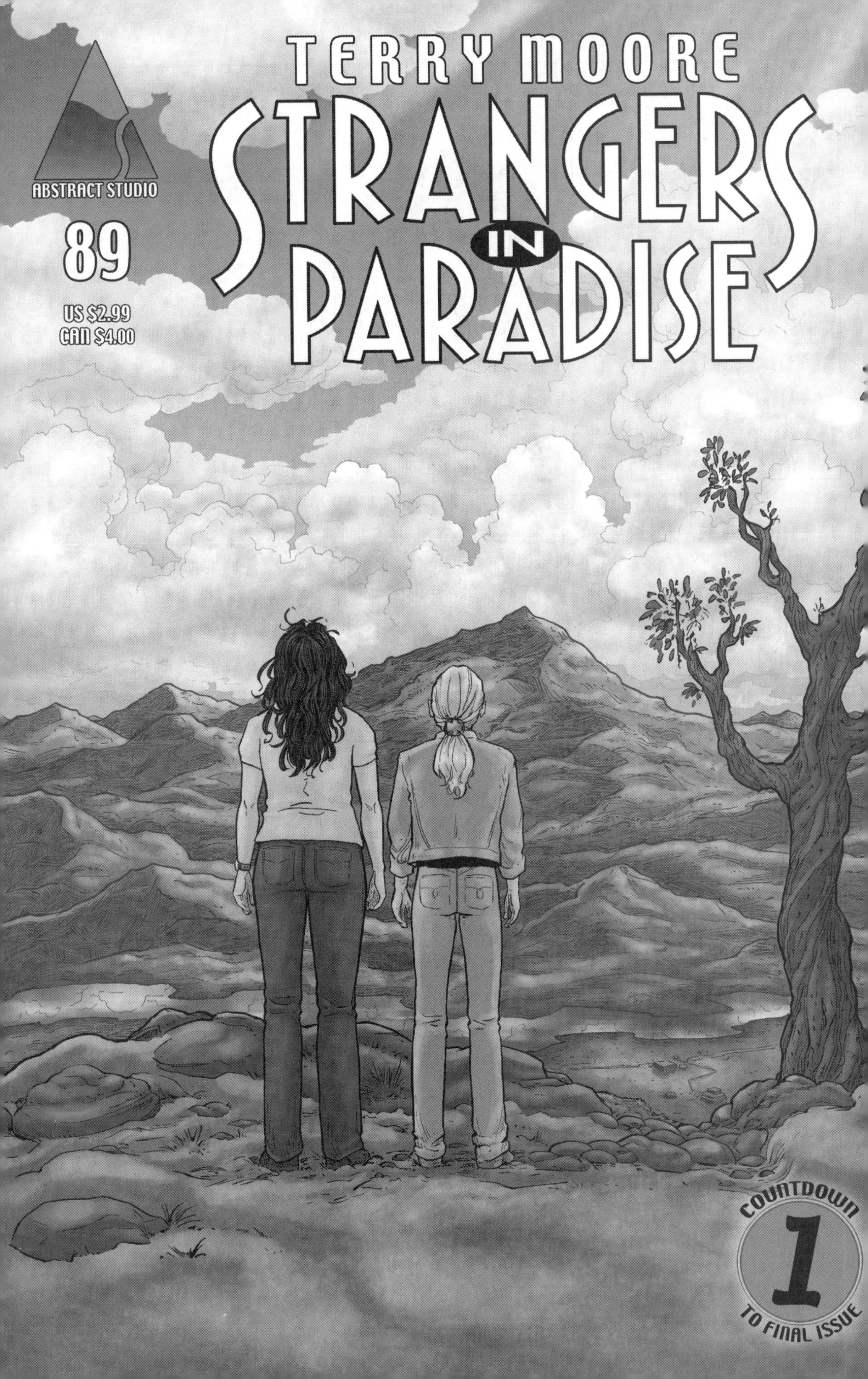
ABSTRACT STUDIO
TERRY MOORE
STRANGERS IN PARADISE
89
US $2.99
CAN $4.00
COUNTDOWN
1
TO FINAL ISSUE

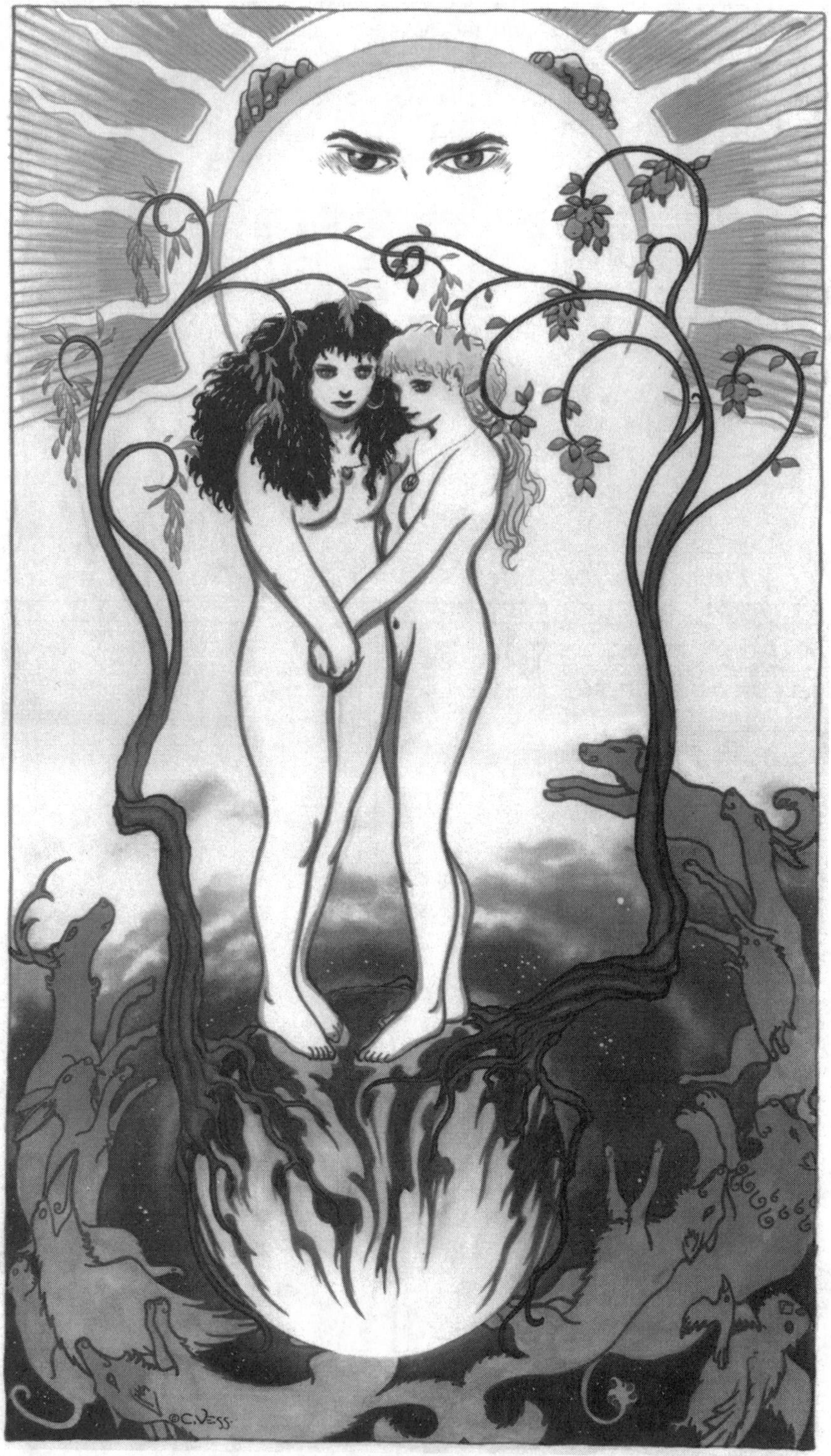
©C.VESS

I've been without you
I've been so deep within you
And the feeling's still the same
When I'm holding you
I can't even remember my name

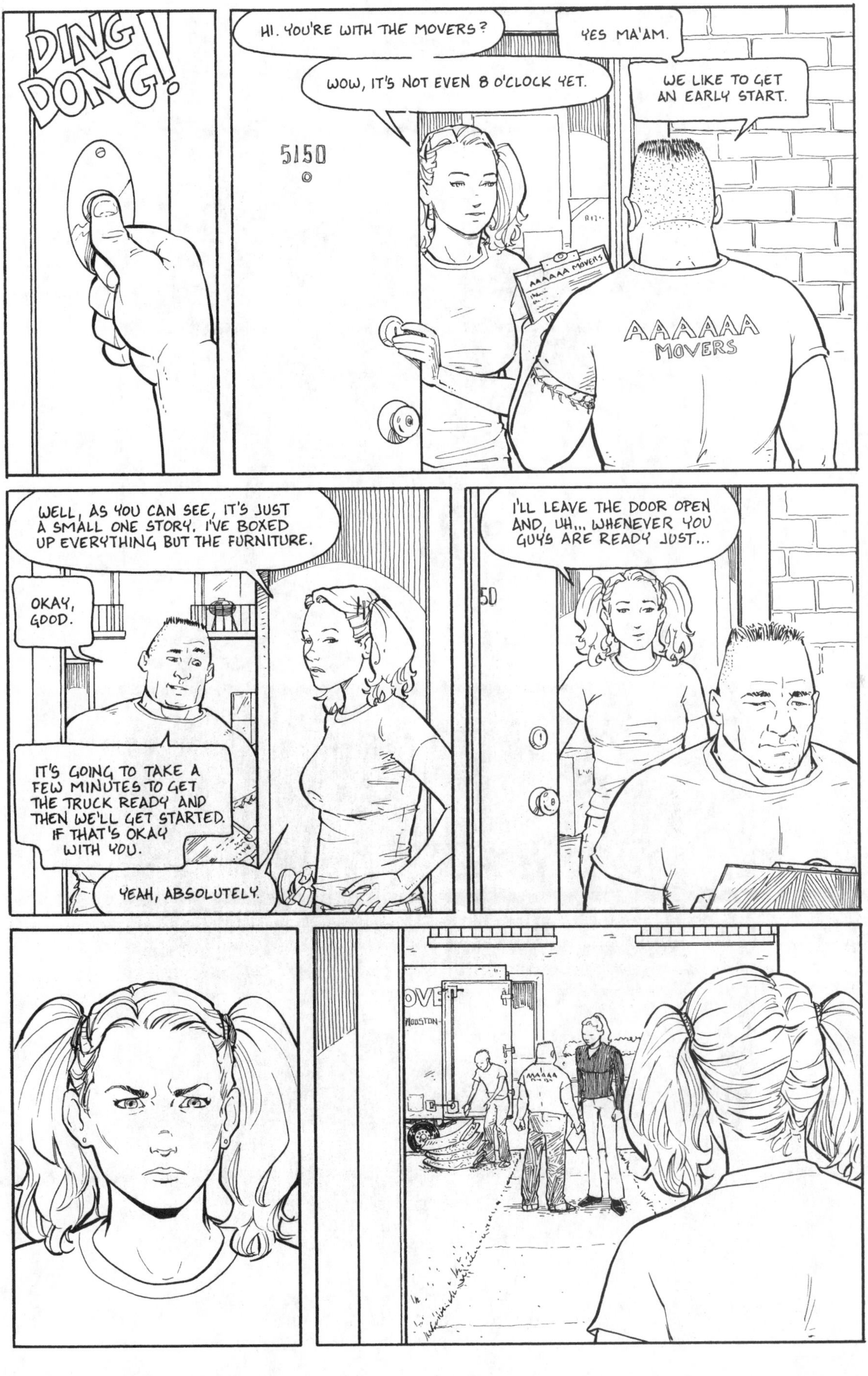
DING DONG!
HI. YOU'RE WITH THE MOVERS?
YES MA'AM.
WOW, IT'S NOT EVEN 8 O'CLOCK YET.
WE LIKE TO GET AN EARLY START.
5150
AAAAAA MOVERS
AAAAAA MOVERS
WELL, AS YOU CAN SEE, IT'S JUST A SMALL ONE STORY. I'VE BOXED UP EVERYTHING BUT THE FURNITURE.
OKAY, GOOD.
IT'S GOING TO TAKE A FEW MINUTES TO GET THE TRUCK READY AND THEN WE'LL GET STARTED. IF THAT'S OKAY WITH YOU.
YEAH, ABSOLUTELY.
I'LL LEAVE THE DOOR OPEN AND, UH... WHENEVER YOU GUYS ARE READY JUST...
50
HOUSTON

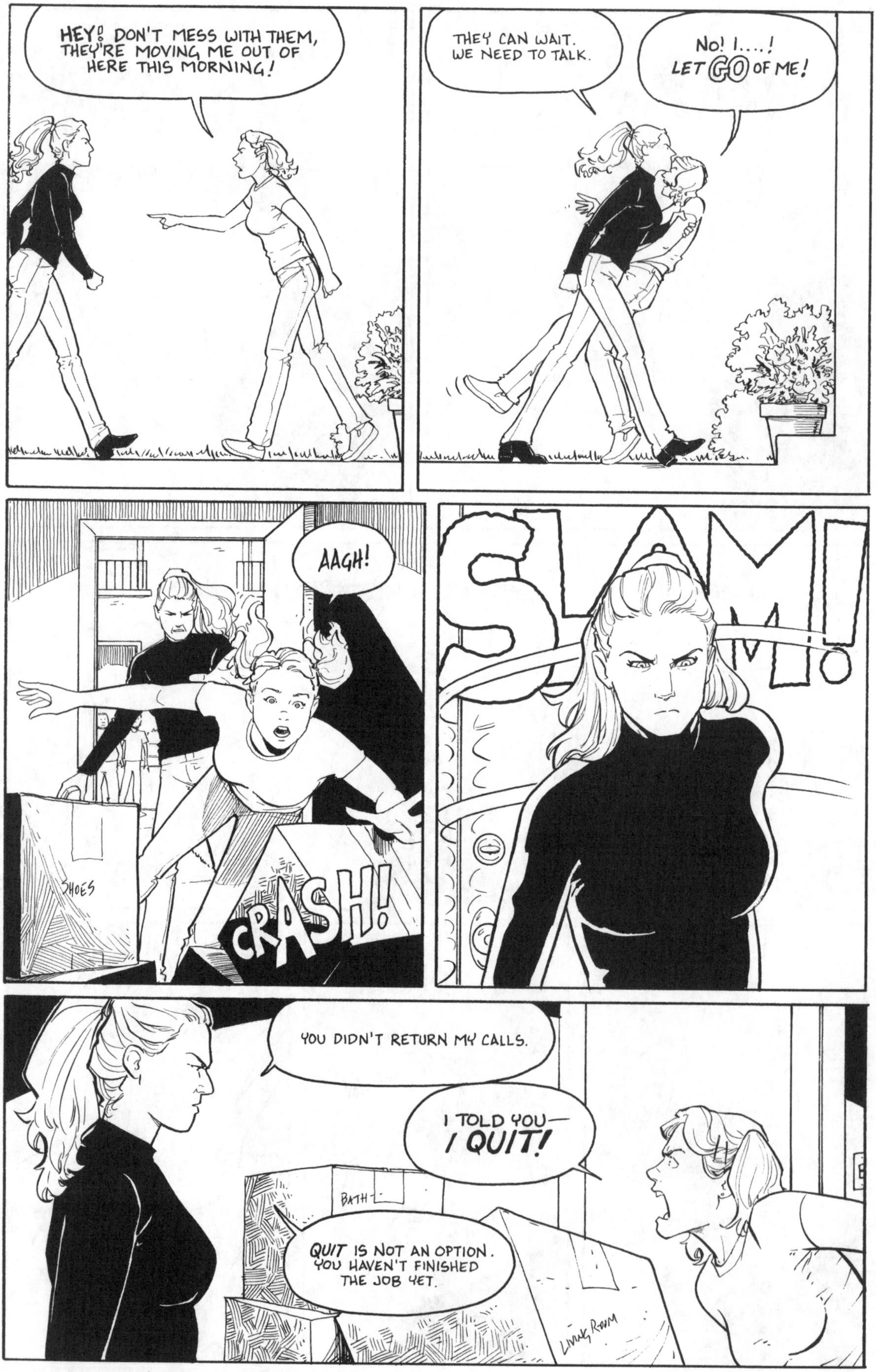
HEY! DON'T MESS WITH THEM, THEY'RE MOVING ME OUT OF HERE THIS MORNING!
THEY CAN WAIT. WE NEED TO TALK.
NO! I....! LET GO OF ME!
AAGH!
SHOES
CRASH!
SLAM!
YOU DIDN'T RETURN MY CALLS.
I TOLD YOU— I QUIT!
BATH
QUIT IS NOT AN OPTION. YOU HAVEN'T FINISHED THE JOB YET.
LIVING ROOM

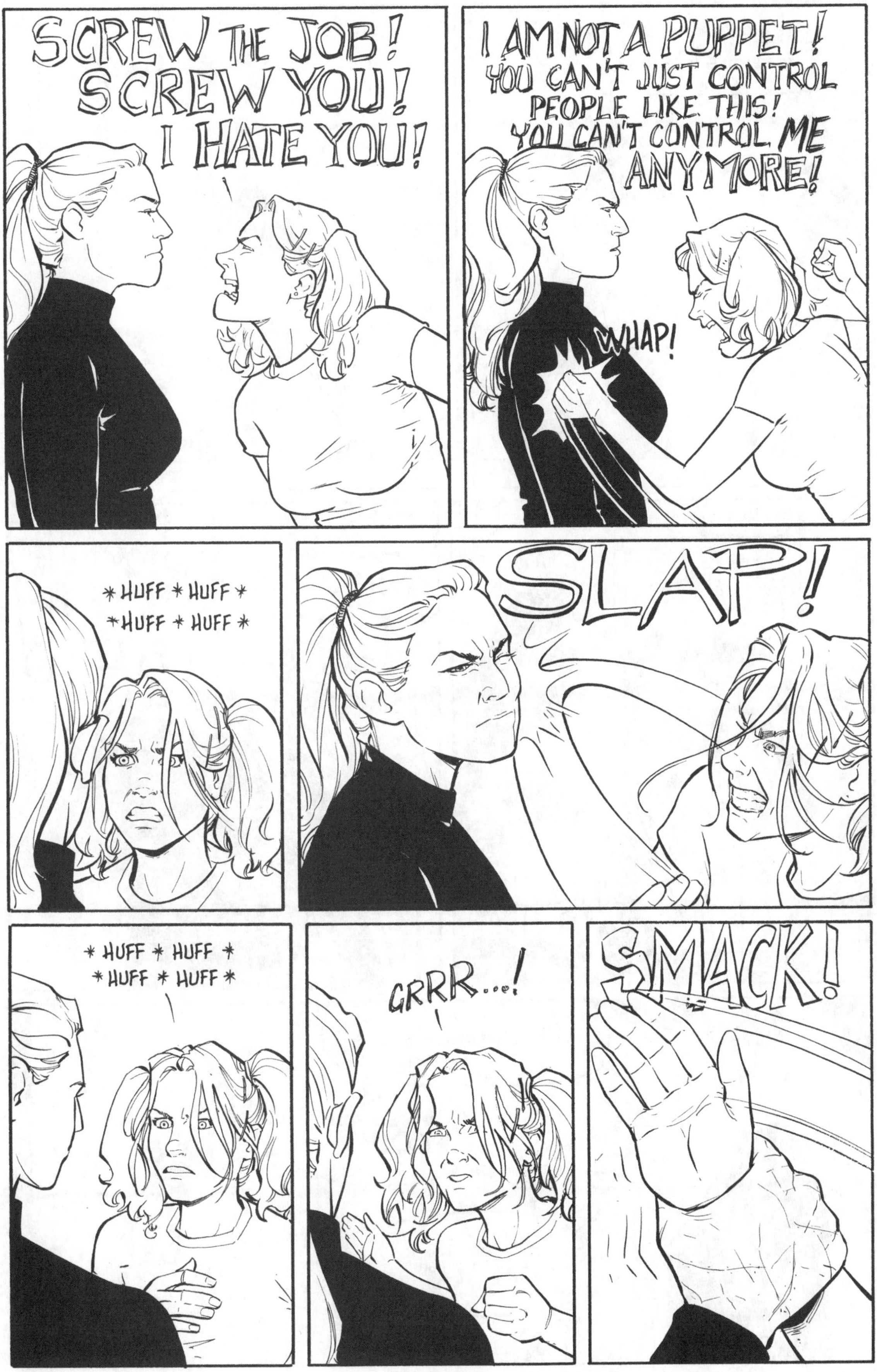
SCREW THE JOB! SCREW YOU! I HATE YOU!
I AM NOT A PUPPET! YOU CAN'T JUST CONTROL PEOPLE LIKE THIS! YOU CAN'T CONTROL ME ANYMORE!
WHAP!
* HUFF * HUFF * * HUFF * HUFF *
SLAP!
* HUFF * HUFF * * HUFF * HUFF *
GRRR...!
SMACK!

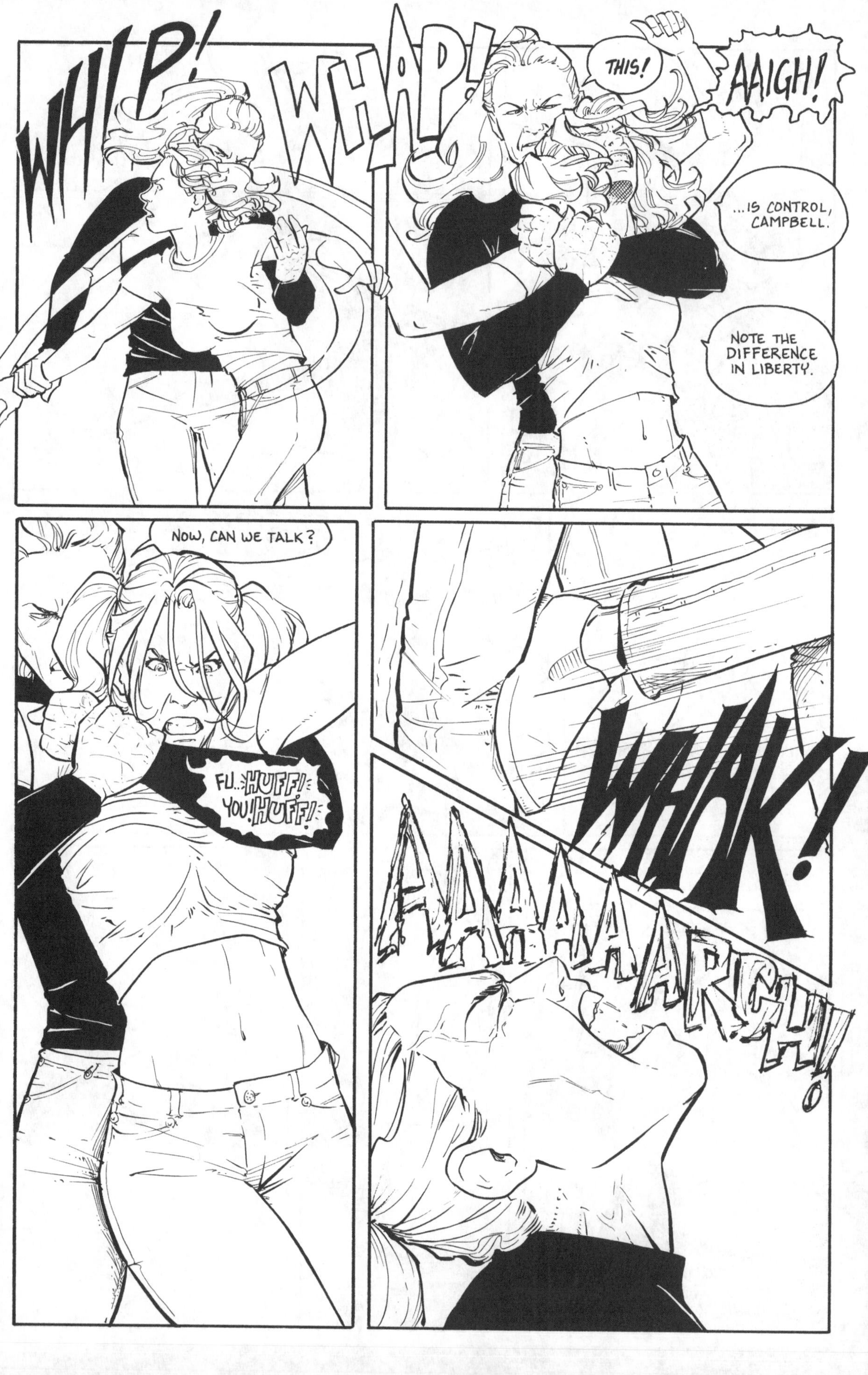
WHIP!
WHAP!
THIS!
AAIGH!
...IS CONTROL, CAMPBELL.
NOTE THE DIFFERENCE IN LIBERTY.
NOW, CAN WE TALK?
FU..HUFF! YOU!HUFF!
WHAK!
AAAAAARGH!!

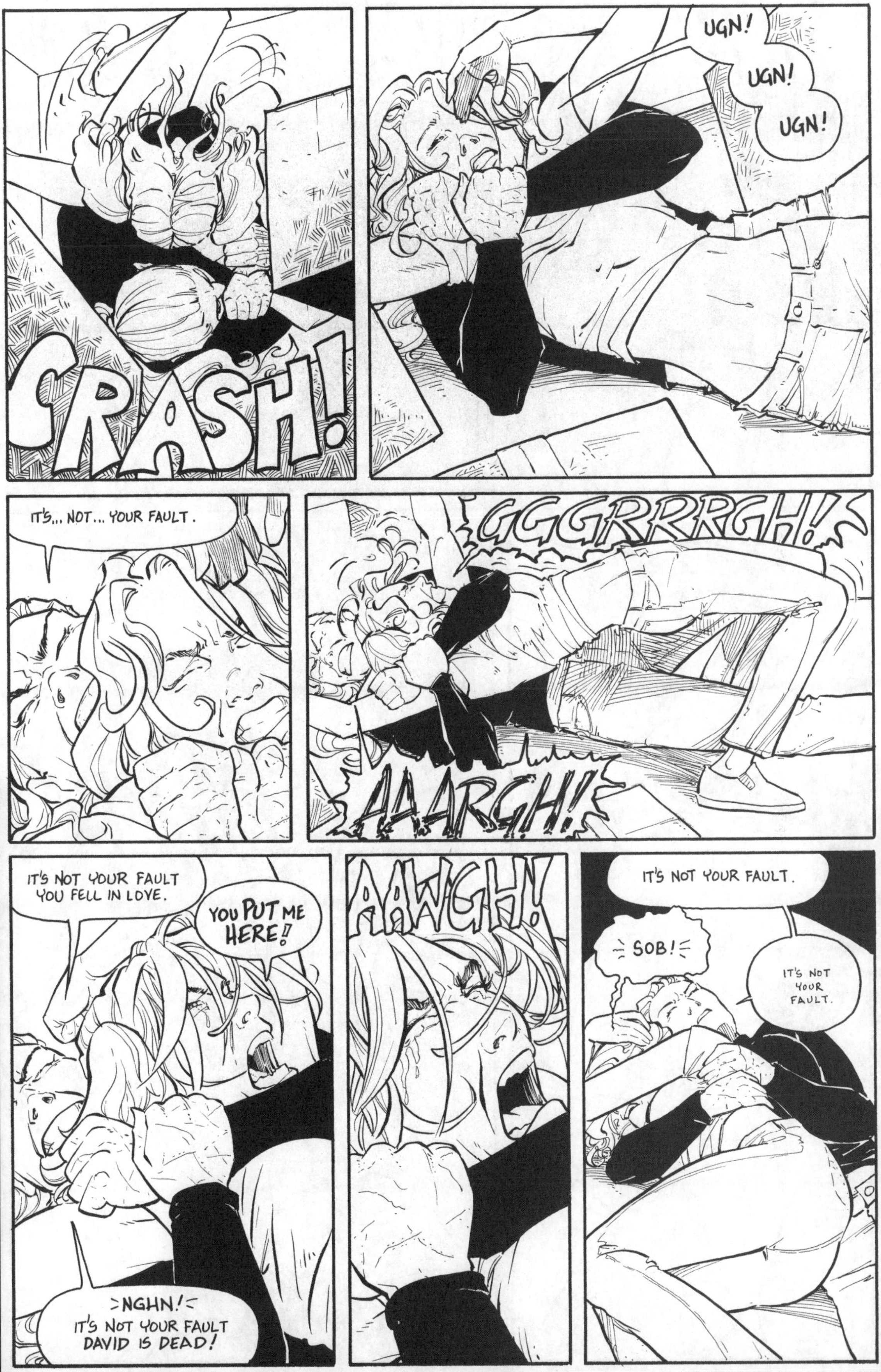
CRASH!
UGN!
UGN!
UGN!
IT'S... NOT... YOUR FAULT.
GGGRRRRGH!
AAARGH!
IT'S NOT YOUR FAULT YOU FELL IN LOVE.
YOU PUT ME HERE!
NGHN! IT'S NOT YOUR FAULT DAVID IS DEAD!
AAWGH!
IT'S NOT YOUR FAULT.
SOB!
IT'S NOT YOUR FAULT.

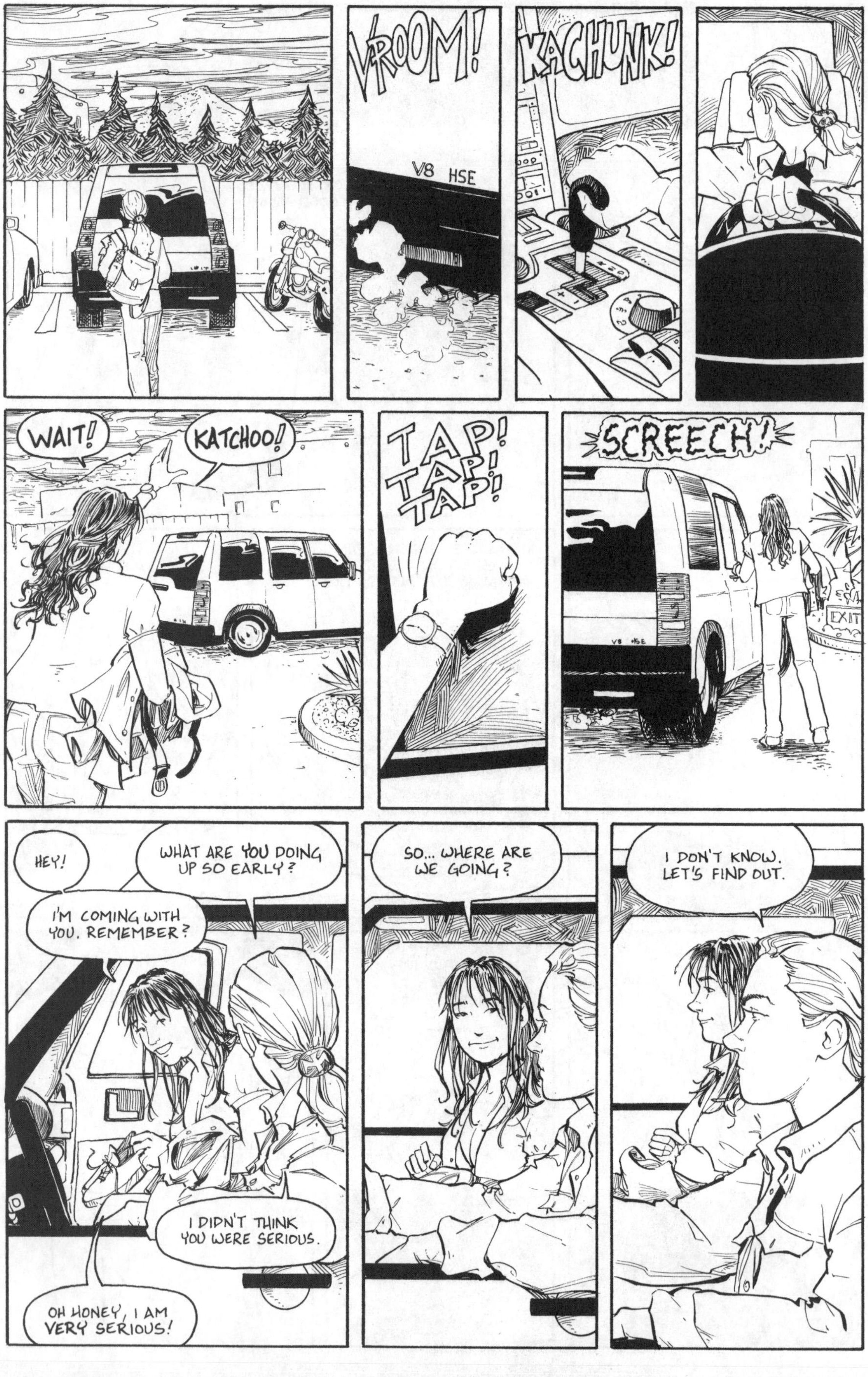
VROOM!
V8 HSE
KACHUNK!
WAIT!
KATCHOO!
TAP! TAP! TAP!
SCREECH!
V8 HSE
EXIT
HEY!
WHAT ARE YOU DOING UP SO EARLY?
I'M COMING WITH YOU. REMEMBER?
I DIDN'T THINK YOU WERE SERIOUS.
OH HONEY, I AM VERY SERIOUS!
SO... WHERE ARE WE GOING?
I DON'T KNOW. LET'S FIND OUT.

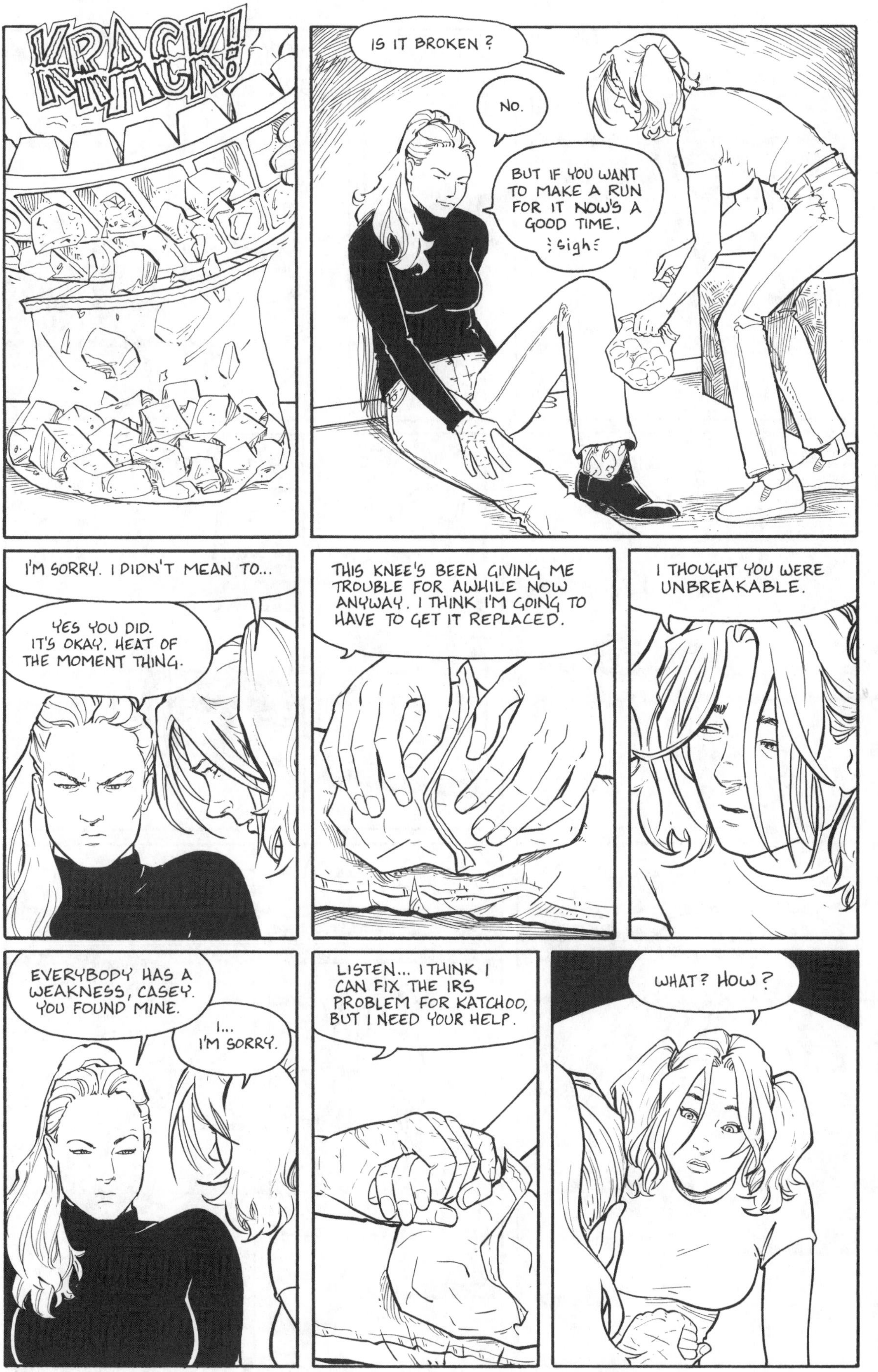
KRACK!
IS IT BROKEN?
NO.
BUT IF YOU WANT TO MAKE A RUN FOR IT NOW'S A GOOD TIME.
sigh
I'M SORRY. I DIDN'T MEAN TO...
YES YOU DID. IT'S OKAY. HEAT OF THE MOMENT THING.
THIS KNEE'S BEEN GIVING ME TROUBLE FOR AWHILE NOW ANYWAY. I THINK I'M GOING TO HAVE TO GET IT REPLACED.
I THOUGHT YOU WERE UNBREAKABLE.
EVERYBODY HAS A WEAKNESS, CASEY. YOU FOUND MINE.
I... I'M SORRY.
LISTEN... I THINK I CAN FIX THE IRS PROBLEM FOR KATCHOO, BUT I NEED YOUR HELP.
WHAT? HOW?

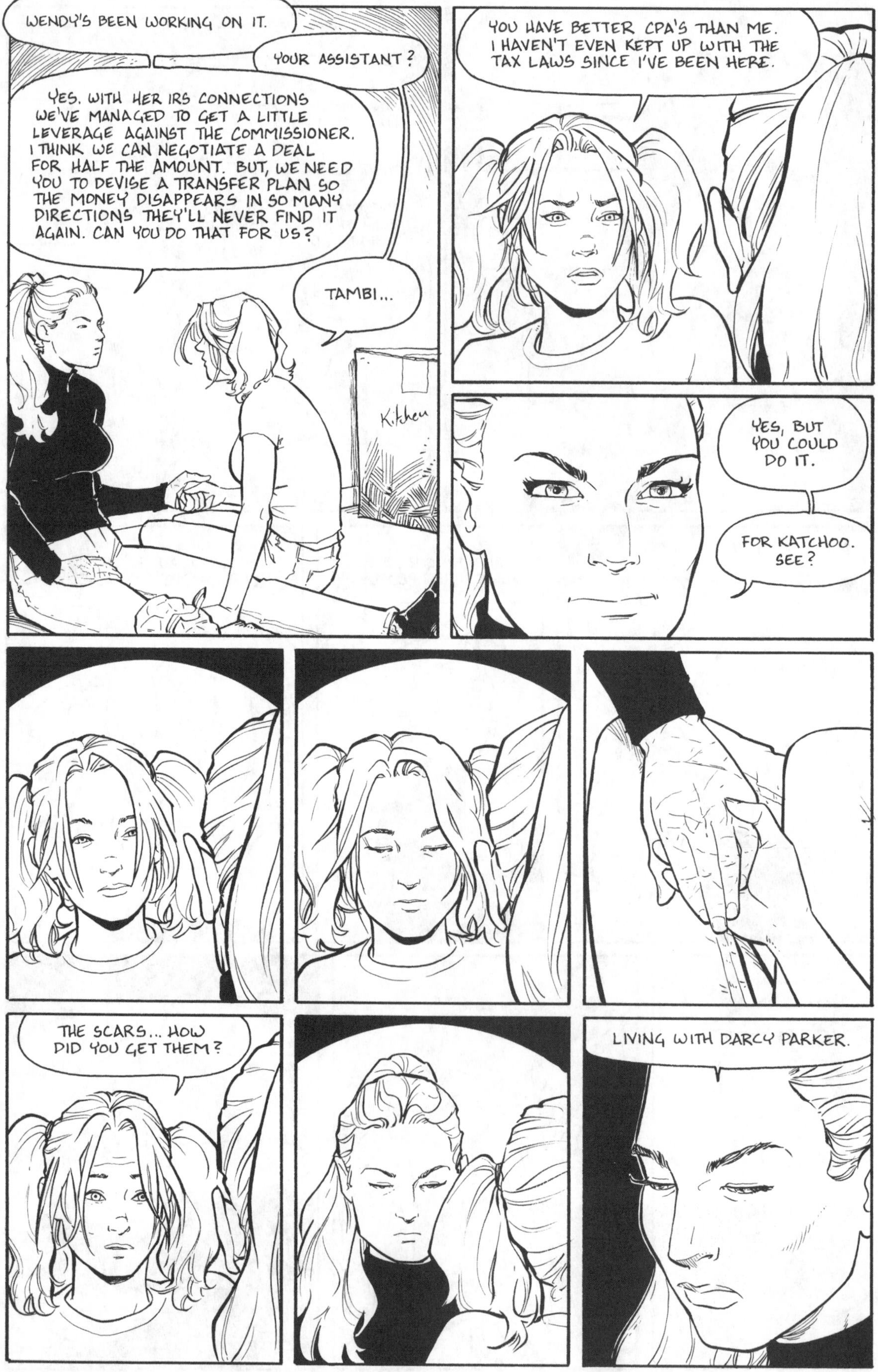
WENDY'S BEEN WORKING ON IT.
YOUR ASSISTANT?
YES. WITH HER IRS CONNECTIONS WE'VE MANAGED TO GET A LITTLE LEVERAGE AGAINST THE COMMISSIONER. I THINK WE CAN NEGOTIATE A DEAL FOR HALF THE AMOUNT. BUT, WE NEED YOU TO DEVISE A TRANSFER PLAN SO THE MONEY DISAPPEARS IN SO MANY DIRECTIONS THEY'LL NEVER FIND IT AGAIN. CAN YOU DO THAT FOR US?
TAMBI...
Kitchen
YOU HAVE BETTER CPA'S THAN ME. I HAVEN'T EVEN KEPT UP WITH THE TAX LAWS SINCE I'VE BEEN HERE.
YES, BUT YOU COULD DO IT.
FOR KATCHOO. SEE?
THE SCARS... HOW DID YOU GET THEM?
LIVING WITH DARCY PARKER.

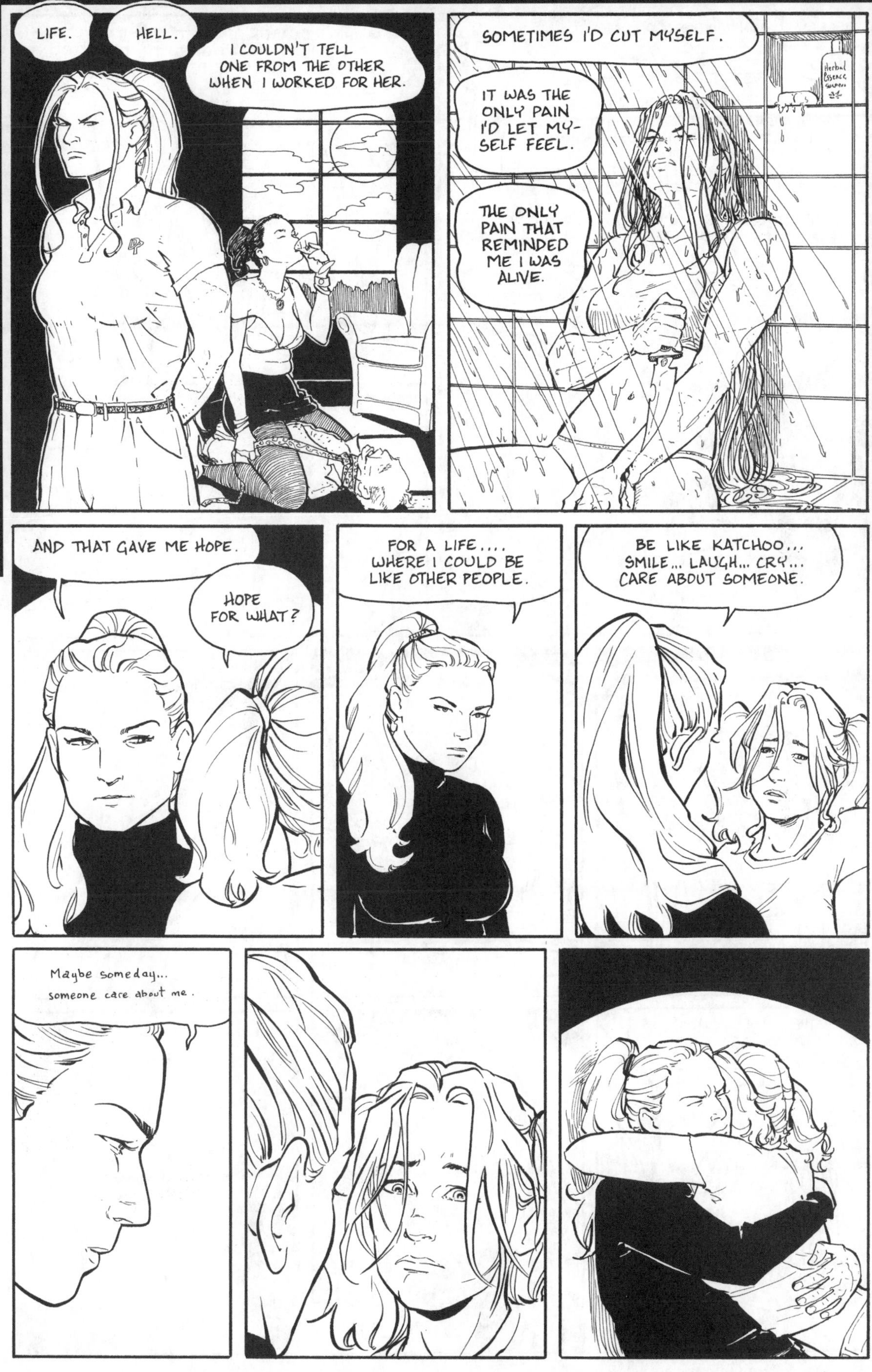
LIFE.
HELL.
I COULDN'T TELL ONE FROM THE OTHER WHEN I WORKED FOR HER.
SOMETIMES I'D CUT MYSELF.
IT WAS THE ONLY PAIN I'D LET MY-SELF FEEL.
THE ONLY PAIN THAT REMINDED ME I WAS ALIVE.
AND THAT GAVE ME HOPE.
HOPE FOR WHAT?
FOR A LIFE.... WHERE I COULD BE LIKE OTHER PEOPLE.
BE LIKE KATCHOO... SMILE... LAUGH... CRY... CARE ABOUT SOMEONE.
Maybe someday... someone care about me.

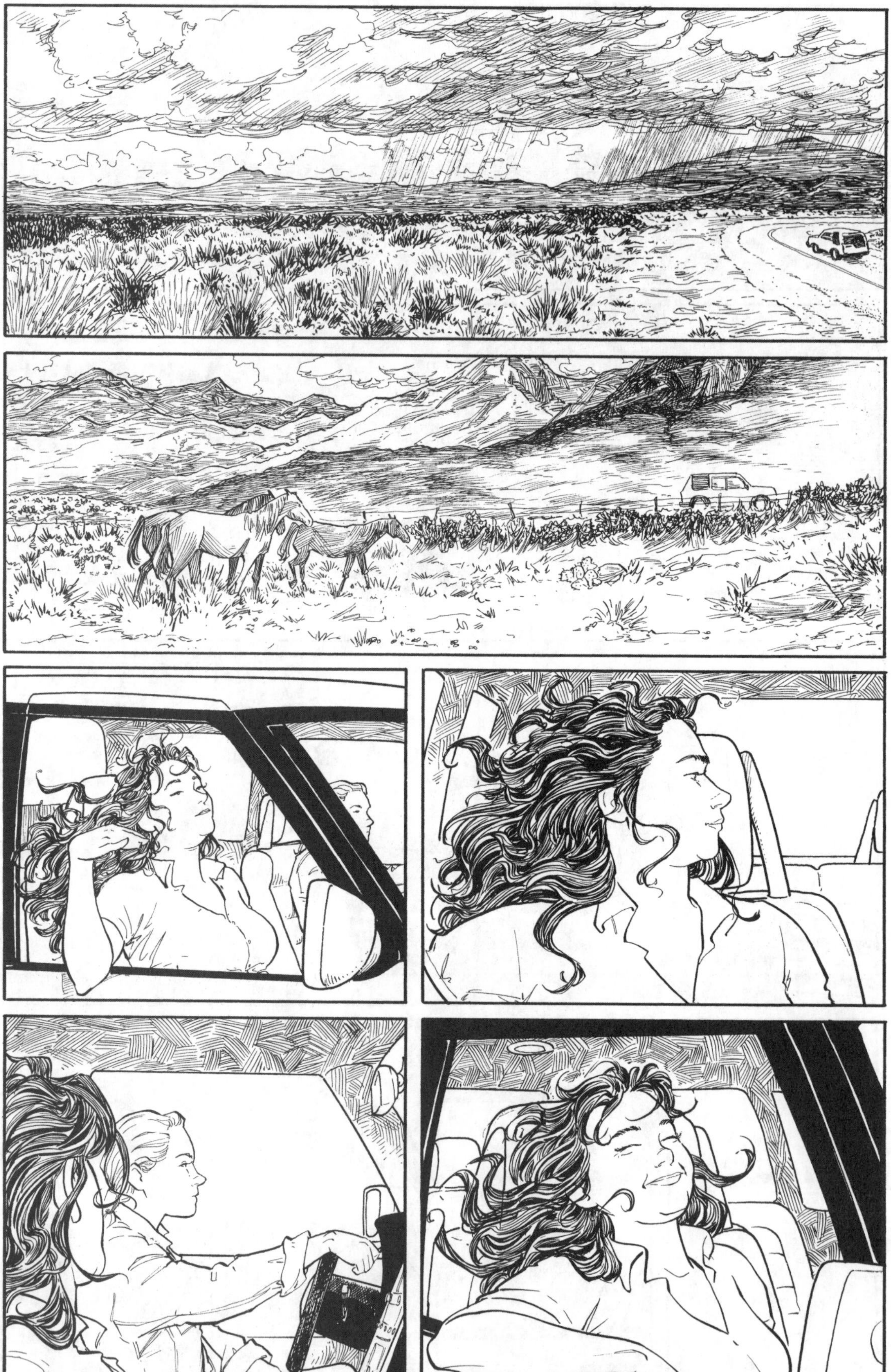

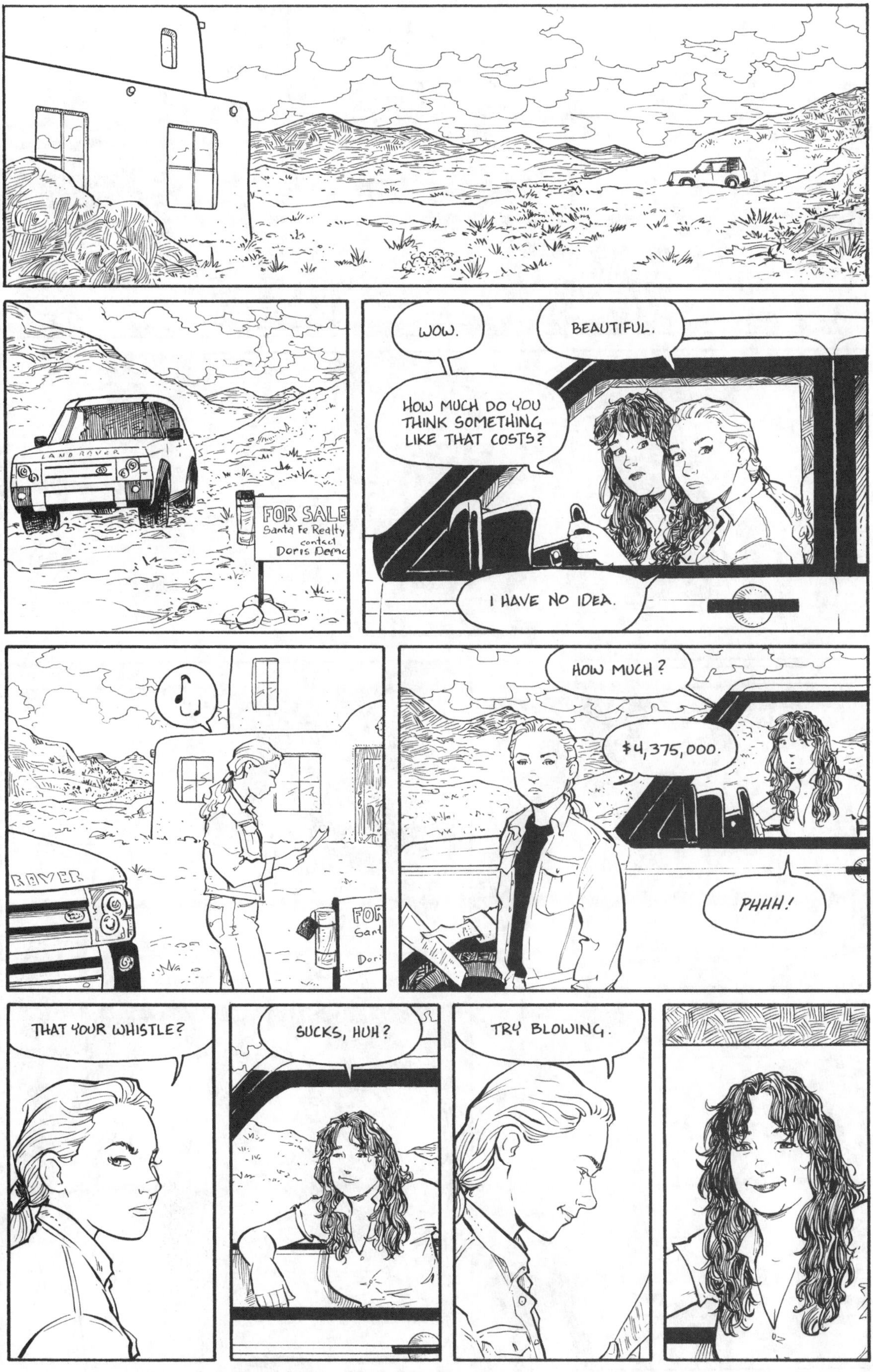

FOR SALE
Santa Fe Realty
contact
Doris Demc
WOW.
BEAUTIFUL.
HOW MUCH DO YOU THINK SOMETHING LIKE THAT COSTS?
I HAVE NO IDEA.
HOW MUCH?
$4,375,000.
PHHH!
THAT YOUR WHISTLE?
SUCKS, HUH?
TRY BLOWING.

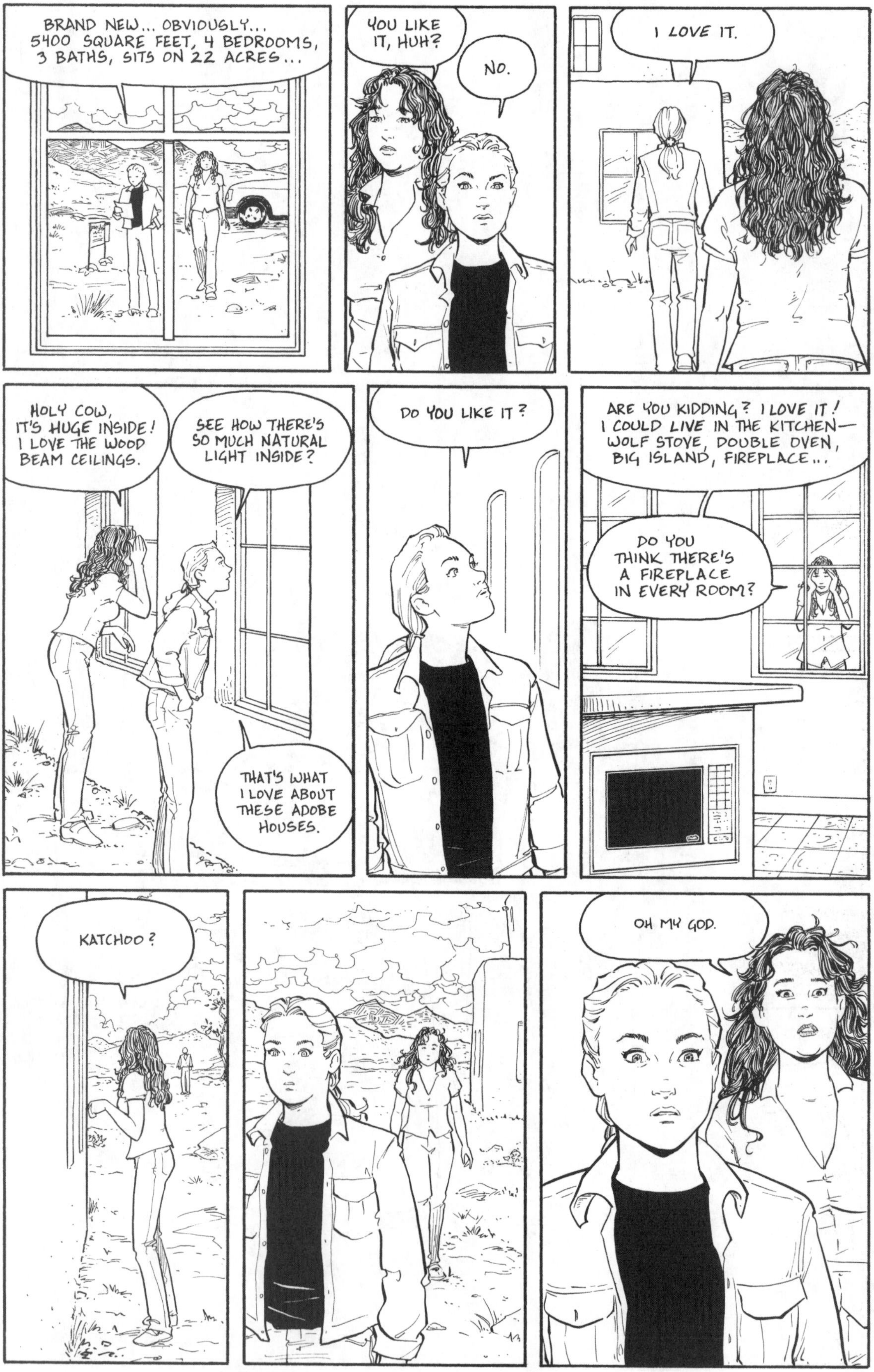
BRAND NEW... OBVIOUSLY... 5400 SQUARE FEET, 4 BEDROOMS, 3 BATHS, SITS ON 22 ACRES...
YOU LIKE IT, HUH?
NO.
I LOVE IT.
HOLY COW, IT'S HUGE INSIDE! I LOVE THE WOOD BEAM CEILINGS.
SEE HOW THERE'S SO MUCH NATURAL LIGHT INSIDE?
THAT'S WHAT I LOVE ABOUT THESE ADOBE HOUSES.
DO YOU LIKE IT?
ARE YOU KIDDING? I LOVE IT! I COULD LIVE IN THE KITCHEN— WOLF STOVE, DOUBLE OVEN, BIG ISLAND, FIREPLACE...
DO YOU THINK THERE'S A FIREPLACE IN EVERY ROOM?
KATCHOO?
OH MY GOD.

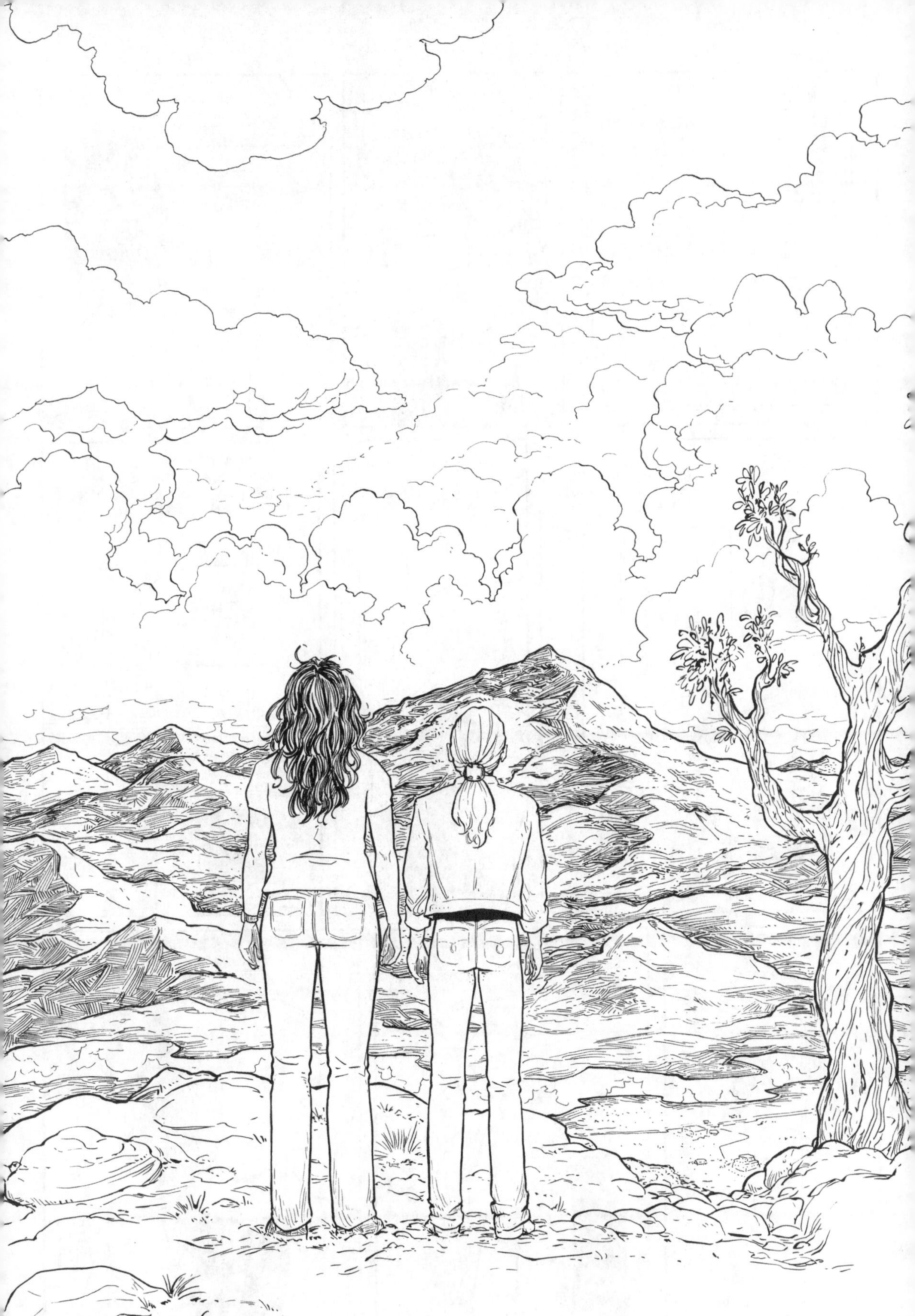

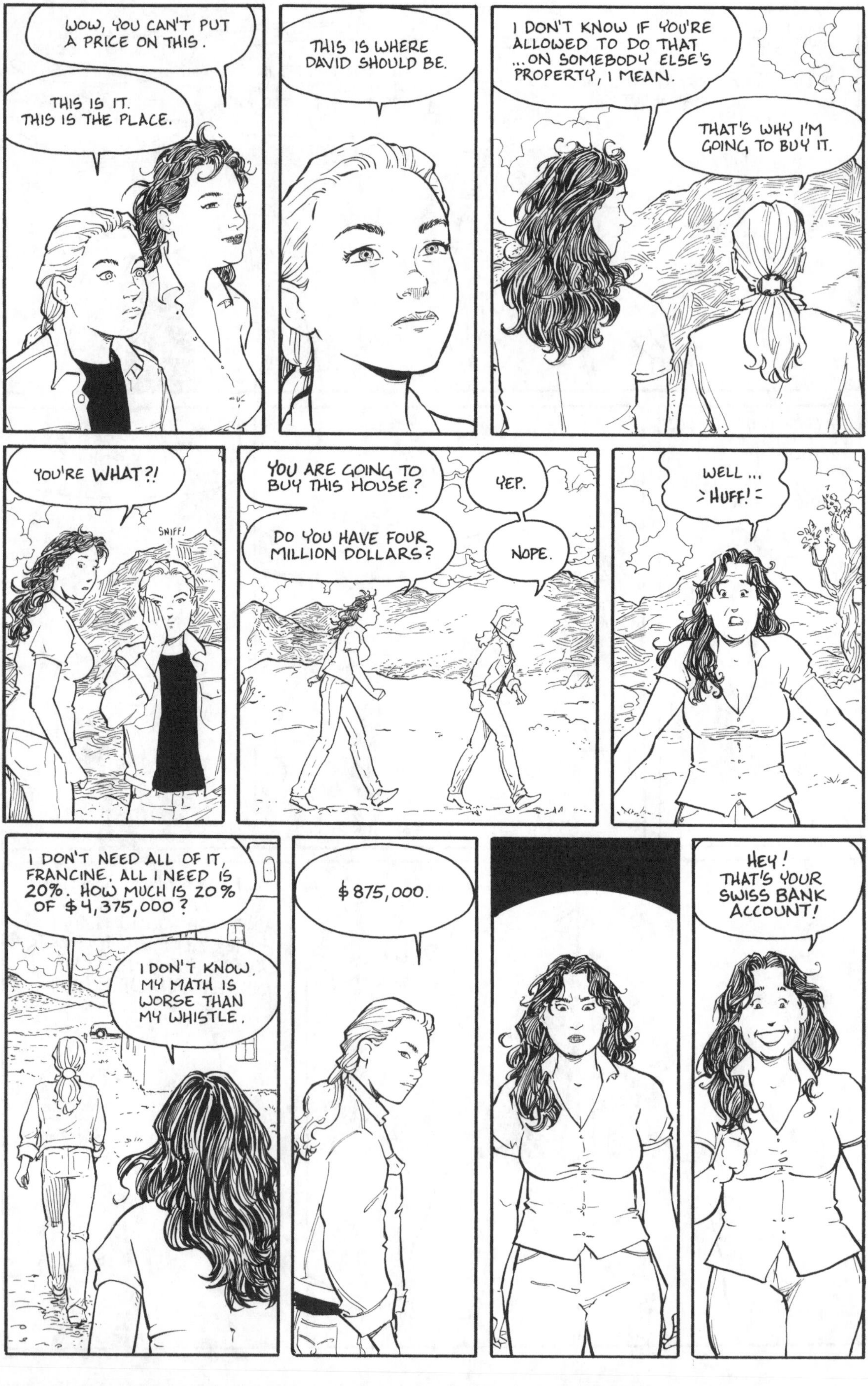
WOW, YOU CAN'T PUT A PRICE ON THIS.
THIS IS IT. THIS IS THE PLACE.
THIS IS WHERE DAVID SHOULD BE.
I DON'T KNOW IF YOU'RE ALLOWED TO DO THAT ...ON SOMEBODY ELSE'S PROPERTY, I MEAN.
THAT'S WHY I'M GOING TO BUY IT.
YOU'RE WHAT?!
SNIFF!
YOU ARE GOING TO BUY THIS HOUSE?
YEP.
DO YOU HAVE FOUR MILLION DOLLARS?
NOPE.
WELL ...
HUFF!
I DON'T NEED ALL OF IT, FRANCINE. ALL I NEED IS 20%. HOW MUCH IS 20% OF $4,375,000?
I DON'T KNOW. MY MATH IS WORSE THAN MY WHISTLE.
$875,000.
HEY! THAT'S YOUR SWISS BANK ACCOUNT!

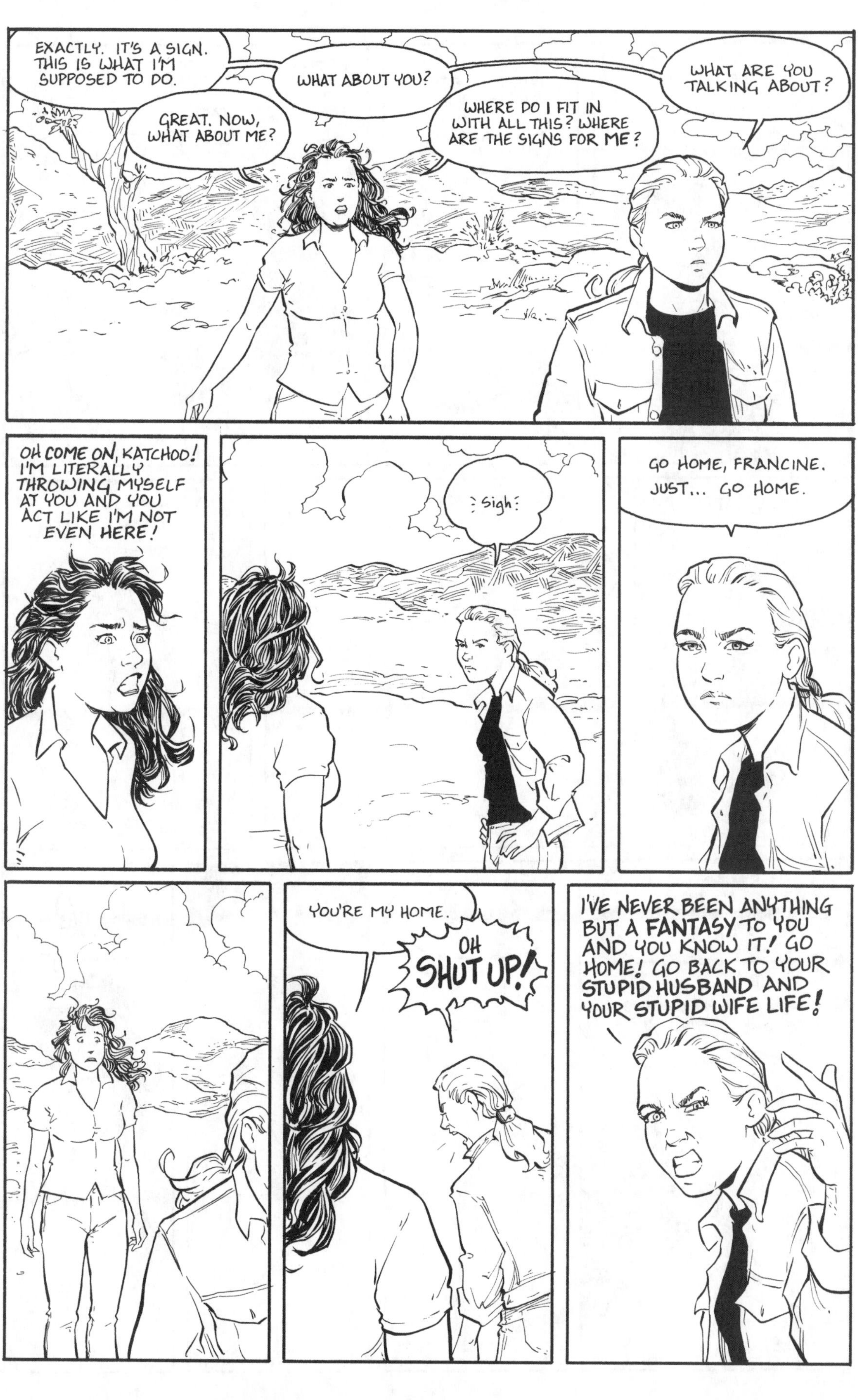
EXACTLY. IT'S A SIGN. THIS IS WHAT I'M SUPPOSED TO DO.
GREAT. NOW, WHAT ABOUT ME?
WHAT ABOUT YOU?
WHERE DO I FIT IN WITH ALL THIS? WHERE ARE THE SIGNS FOR ME?
WHAT ARE YOU TALKING ABOUT?
OH COME ON, KATCHOO! I'M LITERALLY THROWING MYSELF AT YOU AND YOU ACT LIKE I'M NOT EVEN HERE!
Sigh
GO HOME, FRANCINE. JUST... GO HOME.
YOU'RE MY HOME.
OH SHUT UP!
I'VE NEVER BEEN ANYTHING BUT A FANTASY TO YOU AND YOU KNOW IT! GO HOME! GO BACK TO YOUR STUPID HUSBAND AND YOUR STUPID WIFE LIFE!

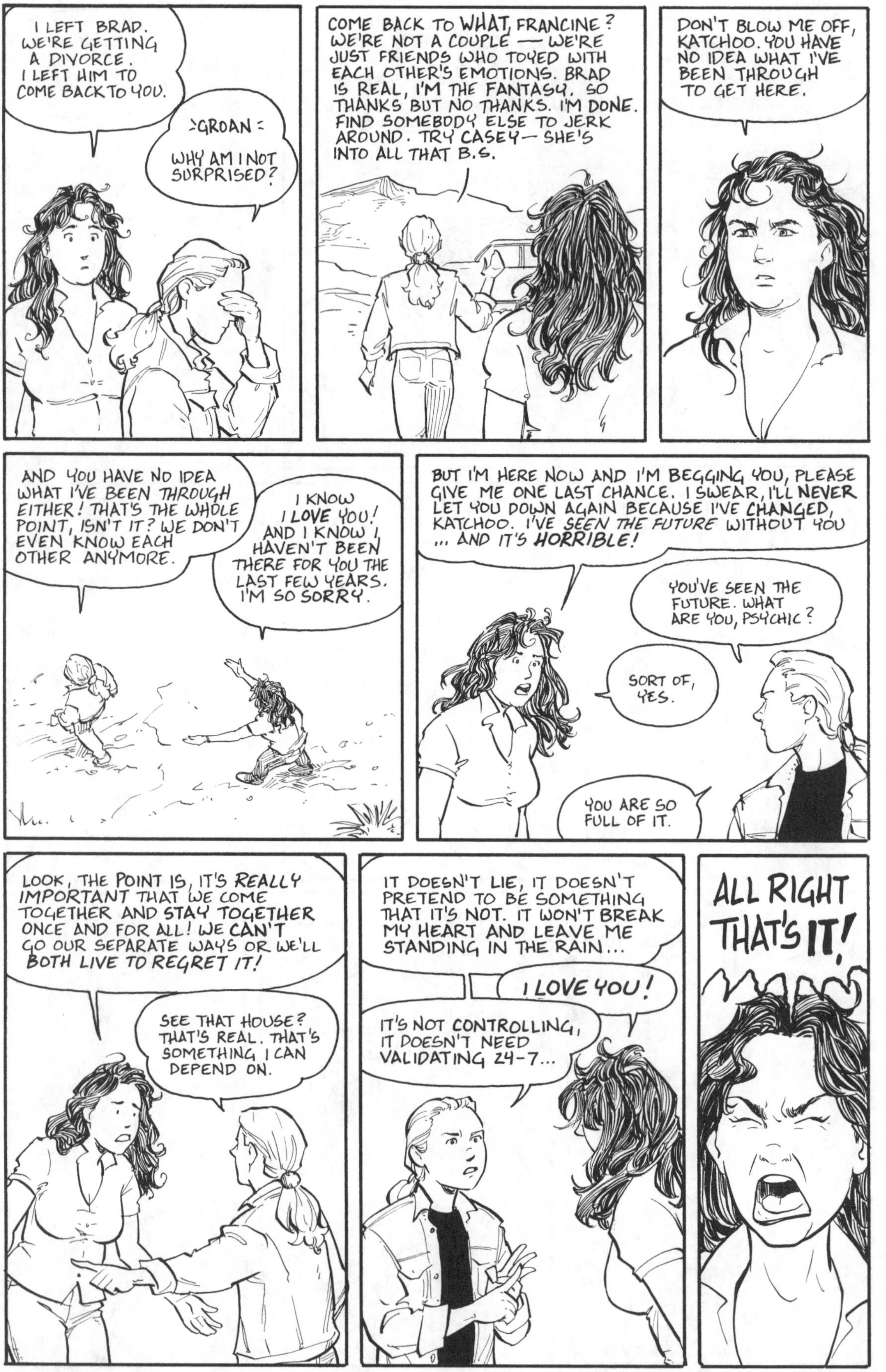
I LEFT BRAD. WE'RE GETTING A DIVORCE. I LEFT HIM TO COME BACK TO YOU.
=GROAN= WHY AM I NOT SURPRISED?
COME BACK TO WHAT, FRANCINE? WE'RE NOT A COUPLE — WE'RE JUST FRIENDS WHO TOYED WITH EACH OTHER'S EMOTIONS. BRAD IS REAL, I'M THE FANTASY. SO THANKS BUT NO THANKS. I'M DONE. FIND SOMEBODY ELSE TO JERK AROUND. TRY CASEY— SHE'S INTO ALL THAT B.S.
DON'T BLOW ME OFF, KATCHOO. YOU HAVE NO IDEA WHAT I'VE BEEN THROUGH TO GET HERE.
AND YOU HAVE NO IDEA WHAT I'VE BEEN THROUGH EITHER! THAT'S THE WHOLE POINT, ISN'T IT? WE DON'T EVEN KNOW EACH OTHER ANYMORE.
I KNOW I LOVE YOU! AND I KNOW I HAVEN'T BEEN THERE FOR YOU THE LAST FEW YEARS. I'M SO SORRY.
BUT I'M HERE NOW AND I'M BEGGING YOU, PLEASE GIVE ME ONE LAST CHANCE. I SWEAR, I'LL NEVER LET YOU DOWN AGAIN BECAUSE I'VE CHANGED, KATCHOO. I'VE SEEN THE FUTURE WITHOUT YOU ... AND IT'S HORRIBLE!
YOU'VE SEEN THE FUTURE. WHAT ARE YOU, PSYCHIC?
SORT OF, YES.
YOU ARE SO FULL OF IT.
LOOK, THE POINT IS, IT'S REALLY IMPORTANT THAT WE COME TOGETHER AND STAY TOGETHER ONCE AND FOR ALL! WE CAN'T GO OUR SEPARATE WAYS OR WE'LL BOTH LIVE TO REGRET IT!
SEE THAT HOUSE? THAT'S REAL. THAT'S SOMETHING I CAN DEPEND ON.
IT DOESN'T LIE, IT DOESN'T PRETEND TO BE SOMETHING THAT IT'S NOT. IT WON'T BREAK MY HEART AND LEAVE ME STANDING IN THE RAIN...
I LOVE YOU!
IT'S NOT CONTROLLING, IT DOESN'T NEED VALIDATING 24-7...
ALL RIGHT THAT'S IT!

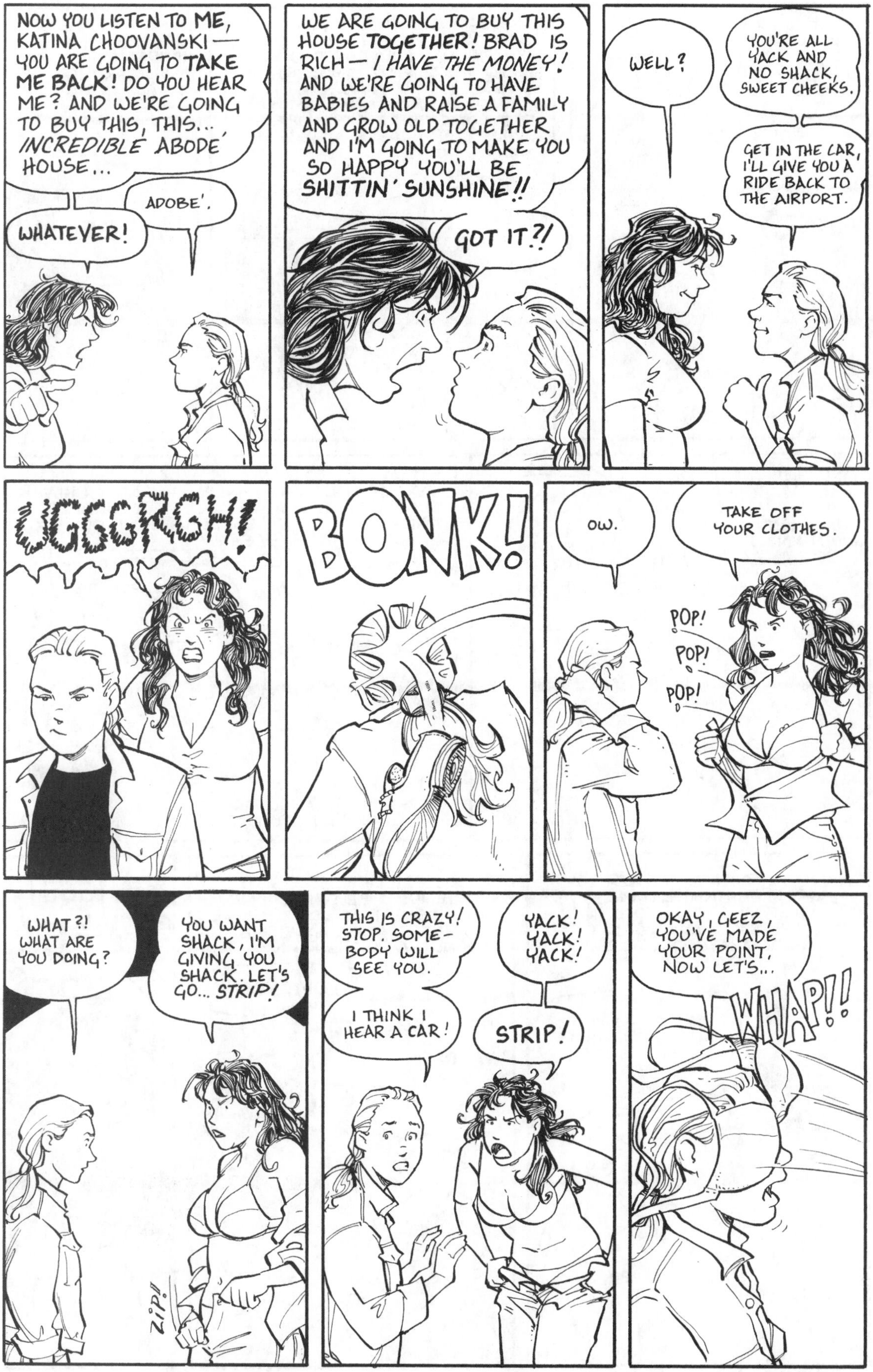
NOW YOU LISTEN TO ME, KATINA CHOOVANSKI — YOU ARE GOING TO TAKE ME BACK! DO YOU HEAR ME? AND WE'RE GOING TO BUY THIS, THIS... INCREDIBLE ABODE HOUSE...
ADOBE'.
WHATEVER!
WE ARE GOING TO BUY THIS HOUSE TOGETHER! BRAD IS RICH — I HAVE THE MONEY! AND WE'RE GOING TO HAVE BABIES AND RAISE A FAMILY AND GROW OLD TOGETHER AND I'M GOING TO MAKE YOU SO HAPPY YOU'LL BE SHITTIN' SUNSHINE!!
GOT IT?!
WELL?
YOU'RE ALL YACK AND NO SHACK, SWEET CHEEKS.
GET IN THE CAR, I'LL GIVE YOU A RIDE BACK TO THE AIRPORT.
UGGGRGH!
BONK!
OW.
TAKE OFF YOUR CLOTHES.
POP!
POP!
POP!
WHAT?! WHAT ARE YOU DOING?
YOU WANT SHACK, I'M GIVING YOU SHACK. LET'S GO... STRIP!
ZIP!
THIS IS CRAZY! STOP. SOMEBODY WILL SEE YOU.
YACK! YACK! YACK!
I THINK I HEAR A CAR!
STRIP!
OKAY, GEEZ, YOU'VE MADE YOUR POINT, NOW LET'S...
WHAP!!

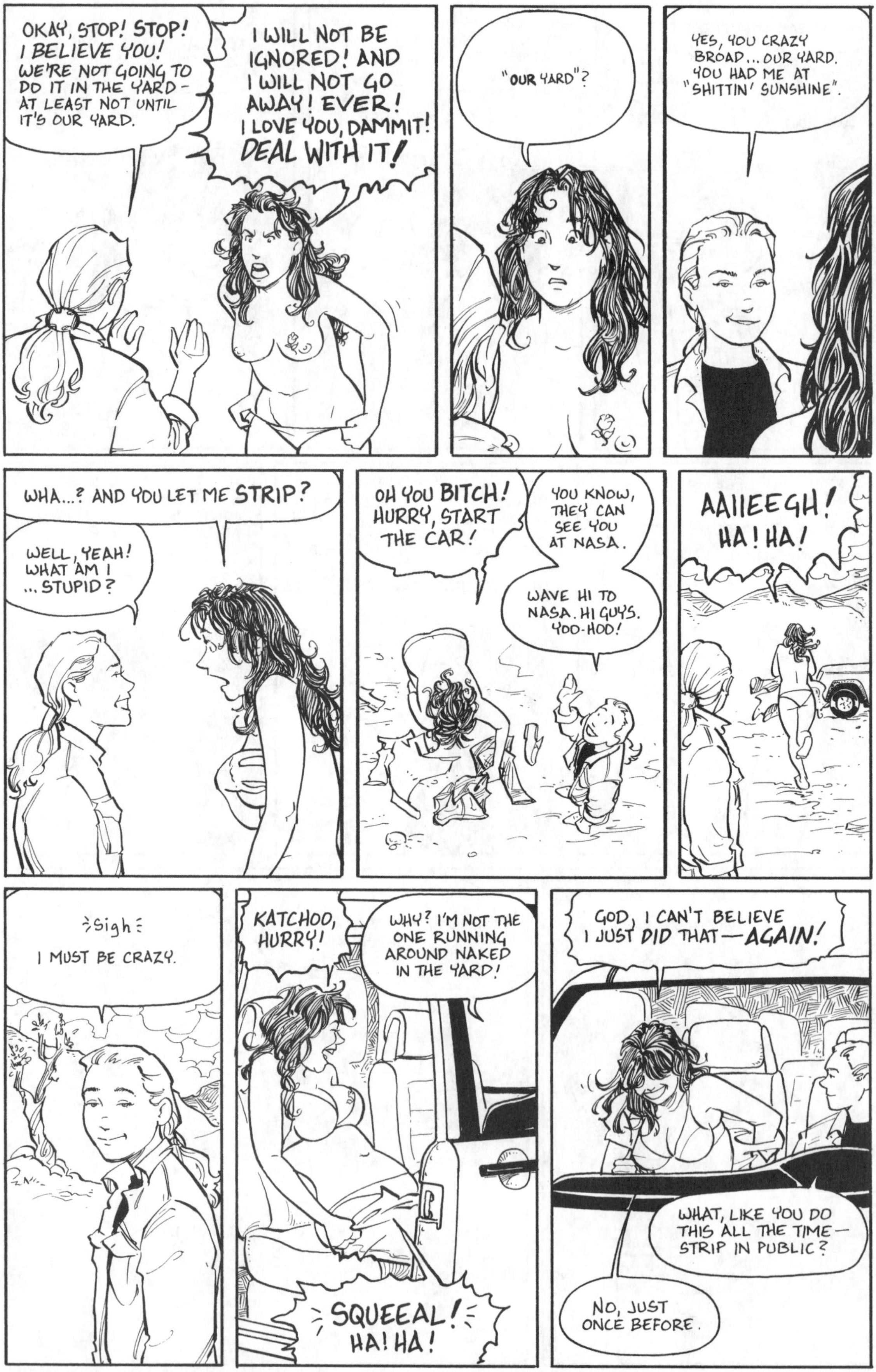
OKAY, STOP! STOP! I BELIEVE YOU! WE'RE NOT GOING TO DO IT IN THE YARD - AT LEAST NOT UNTIL IT'S OUR YARD.
I WILL NOT BE IGNORED! AND I WILL NOT GO AWAY! EVER! I LOVE YOU, DAMMIT! DEAL WITH IT!
"OUR YARD"?
YES, YOU CRAZY BROAD... OUR YARD. YOU HAD ME AT "SHITTIN' SUNSHINE".
WHA...? AND YOU LET ME STRIP?
WELL, YEAH! WHAT AM I ... STUPID?
OH YOU BITCH! HURRY, START THE CAR!
YOU KNOW, THEY CAN SEE YOU AT NASA.
WAVE HI TO NASA. HI GUYS. YOO-HOO!
AAIIEEGH! HA! HA!
Sigh
I MUST BE CRAZY.
KATCHOO, HURRY!
WHY? I'M NOT THE ONE RUNNING AROUND NAKED IN THE YARD!
SQUEEAL! HA! HA!
GOD, I CAN'T BELIEVE I JUST DID THAT—AGAIN!
WHAT, LIKE YOU DO THIS ALL THE TIME— STRIP IN PUBLIC?
NO, JUST ONCE BEFORE.

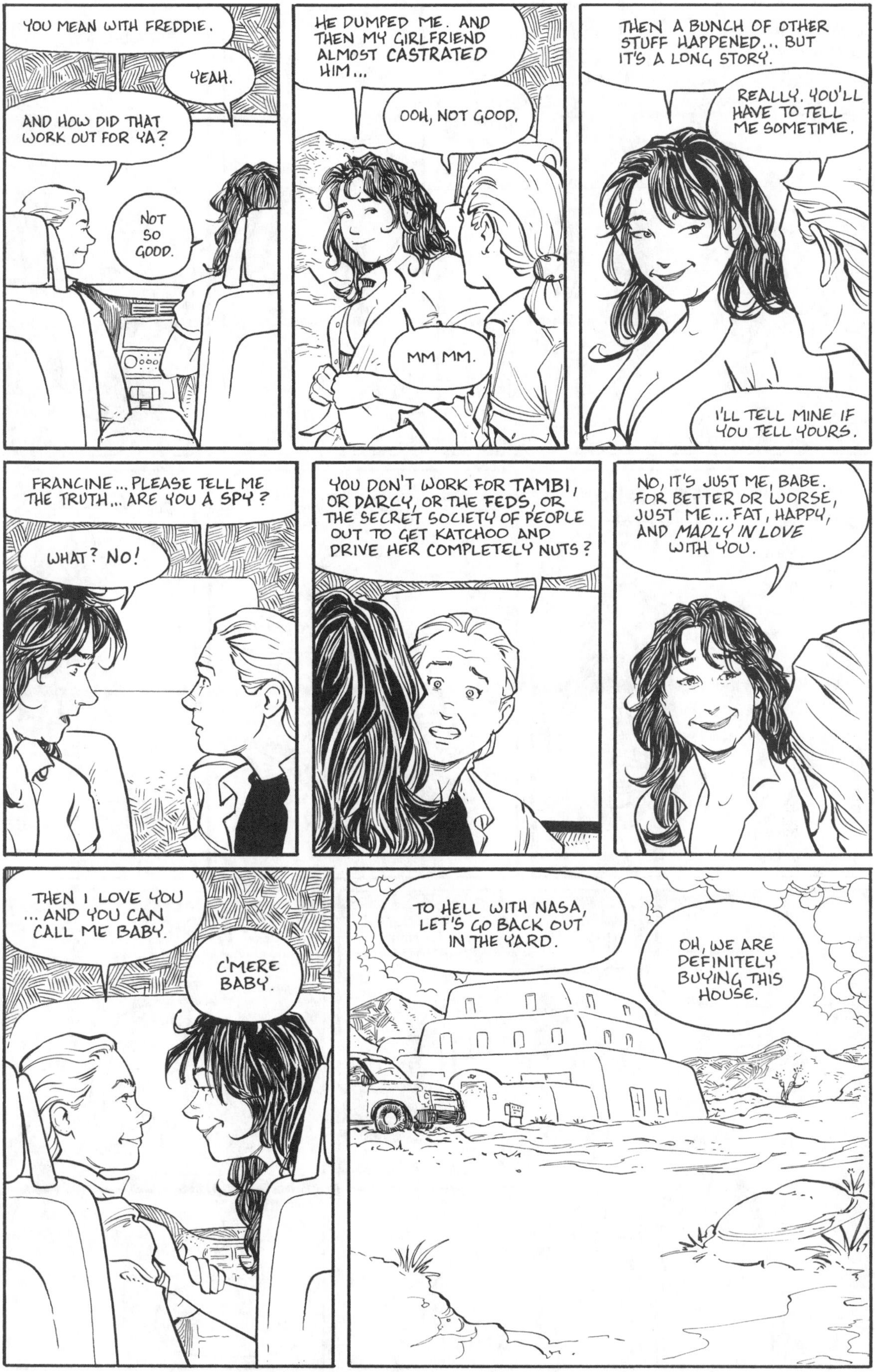
YOU MEAN WITH FREDDIE.
YEAH.
AND HOW DID THAT WORK OUT FOR YA?
NOT SO GOOD.
HE DUMPED ME. AND THEN MY GIRLFRIEND ALMOST CASTRATED HIM...
OOH, NOT GOOD.
MM MM.
THEN A BUNCH OF OTHER STUFF HAPPENED... BUT IT'S A LONG STORY.
REALLY. YOU'LL HAVE TO TELL ME SOMETIME.
I'LL TELL MINE IF YOU TELL YOURS.
FRANCINE... PLEASE TELL ME THE TRUTH... ARE YOU A SPY?
WHAT? NO!
YOU DON'T WORK FOR TAMBI, OR DARCY, OR THE FEDS, OR THE SECRET SOCIETY OF PEOPLE OUT TO GET KATCHOO AND DRIVE HER COMPLETELY NUTS?
NO, IT'S JUST ME, BABE. FOR BETTER OR WORSE, JUST ME... FAT, HAPPY, AND MADLY IN LOVE WITH YOU.
THEN I LOVE YOU ...AND YOU CAN CALL ME BABY.
C'MERE BABY.
TO HELL WITH NASA, LET'S GO BACK OUT IN THE YARD.
OH, WE ARE DEFINITELY BUYING THIS HOUSE.

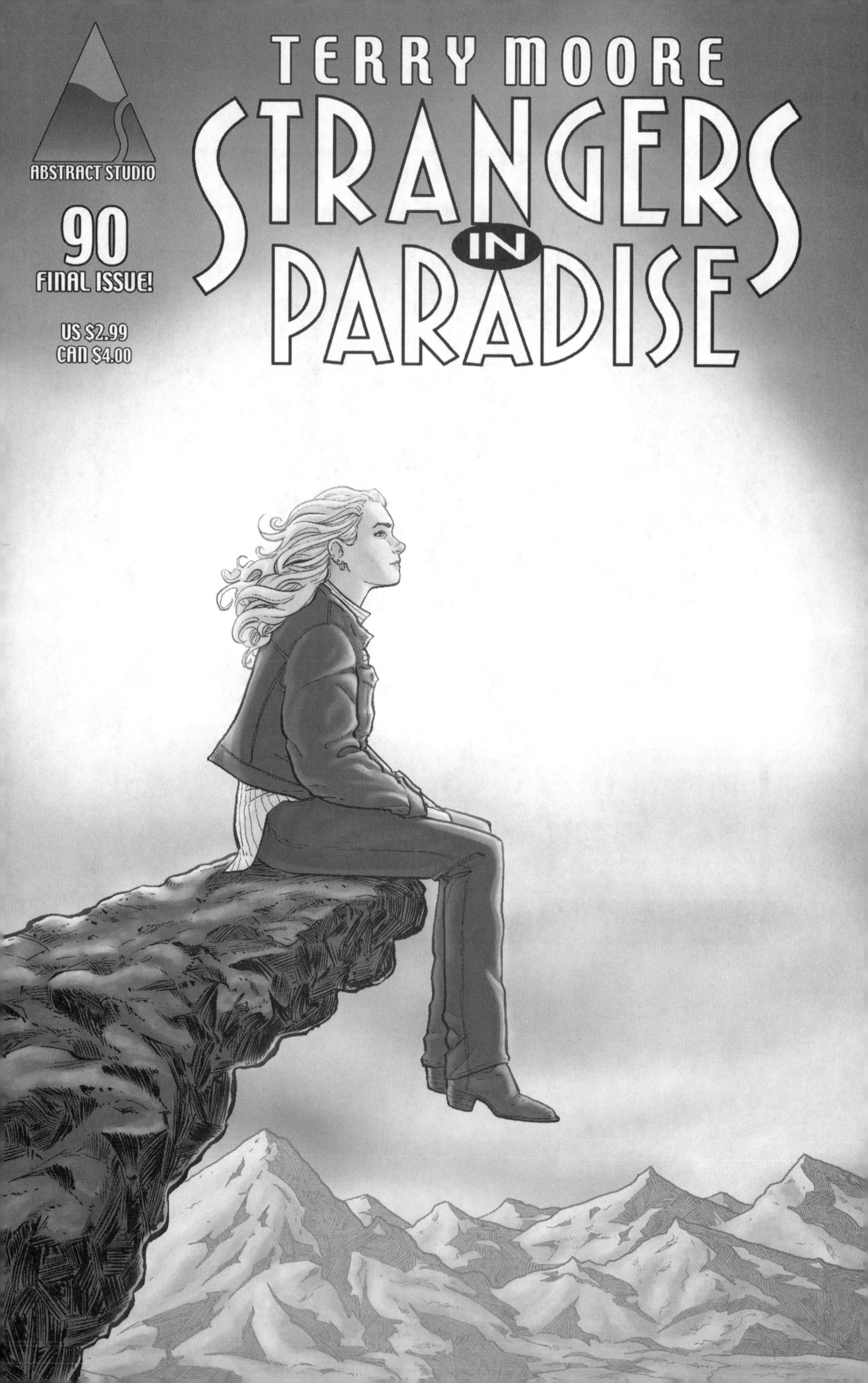
ABSTRACT STUDIO
90
FINAL ISSUE!
US $2.99
CAN $4.00
TERRY MOORE
STRANGERS IN PARADISE

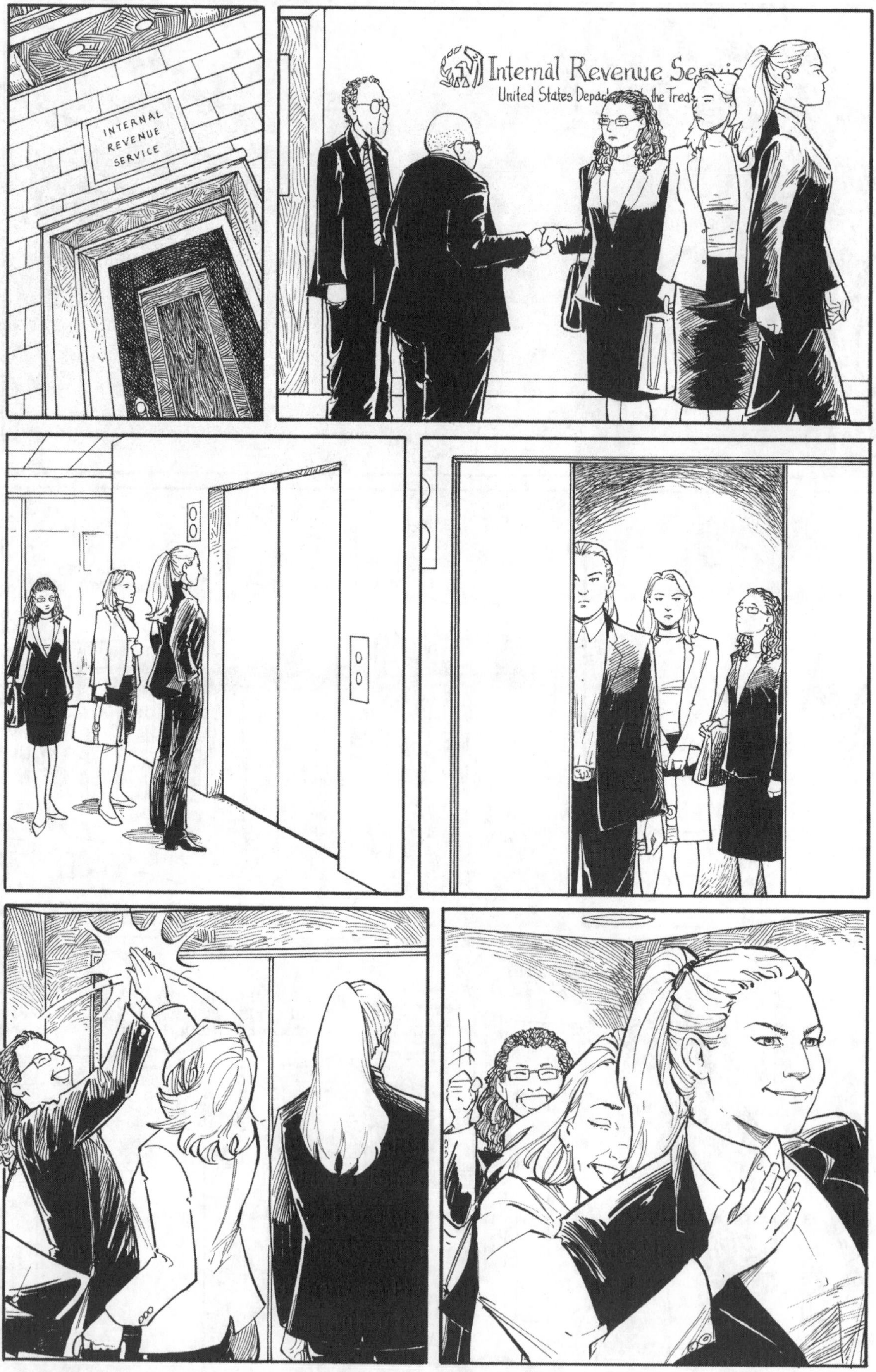
INTERNAL REVENUE SERVICE
Internal Revenue Servic
United States Depar the Trea

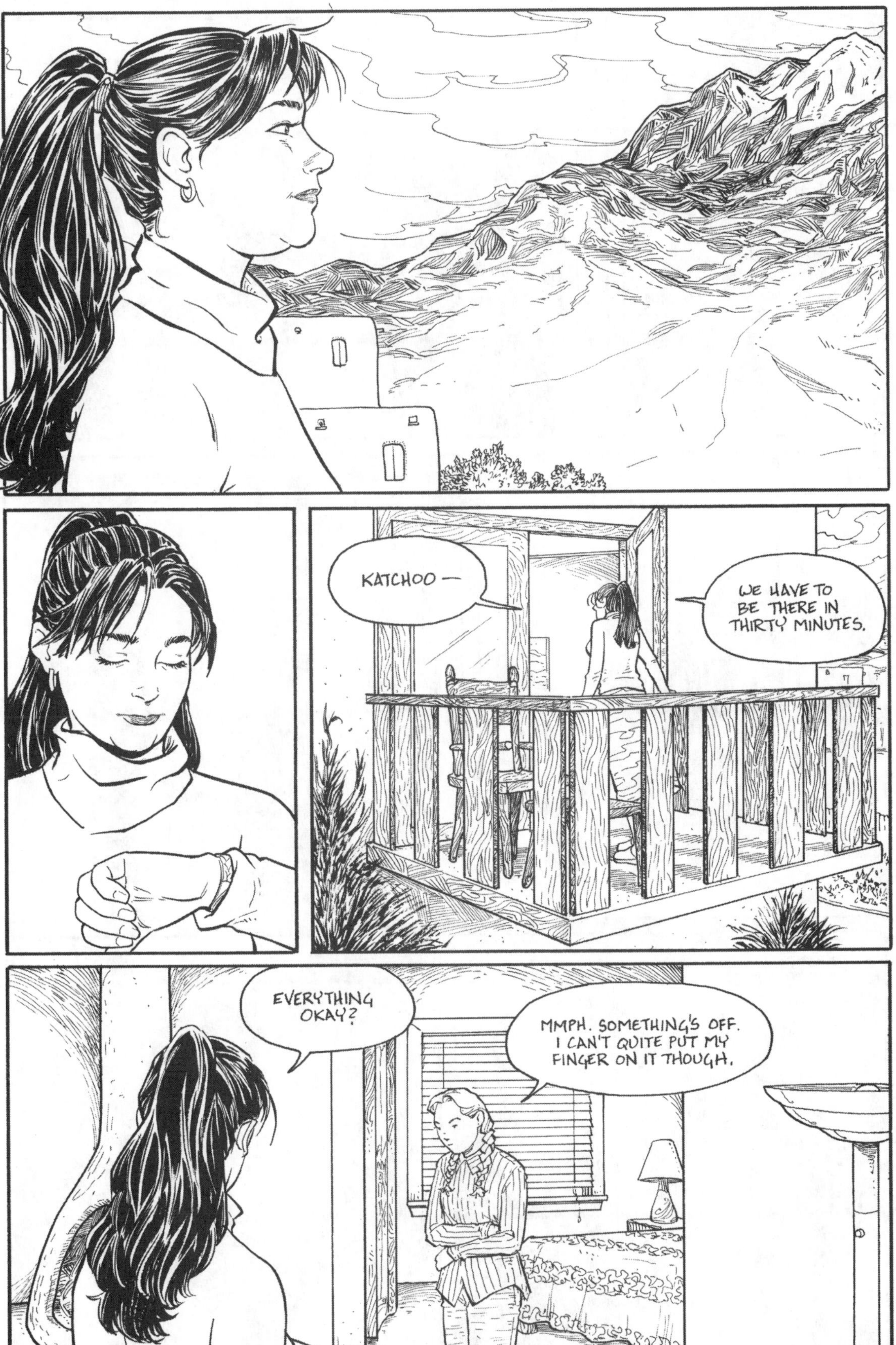
KATCHOO —
WE HAVE TO BE THERE IN THIRTY MINUTES.
EVERYTHING OKAY?
MMPH. SOMETHING'S OFF. I CAN'T QUITE PUT MY FINGER ON IT THOUGH.

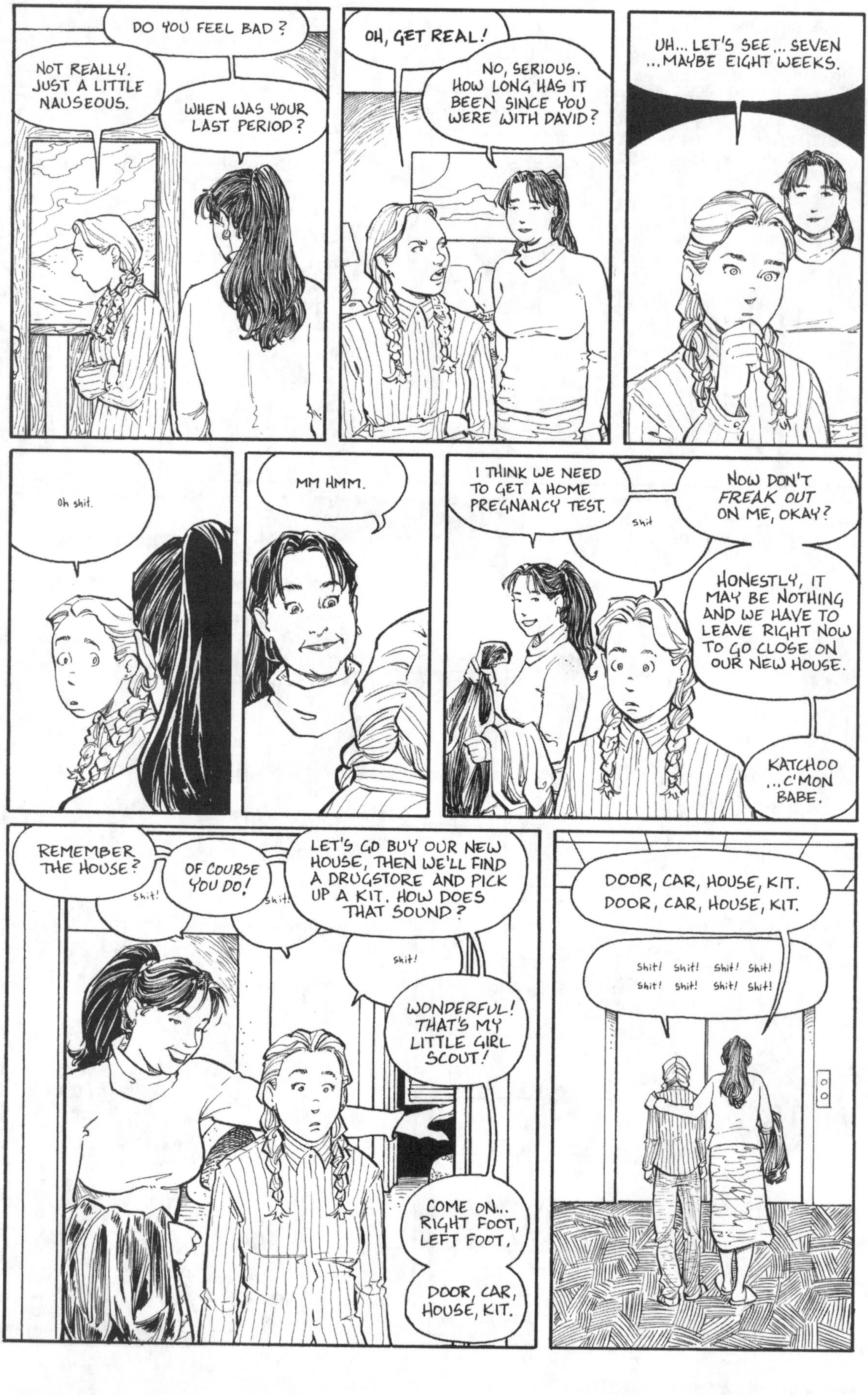
DO YOU FEEL BAD?
NOT REALLY. JUST A LITTLE NAUSEOUS.
WHEN WAS YOUR LAST PERIOD?
OH, GET REAL!
NO, SERIOUS. HOW LONG HAS IT BEEN SINCE YOU WERE WITH DAVID?
UH... LET'S SEE... SEVEN ...MAYBE EIGHT WEEKS.
Oh shit.
MM HMM.
I THINK WE NEED TO GET A HOME PREGNANCY TEST.
shit
NOW DON'T FREAK OUT ON ME, OKAY?
HONESTLY, IT MAY BE NOTHING AND WE HAVE TO LEAVE RIGHT NOW TO GO CLOSE ON OUR NEW HOUSE.
KATCHOO ...C'MON BABE.
REMEMBER THE HOUSE?
shit!
OF COURSE YOU DO!
shit!
LET'S GO BUY OUR NEW HOUSE, THEN WE'LL FIND A DRUGSTORE AND PICK UP A KIT. HOW DOES THAT SOUND?
shit!
WONDERFUL! THAT'S MY LITTLE GIRL SCOUT!
COME ON... RIGHT FOOT, LEFT FOOT.
DOOR, CAR, HOUSE, KIT.
DOOR, CAR, HOUSE, KIT. DOOR, CAR, HOUSE, KIT.
Shit! Shit! Shit! Shit! Shit! Shit! Shit! Shit!

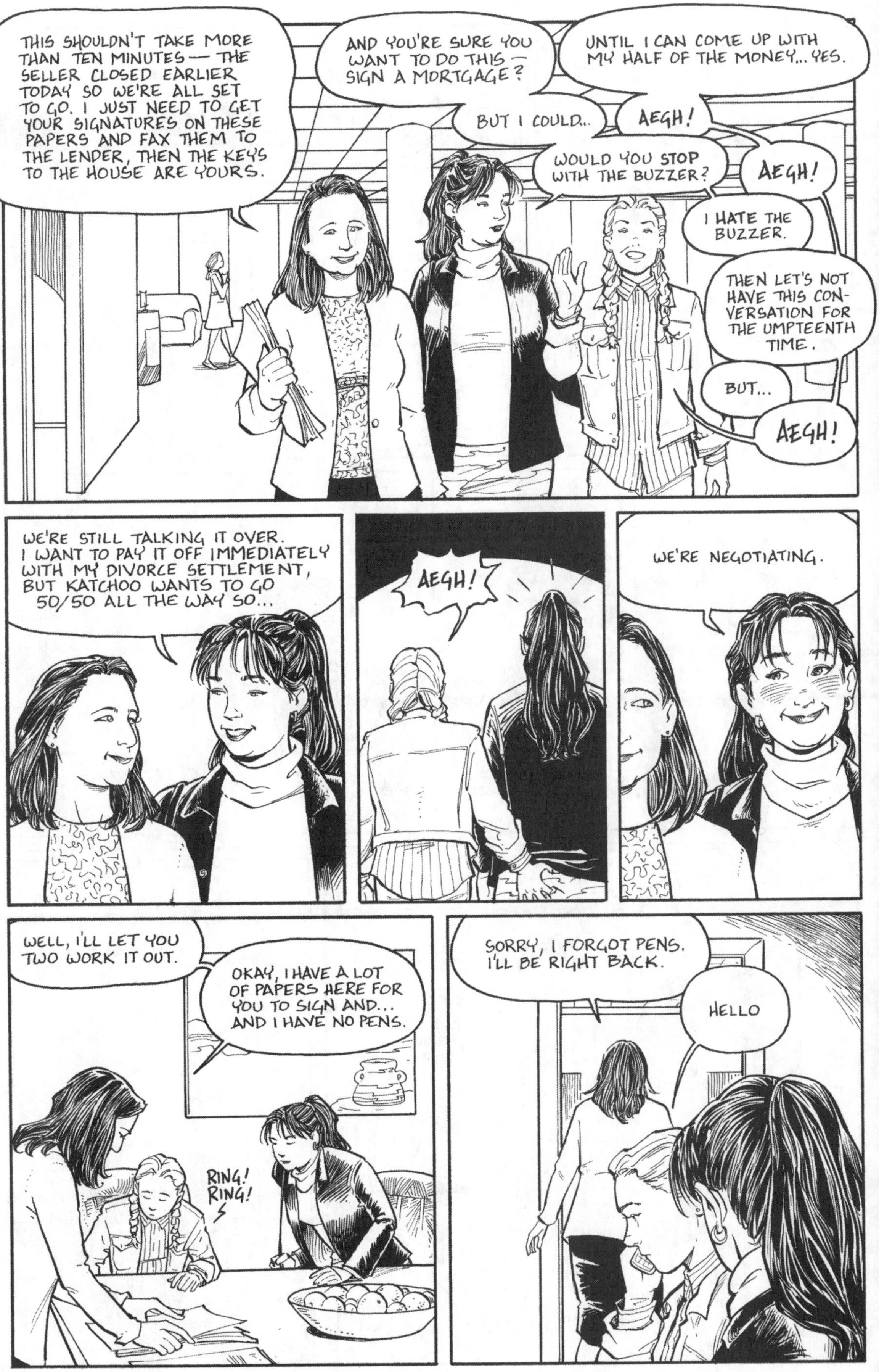
THIS SHOULDN'T TAKE MORE THAN TEN MINUTES — THE SELLER CLOSED EARLIER TODAY SO WE'RE ALL SET TO GO. I JUST NEED TO GET YOUR SIGNATURES ON THESE PAPERS AND FAX THEM TO THE LENDER, THEN THE KEYS TO THE HOUSE ARE YOURS.
AND YOU'RE SURE YOU WANT TO DO THIS — SIGN A MORTGAGE?
UNTIL I CAN COME UP WITH MY HALF OF THE MONEY... YES.
BUT I COULD..
AEGH!
WOULD YOU STOP WITH THE BUZZER?
AEGH!
I HATE THE BUZZER.
THEN LET'S NOT HAVE THIS CONVERSATION FOR THE UMPTEENTH TIME.
BUT...
AEGH!
WE'RE STILL TALKING IT OVER. I WANT TO PAY IT OFF IMMEDIATELY WITH MY DIVORCE SETTLEMENT, BUT KATCHOO WANTS TO GO 50/50 ALL THE WAY SO...
AEGH!
WE'RE NEGOTIATING.
WELL, I'LL LET YOU TWO WORK IT OUT.
OKAY, I HAVE A LOT OF PAPERS HERE FOR YOU TO SIGN AND... AND I HAVE NO PENS.
RING! RING!
SORRY, I FORGOT PENS. I'LL BE RIGHT BACK.
HELLO

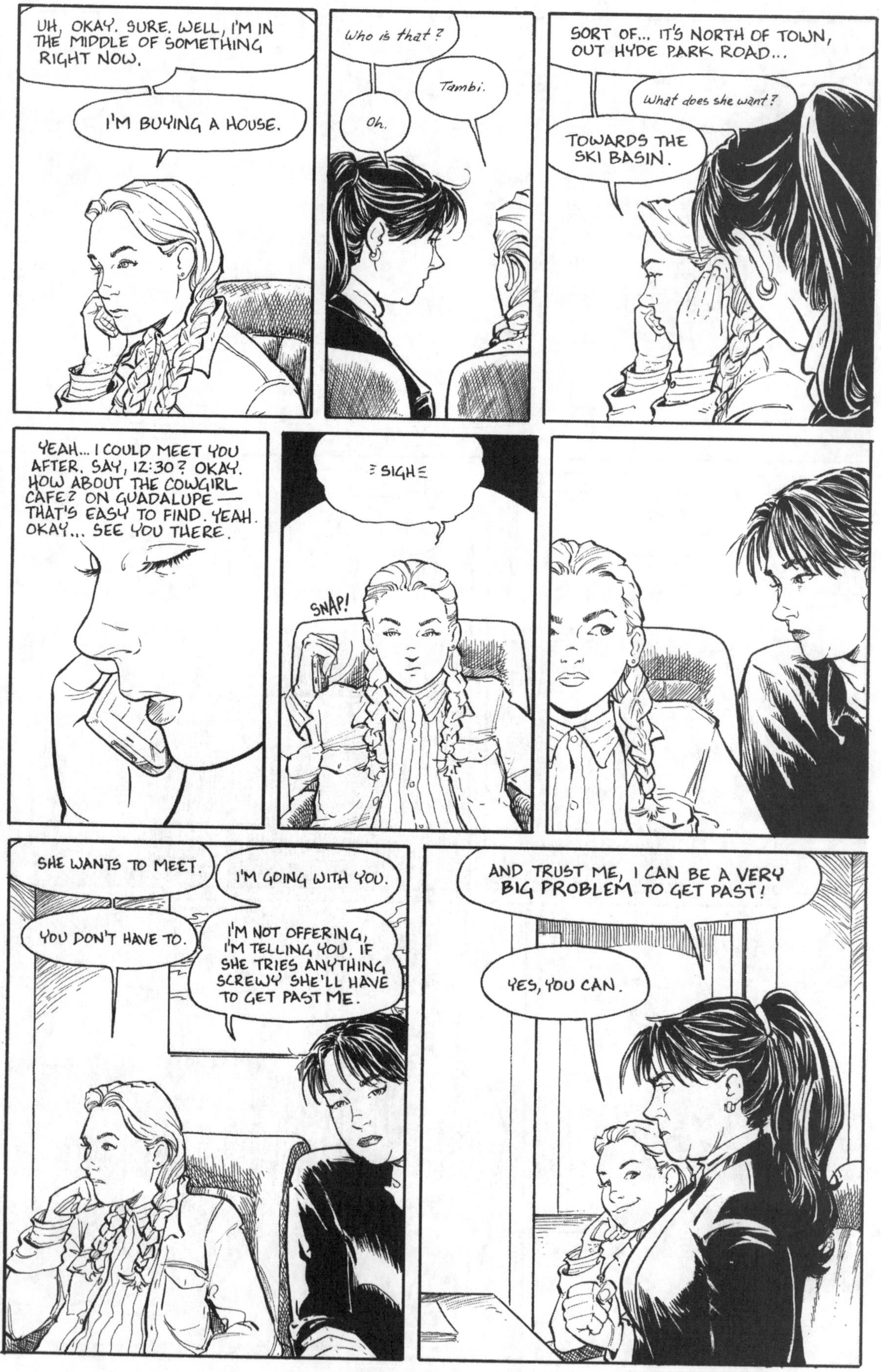
UH, OKAY. SURE. WELL, I'M IN THE MIDDLE OF SOMETHING RIGHT NOW.
I'M BUYING A HOUSE.
Who is that?
Tambi.
Oh.
SORT OF... IT'S NORTH OF TOWN, OUT HYDE PARK ROAD...
What does she want?
TOWARDS THE SKI BASIN.
YEAH... I COULD MEET YOU AFTER. SAY, 12:30? OKAY. HOW ABOUT THE COWGIRL CAFE? ON GUADALUPE — THAT'S EASY TO FIND. YEAH. OKAY... SEE YOU THERE.
SIGH
SNAP!
SHE WANTS TO MEET.
I'M GOING WITH YOU.
YOU DON'T HAVE TO.
I'M NOT OFFERING, I'M TELLING YOU. IF SHE TRIES ANYTHING SCREWY SHE'LL HAVE TO GET PAST ME.
AND TRUST ME, I CAN BE A VERY BIG PROBLEM TO GET PAST!
YES, YOU CAN.

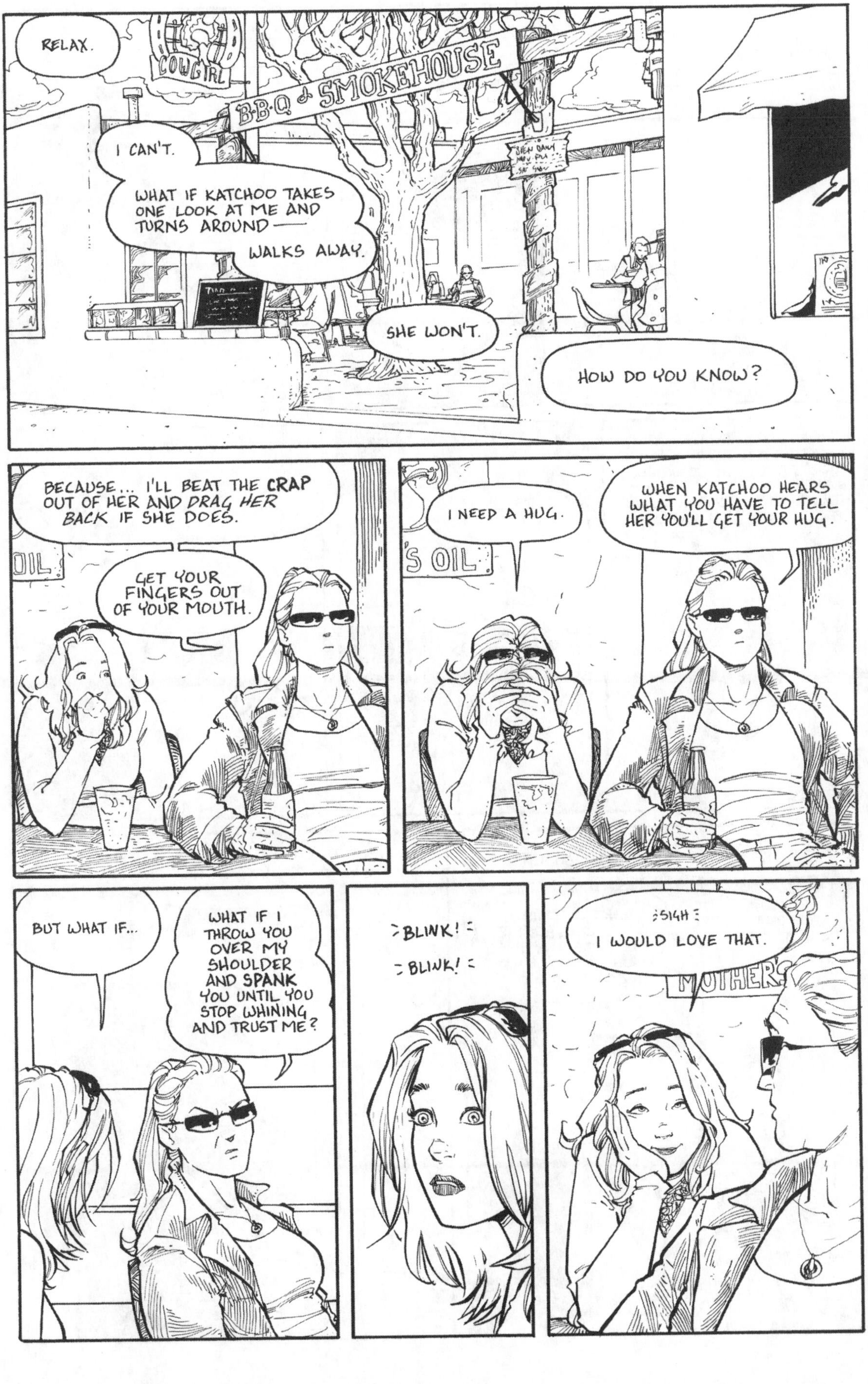
RELAX.
COWGIRL
B·B·Q & SMOKEHOUSE
I CAN'T.
WHAT IF KATCHOO TAKES ONE LOOK AT ME AND TURNS AROUND—
WALKS AWAY.
SHE WON'T.
HOW DO YOU KNOW?
BECAUSE... I'LL BEAT THE **CRAP** OUT OF HER AND *DRAG HER BACK* IF SHE DOES.
GET YOUR FINGERS OUT OF YOUR MOUTH.
I NEED A HUG.
WHEN KATCHOO HEARS WHAT YOU HAVE TO TELL HER YOU'LL GET YOUR HUG.
BUT WHAT IF...
WHAT IF I THROW YOU OVER MY SHOULDER AND **SPANK** YOU UNTIL YOU STOP WHINING AND TRUST ME?
BLINK!
BLINK!
SIGH
I WOULD LOVE THAT.

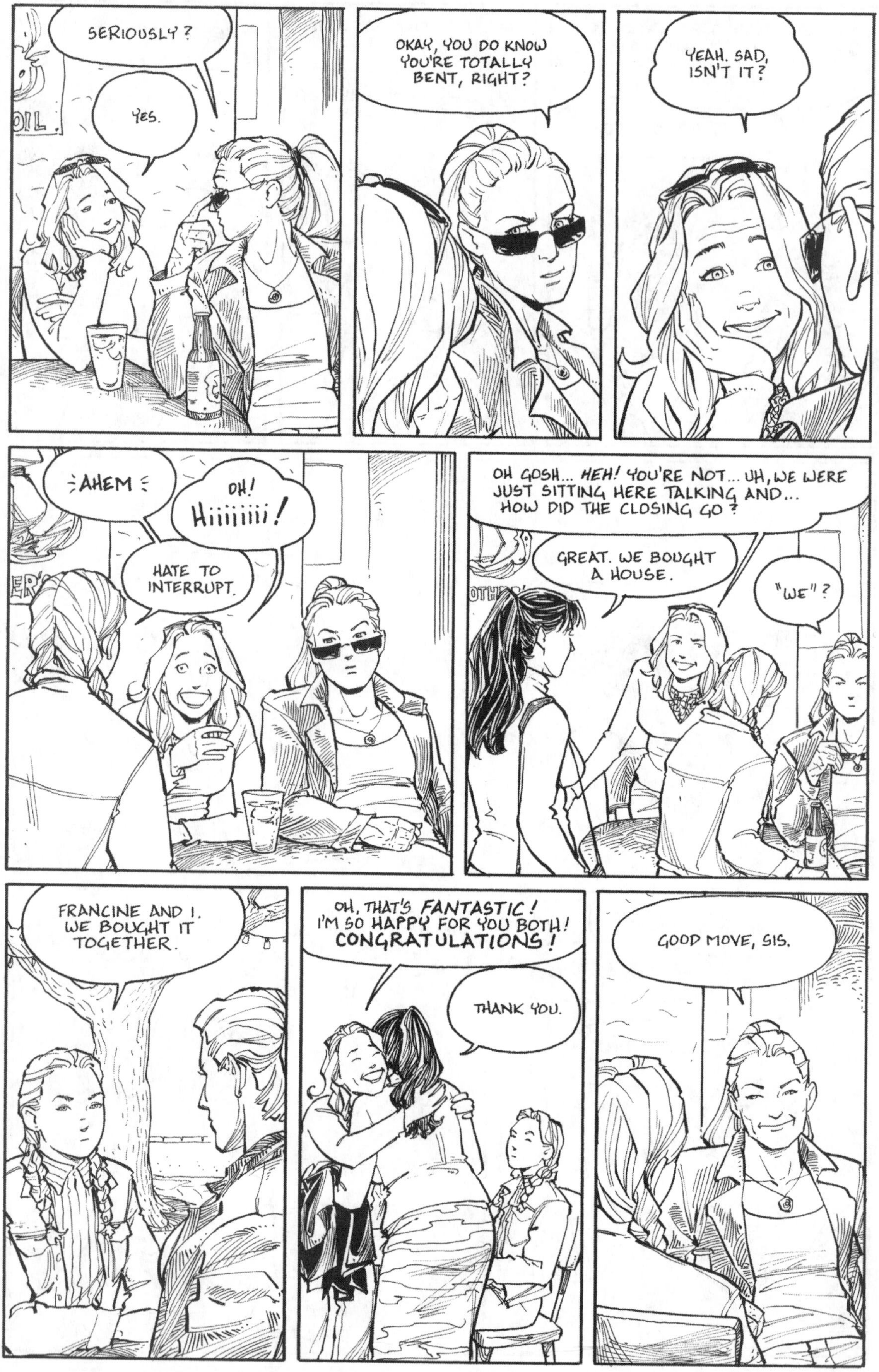
SERIOUSLY?
YES.
OIL.
OKAY, YOU DO KNOW YOU'RE TOTALLY BENT, RIGHT?
YEAH. SAD, ISN'T IT?
AHEM
OH! Hiiiiiii!
HATE TO INTERRUPT.
OH GOSH... HEH! YOU'RE NOT... UH, WE WERE JUST SITTING HERE TALKING AND... HOW DID THE CLOSING GO?
GREAT. WE BOUGHT A HOUSE.
"WE"?
FRANCINE AND I. WE BOUGHT IT TOGETHER.
OH, THAT'S FANTASTIC! I'M SO HAPPY FOR YOU BOTH! CONGRATULATIONS!
THANK YOU.
GOOD MOVE, SIS.

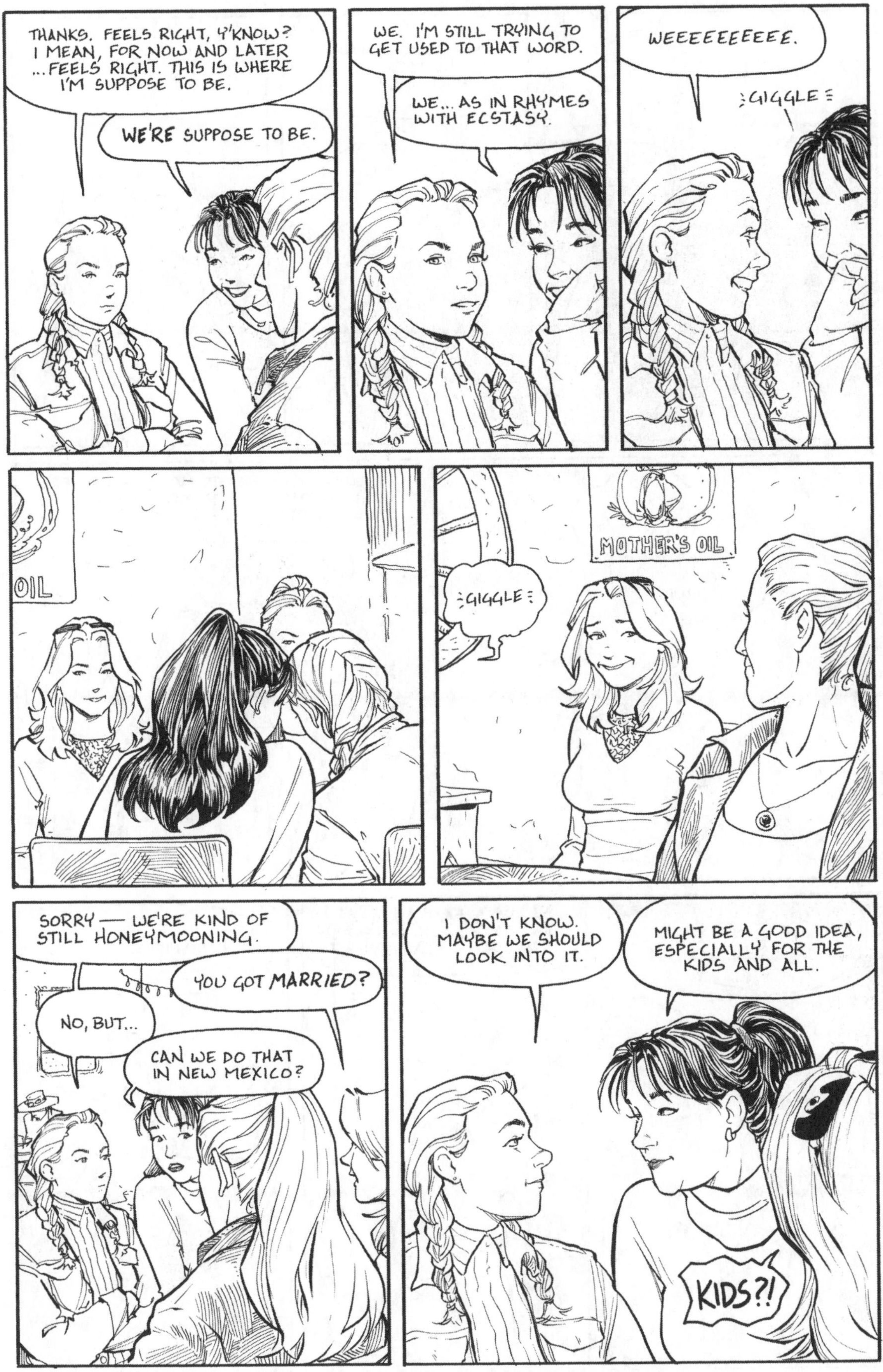
THANKS. FEELS RIGHT, Y'KNOW? I MEAN, FOR NOW AND LATER ...FEELS RIGHT. THIS IS WHERE I'M SUPPOSE TO BE.
WE'RE SUPPOSE TO BE.
WE. I'M STILL TRYING TO GET USED TO THAT WORD.
WE... AS IN RHYMES WITH ECSTASY.
WEEEEEEEEEE.
GIGGLE
OIL
MOTHER'S OIL
GIGGLE
SORRY — WE'RE KIND OF STILL HONEYMOONING.
YOU GOT MARRIED?
NO, BUT...
CAN WE DO THAT IN NEW MEXICO?
I DON'T KNOW. MAYBE WE SHOULD LOOK INTO IT.
MIGHT BE A GOOD IDEA, ESPECIALLY FOR THE KIDS AND ALL.
KIDS?!

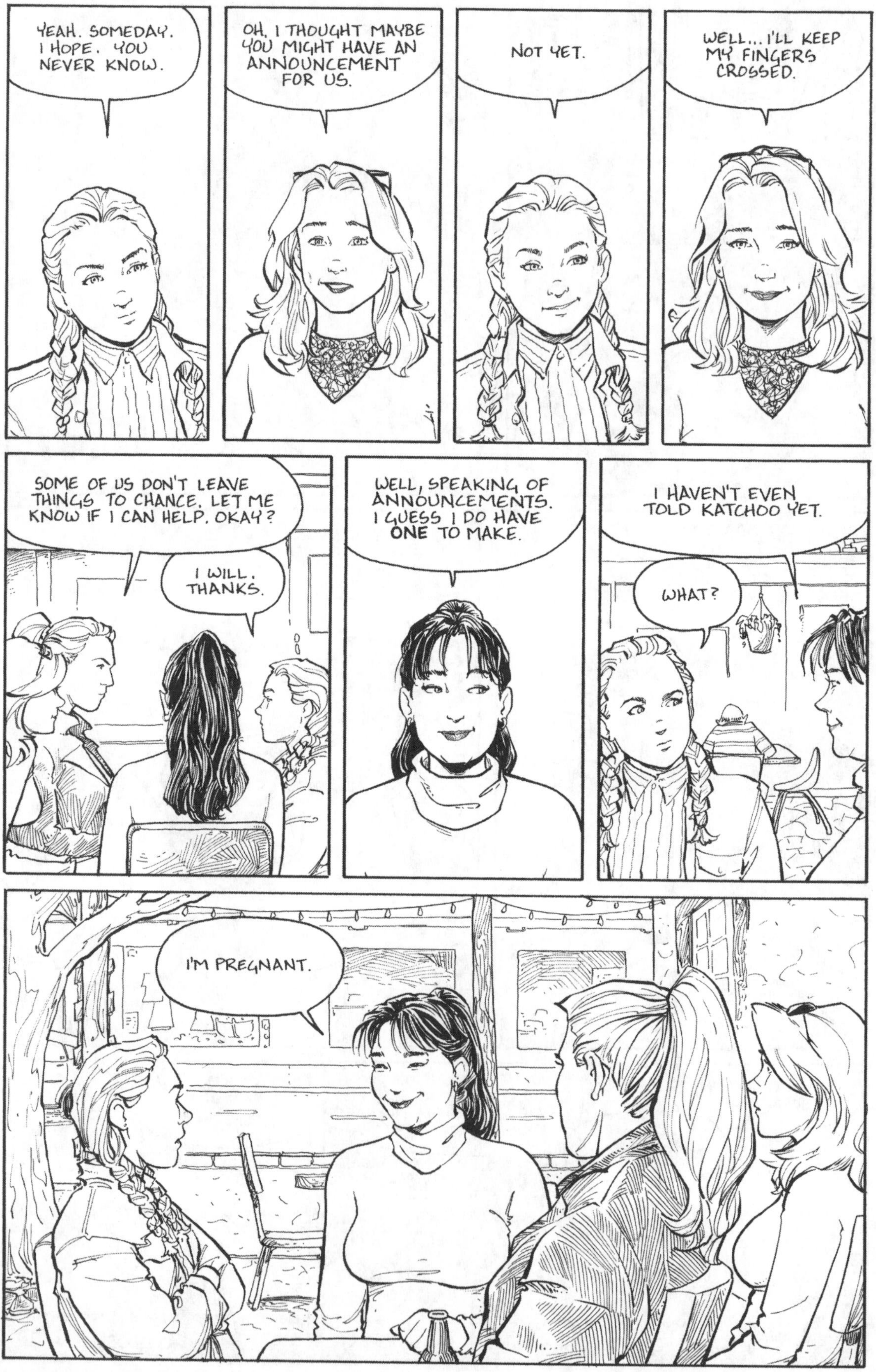
YEAH. SOMEDAY. I HOPE. YOU NEVER KNOW.
OH, I THOUGHT MAYBE YOU MIGHT HAVE AN ANNOUNCEMENT FOR US.
NOT YET.
WELL... I'LL KEEP MY FINGERS CROSSED.
SOME OF US DON'T LEAVE THINGS TO CHANCE. LET ME KNOW IF I CAN HELP, OKAY?
I WILL. THANKS.
WELL, SPEAKING OF ANNOUNCEMENTS. I GUESS I DO HAVE ONE TO MAKE.
I HAVEN'T EVEN TOLD KATCHOO YET.
WHAT?
I'M PREGNANT.

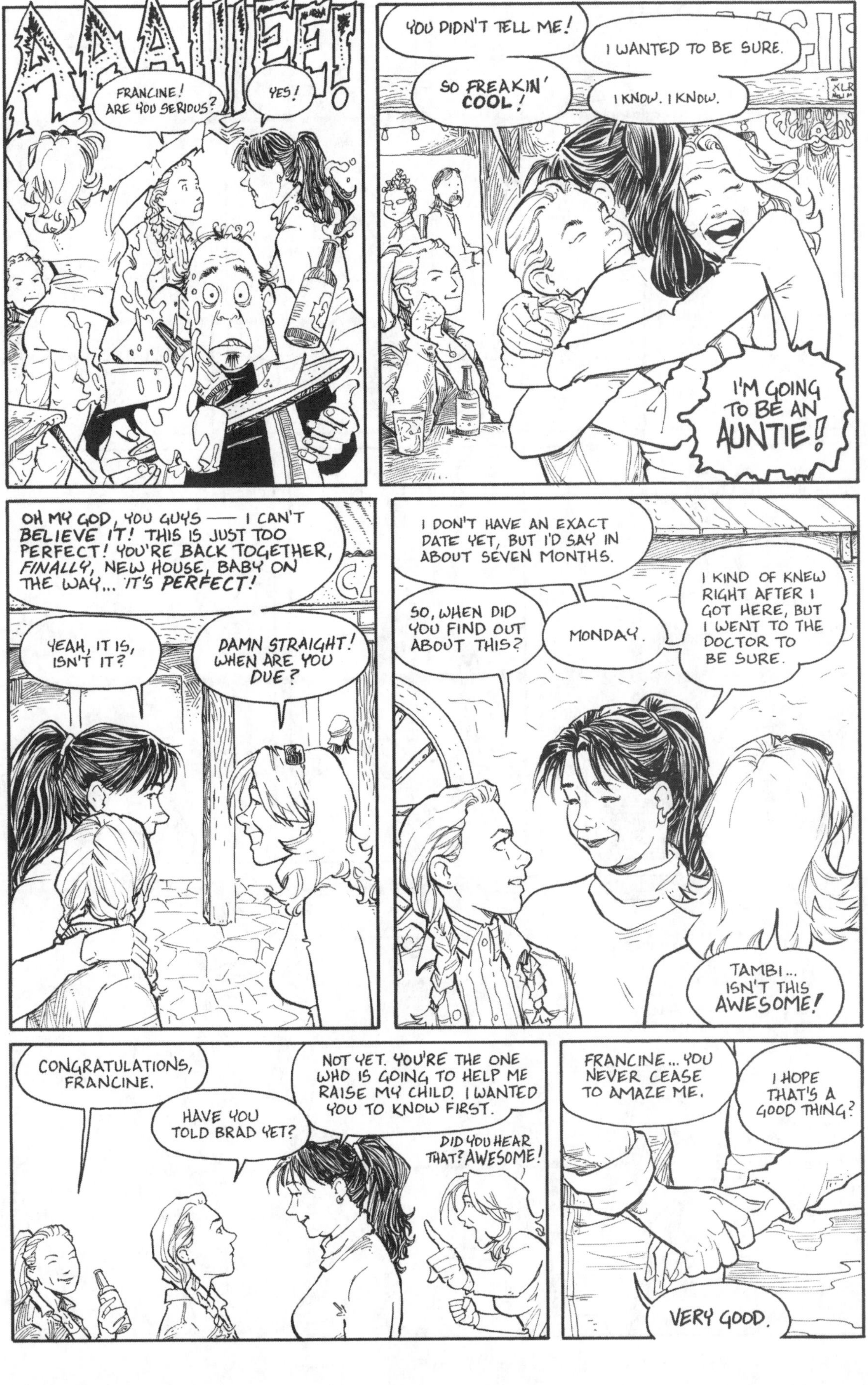
AAAIIIEEE!
FRANCINE! ARE YOU SERIOUS?
YES!
YOU DIDN'T TELL ME!
SO FREAKIN' COOL!
I WANTED TO BE SURE.
I KNOW. I KNOW.
I'M GOING TO BE AN AUNTIE!
OH MY GOD, YOU GUYS — I CAN'T BELIEVE IT! THIS IS JUST TOO PERFECT! YOU'RE BACK TOGETHER, FINALLY, NEW HOUSE, BABY ON THE WAY... IT'S PERFECT!
YEAH, IT IS, ISN'T IT?
DAMN STRAIGHT! WHEN ARE YOU DUE?
I DON'T HAVE AN EXACT DATE YET, BUT I'D SAY IN ABOUT SEVEN MONTHS.
SO, WHEN DID YOU FIND OUT ABOUT THIS?
MONDAY.
I KIND OF KNEW RIGHT AFTER I GOT HERE, BUT I WENT TO THE DOCTOR TO BE SURE.
TAMBI... ISN'T THIS AWESOME!
CONGRATULATIONS, FRANCINE.
HAVE YOU TOLD BRAD YET?
NOT YET. YOU'RE THE ONE WHO IS GOING TO HELP ME RAISE MY CHILD. I WANTED YOU TO KNOW FIRST.
DID YOU HEAR THAT? AWESOME!
FRANCINE... YOU NEVER CEASE TO AMAZE ME.
I HOPE THAT'S A GOOD THING?
VERY GOOD.

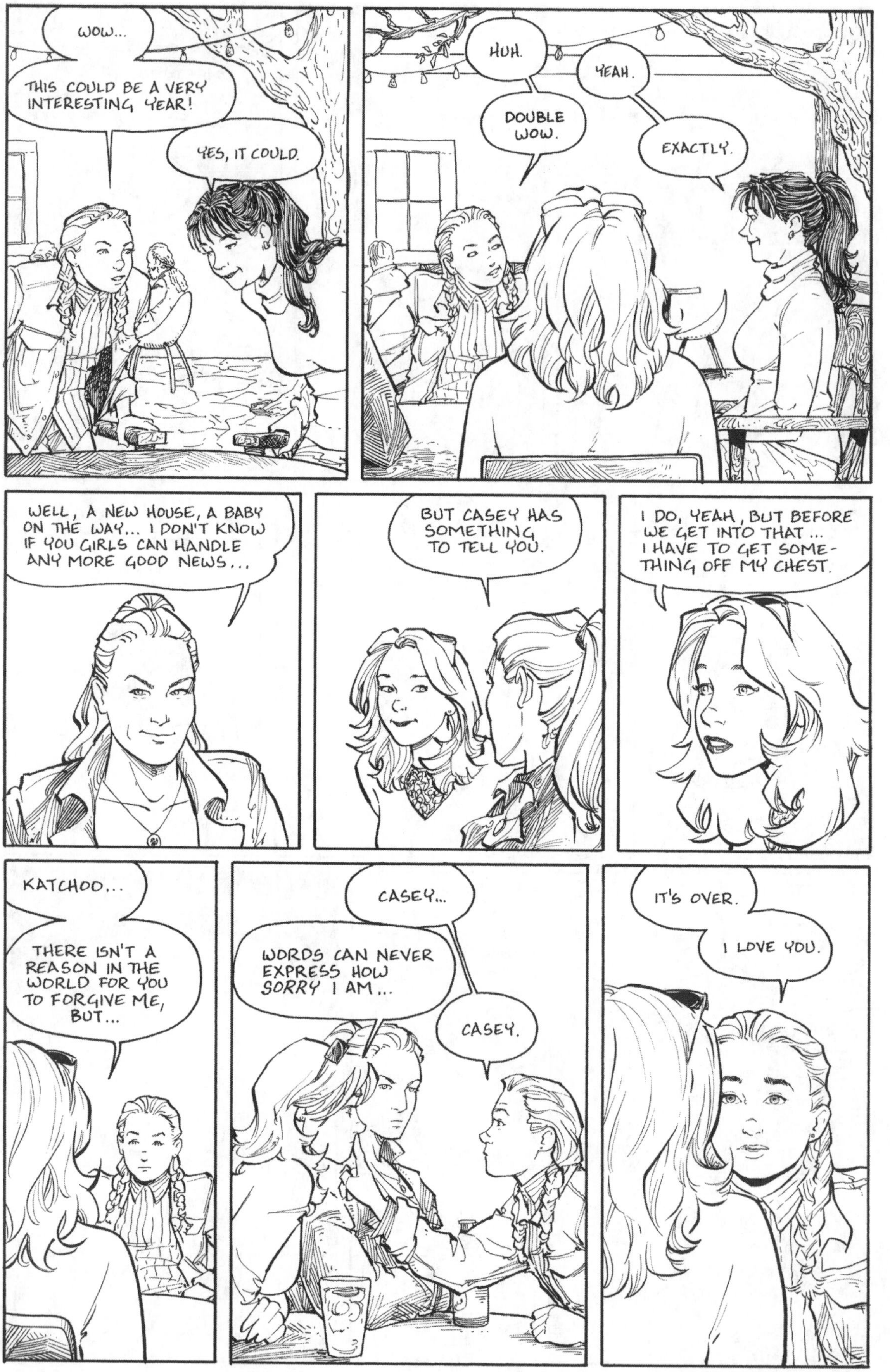
WOW...
THIS COULD BE A VERY INTERESTING YEAR!
YES, IT COULD.
HUH.
DOUBLE WOW.
YEAH.
EXACTLY.
WELL, A NEW HOUSE, A BABY ON THE WAY... I DON'T KNOW IF YOU GIRLS CAN HANDLE ANY MORE GOOD NEWS...
BUT CASEY HAS SOMETHING TO TELL YOU.
I DO, YEAH, BUT BEFORE WE GET INTO THAT... I HAVE TO GET SOME-THING OFF MY CHEST.
KATCHOO...
THERE ISN'T A REASON IN THE WORLD FOR YOU TO FORGIVE ME, BUT...
WORDS CAN NEVER EXPRESS HOW *SORRY* I AM...
CASEY...
CASEY.
IT'S OVER.
I LOVE YOU.

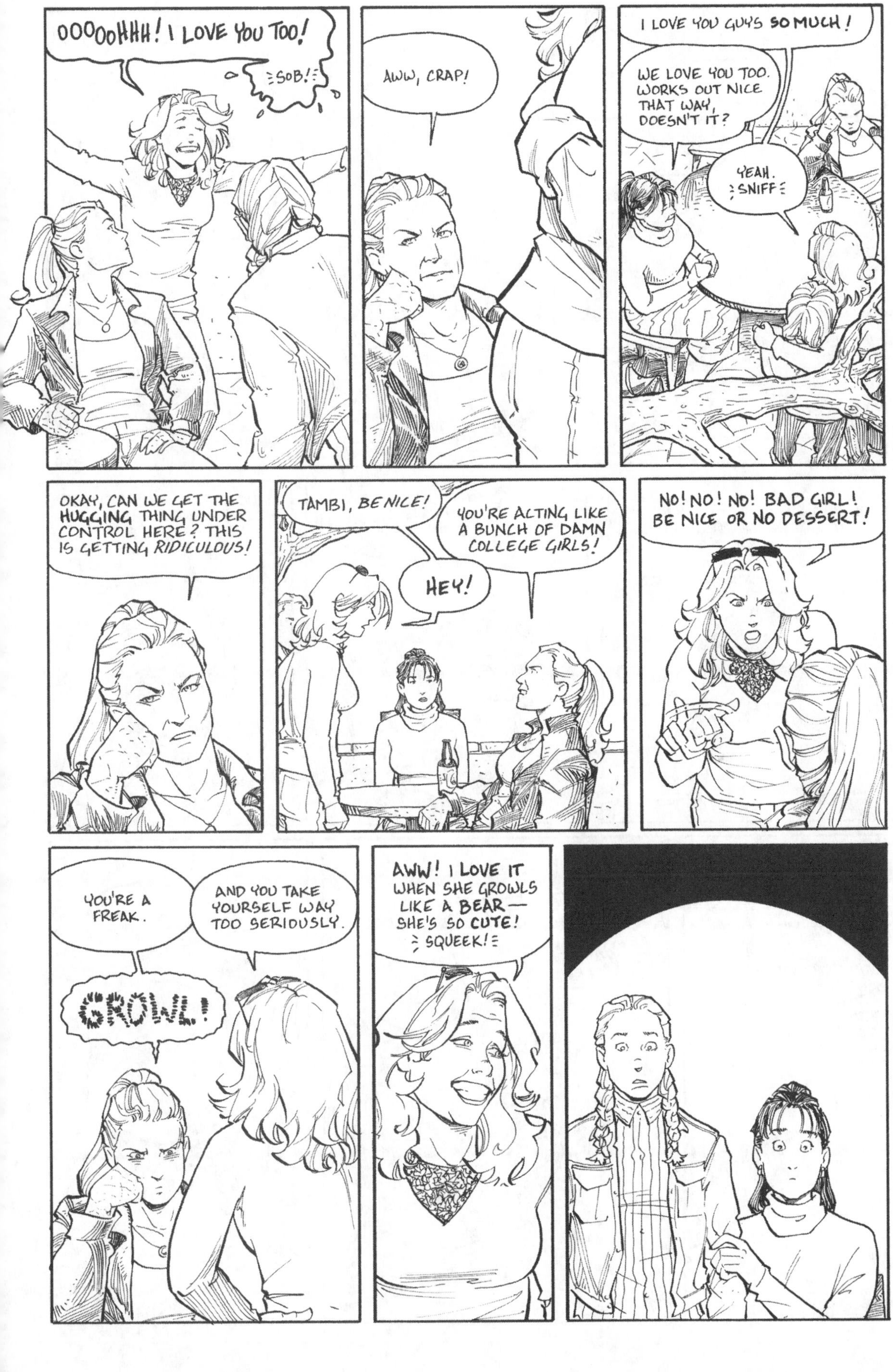

OOOOOHHH! I LOVE YOU TOO!
SOB!
AWW, CRAP!
I LOVE YOU GUYS SO MUCH!
WE LOVE YOU TOO. WORKS OUT NICE THAT WAY, DOESN'T IT?
YEAH. SNIFF
OKAY, CAN WE GET THE HUGGING THING UNDER CONTROL HERE? THIS IS GETTING RIDICULOUS!
TAMBI, BE NICE!
YOU'RE ACTING LIKE A BUNCH OF DAMN COLLEGE GIRLS!
HEY!
NO! NO! NO! BAD GIRL! BE NICE OR NO DESSERT!
YOU'RE A FREAK.
AND YOU TAKE YOURSELF WAY TOO SERIOUSLY.
GROWL!
AWW! I LOVE IT WHEN SHE GROWLS LIKE A BEAR— SHE'S SO CUTE!
SQUEEK!

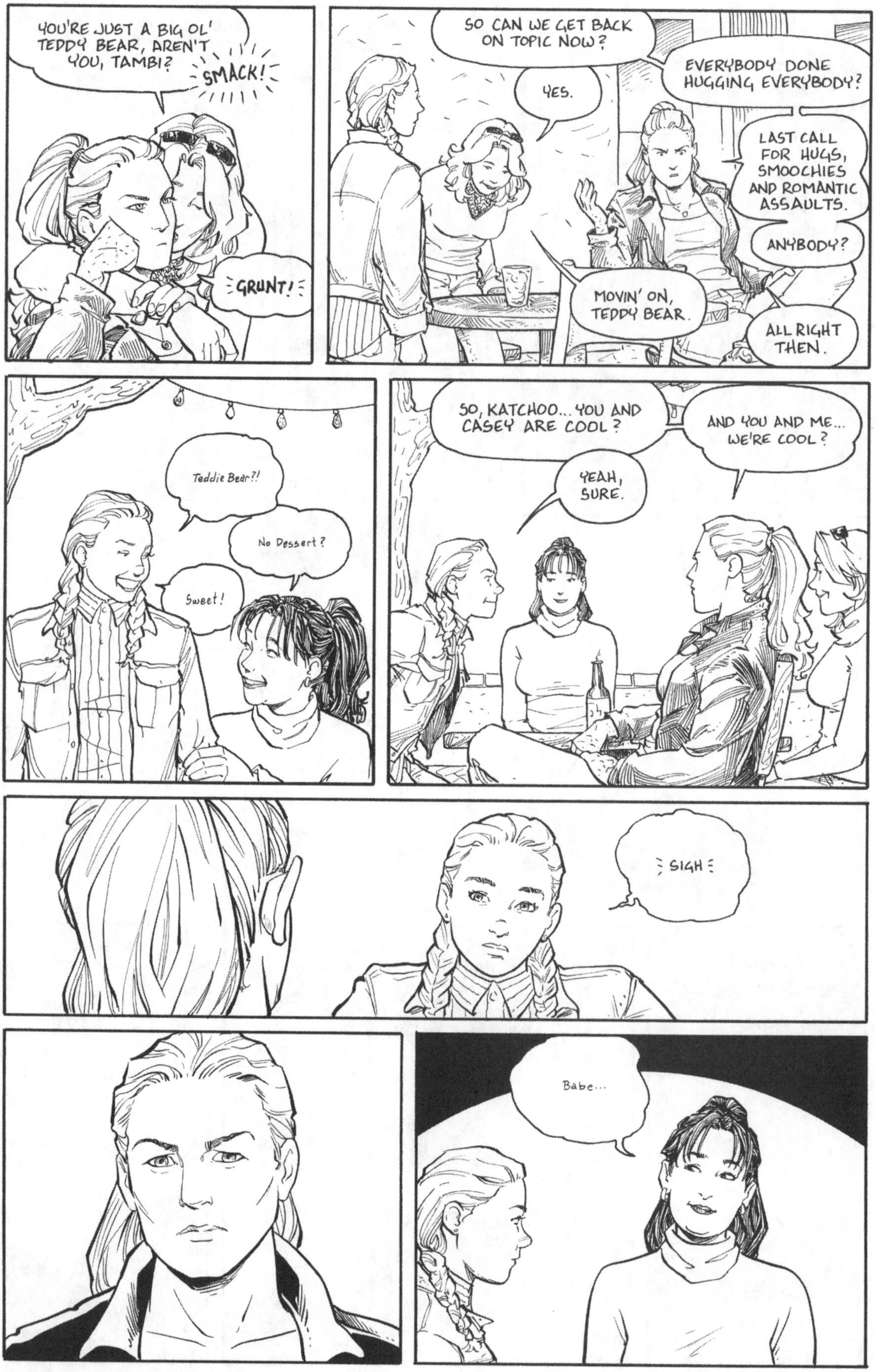
YOU'RE JUST A BIG OL' TEDDY BEAR, AREN'T YOU, TAMBI?
SMACK!
GRUNT!
SO CAN WE GET BACK ON TOPIC NOW?
YES.
EVERYBODY DONE HUGGING EVERYBODY?
LAST CALL FOR HUGS, SMOOCHIES AND ROMANTIC ASSAULTS.
ANYBODY?
MOVIN' ON, TEDDY BEAR.
ALL RIGHT THEN.
Teddie Bear?!
No Dessert?
Sweet!
SO, KATCHOO... YOU AND CASEY ARE COOL?
YEAH, SURE.
AND YOU AND ME... WE'RE COOL?
SIGH
Babe...

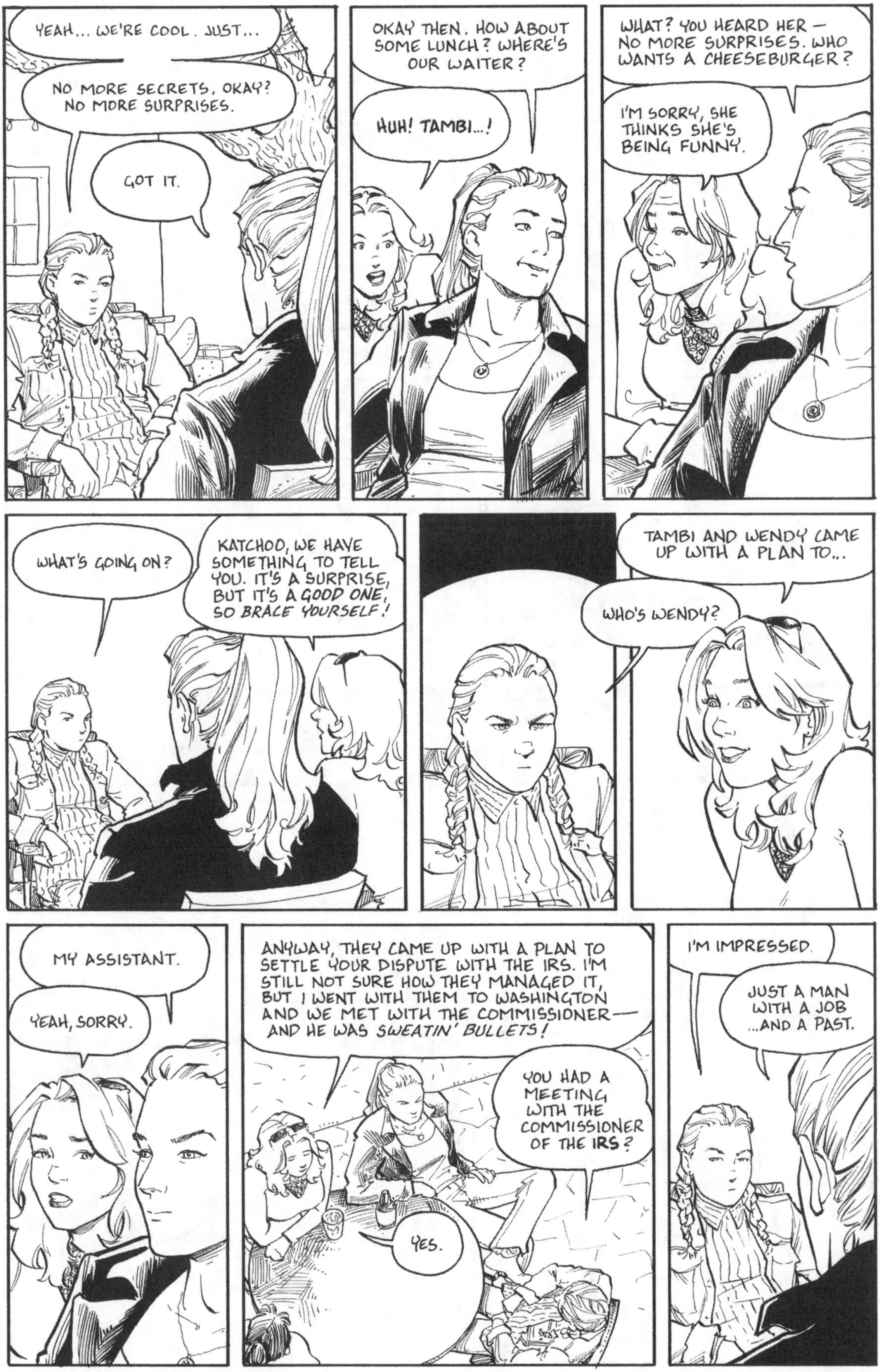
YEAH... WE'RE COOL. JUST...
NO MORE SECRETS, OKAY? NO MORE SURPRISES.
GOT IT.
OKAY THEN. HOW ABOUT SOME LUNCH? WHERE'S OUR WAITER?
HUH! TAMBI...!
WHAT? YOU HEARD HER — NO MORE SURPRISES. WHO WANTS A CHEESEBURGER?
I'M SORRY, SHE THINKS SHE'S BEING FUNNY.
WHAT'S GOING ON?
KATCHOO, WE HAVE SOMETHING TO TELL YOU. IT'S A SURPRISE, BUT IT'S A GOOD ONE, SO BRACE YOURSELF!
TAMBI AND WENDY CAME UP WITH A PLAN TO...
WHO'S WENDY?
MY ASSISTANT.
YEAH, SORRY.
ANYWAY, THEY CAME UP WITH A PLAN TO SETTLE YOUR DISPUTE WITH THE IRS. I'M STILL NOT SURE HOW THEY MANAGED IT, BUT I WENT WITH THEM TO WASHINGTON AND WE MET WITH THE COMMISSIONER — AND HE WAS SWEATIN' BULLETS!
YOU HAD A MEETING WITH THE COMMISSIONER OF THE IRS?
YES.
I'M IMPRESSED.
JUST A MAN WITH A JOB ...AND A PAST.

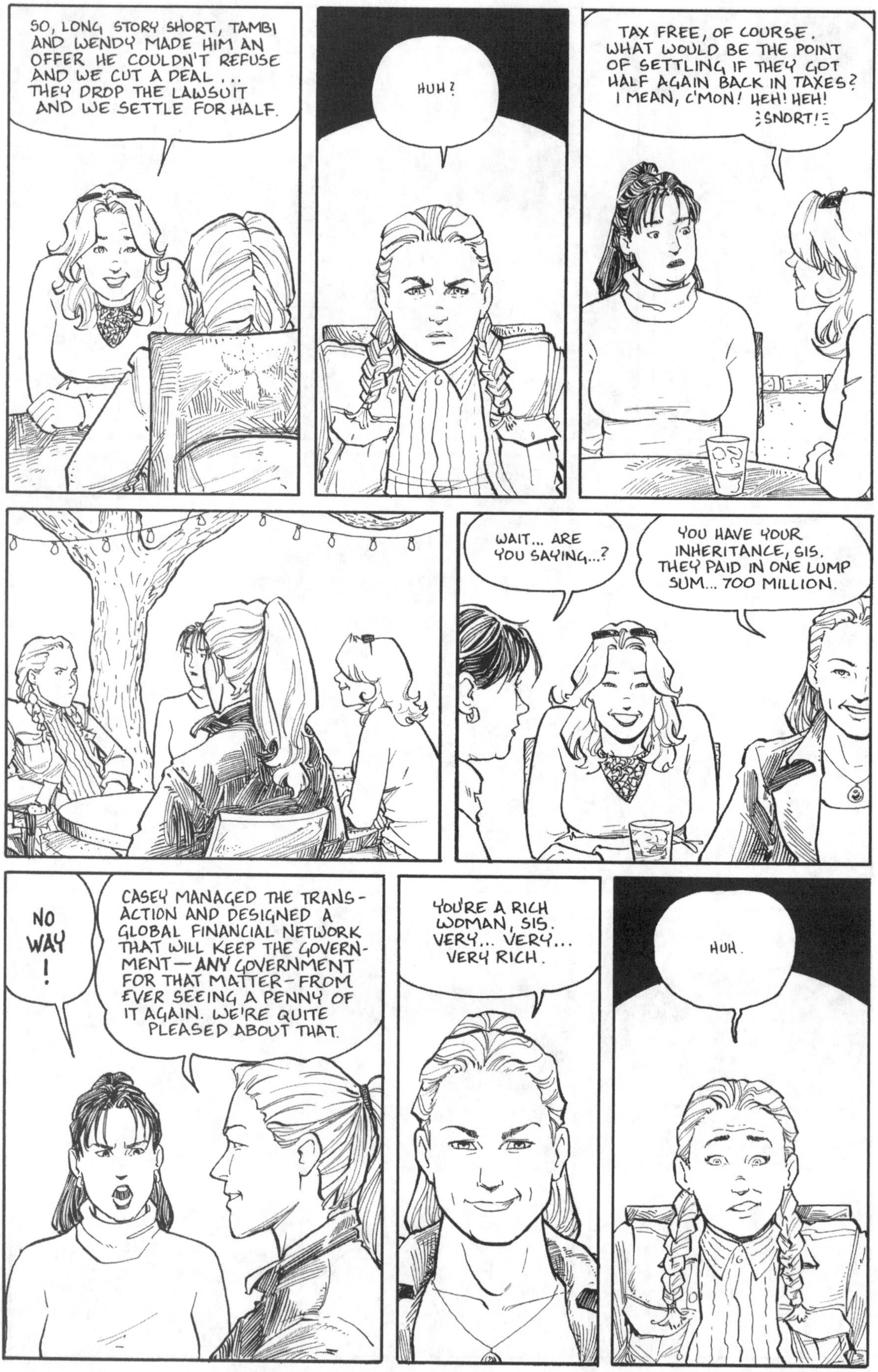
SO, LONG STORY SHORT, TAMBI AND WENDY MADE HIM AN OFFER HE COULDN'T REFUSE AND WE CUT A DEAL... THEY DROP THE LAWSUIT AND WE SETTLE FOR HALF.
HUH?
TAX FREE, OF COURSE. WHAT WOULD BE THE POINT OF SETTLING IF THEY GOT HALF AGAIN BACK IN TAXES? I MEAN, C'MON! HEH! HEH!
SNORT!
WAIT... ARE YOU SAYING...?
YOU HAVE YOUR INHERITANCE, SIS. THEY PAID IN ONE LUMP SUM... 700 MILLION.
NO WAY!
CASEY MANAGED THE TRANS-ACTION AND DESIGNED A GLOBAL FINANCIAL NETWORK THAT WILL KEEP THE GOVERN-MENT—ANY GOVERNMENT FOR THAT MATTER—FROM EVER SEEING A PENNY OF IT AGAIN. WE'RE QUITE PLEASED ABOUT THAT.
YOU'RE A RICH WOMAN, SIS. VERY... VERY... VERY RICH.
HUH.

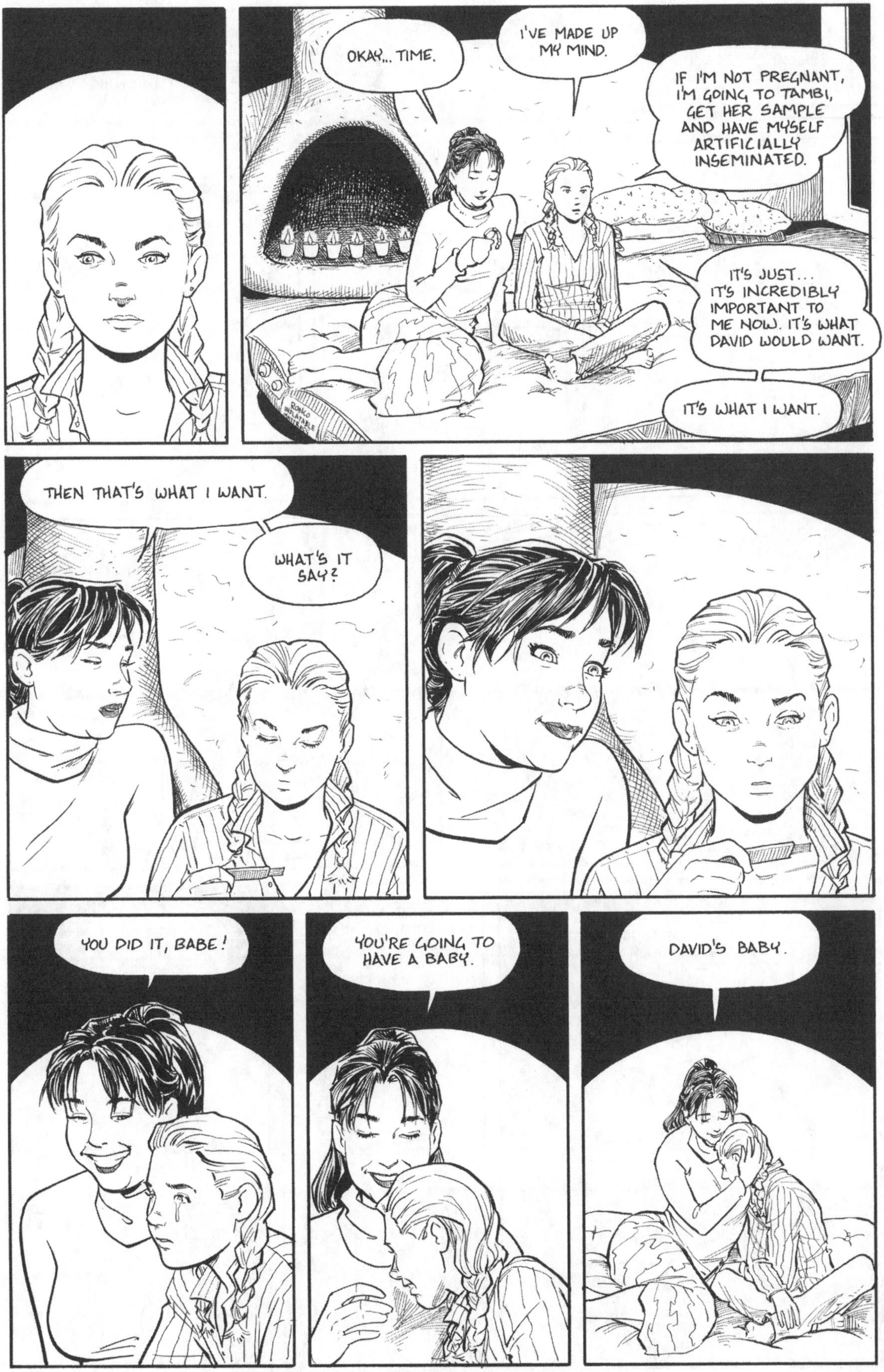
OKAY... TIME.
I'VE MADE UP MY MIND.
IF I'M NOT PREGNANT, I'M GOING TO TAMBI, GET HER SAMPLE AND HAVE MYSELF ARTIFICIALLY INSEMINATED.
IT'S JUST... IT'S INCREDIBLY IMPORTANT TO ME NOW. IT'S WHAT DAVID WOULD WANT.
IT'S WHAT I WANT.
THEN THAT'S WHAT I WANT.
WHAT'S IT SAY?
YOU DID IT, BABE!
YOU'RE GOING TO HAVE A BABY.
DAVID'S BABY.

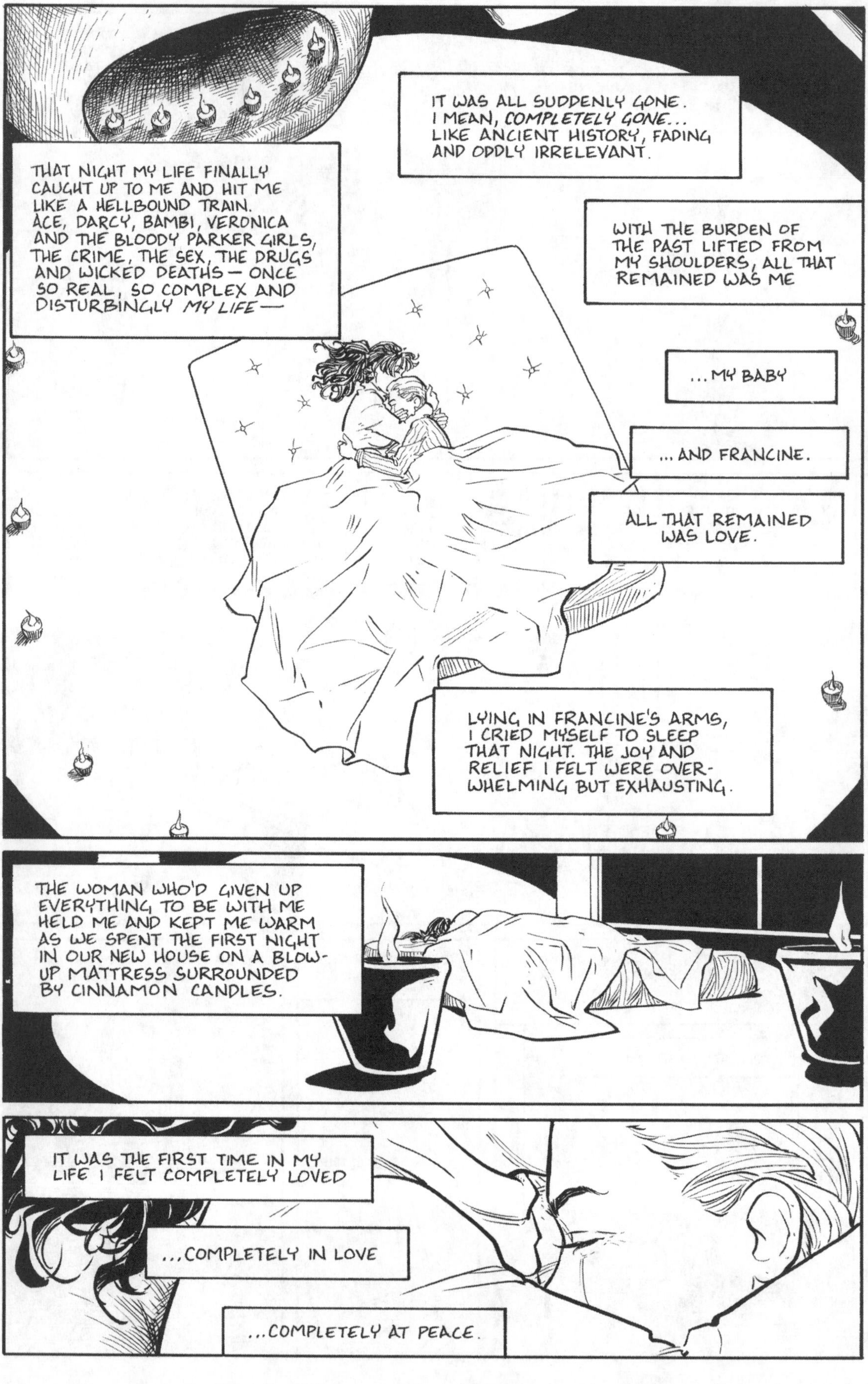
THAT NIGHT MY LIFE FINALLY CAUGHT UP TO ME AND HIT ME LIKE A HELLBOUND TRAIN. ACE, DARCY, BAMBI, VERONICA AND THE BLOODY PARKER GIRLS, THE CRIME, THE SEX, THE DRUGS AND WICKED DEATHS— ONCE SO REAL, SO COMPLEX AND DISTURBINGLY *MY LIFE*—
IT WAS ALL SUDDENLY GONE. I MEAN, *COMPLETELY GONE*... LIKE ANCIENT HISTORY, FADING AND ODDLY IRRELEVANT.
WITH THE BURDEN OF THE PAST LIFTED FROM MY SHOULDERS, ALL THAT REMAINED WAS ME
...MY BABY
...AND FRANCINE.
ALL THAT REMAINED WAS LOVE.
LYING IN FRANCINE'S ARMS, I CRIED MYSELF TO SLEEP THAT NIGHT. THE JOY AND RELIEF I FELT WERE OVER-WHELMING BUT EXHAUSTING.
THE WOMAN WHO'D GIVEN UP EVERYTHING TO BE WITH ME HELD ME AND KEPT ME WARM AS WE SPENT THE FIRST NIGHT IN OUR NEW HOUSE ON A BLOW-UP MATTRESS SURROUNDED BY CINNAMON CANDLES.
IT WAS THE FIRST TIME IN MY LIFE I FELT COMPLETELY LOVED
...COMPLETELY IN LOVE
...COMPLETELY AT PEACE.

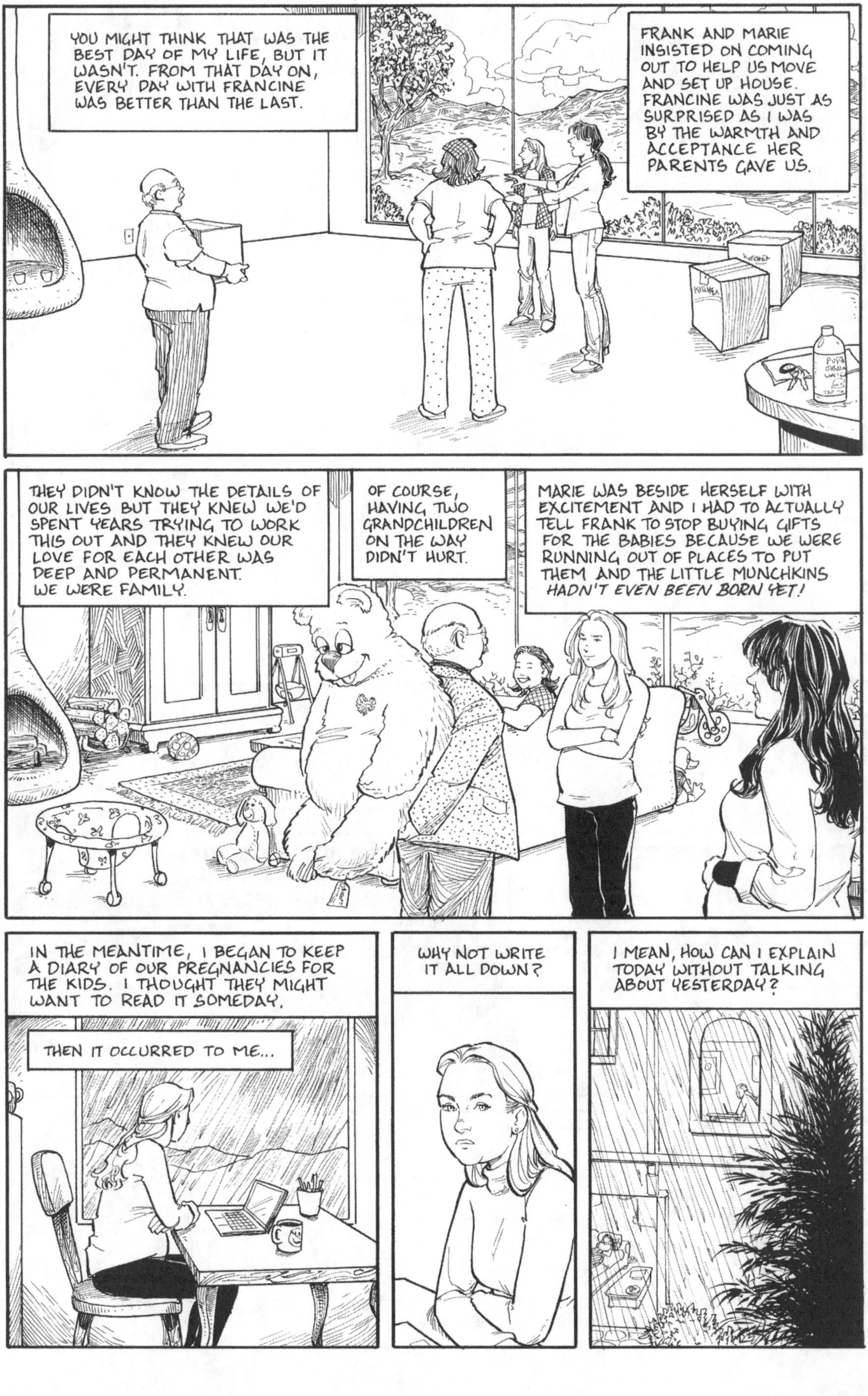
YOU MIGHT THINK THAT WAS THE BEST DAY OF MY LIFE, BUT IT WASN'T. FROM THAT DAY ON, EVERY DAY WITH FRANCINE WAS BETTER THAN THE LAST.
FRANK AND MARIE INSISTED ON COMING OUT TO HELP US MOVE AND SET UP HOUSE. FRANCINE WAS JUST AS SURPRISED AS I WAS BY THE WARMTH AND ACCEPTANCE HER PARENTS GAVE US.
KITCHEN
KITCHEN
THEY DIDN'T KNOW THE DETAILS OF OUR LIVES BUT THEY KNEW WE'D SPENT YEARS TRYING TO WORK THIS OUT AND THEY KNEW OUR LOVE FOR EACH OTHER WAS DEEP AND PERMANENT. WE WERE FAMILY.
OF COURSE, HAVING TWO GRANDCHILDREN ON THE WAY DIDN'T HURT.
MARIE WAS BESIDE HERSELF WITH EXCITEMENT AND I HAD TO ACTUALLY TELL FRANK TO STOP BUYING GIFTS FOR THE BABIES BECAUSE WE WERE RUNNING OUT OF PLACES TO PUT THEM AND THE LITTLE MUNCHKINS *HADN'T EVEN BEEN BORN YET!*
IN THE MEANTIME, I BEGAN TO KEEP A DIARY OF OUR PREGNANCIES FOR THE KIDS. I THOUGHT THEY MIGHT WANT TO READ IT SOMEDAY.
THEN IT OCCURRED TO ME...
WHY NOT WRITE IT ALL DOWN?
I MEAN, HOW CAN I EXPLAIN TODAY WITHOUT TALKING ABOUT YESTERDAY?

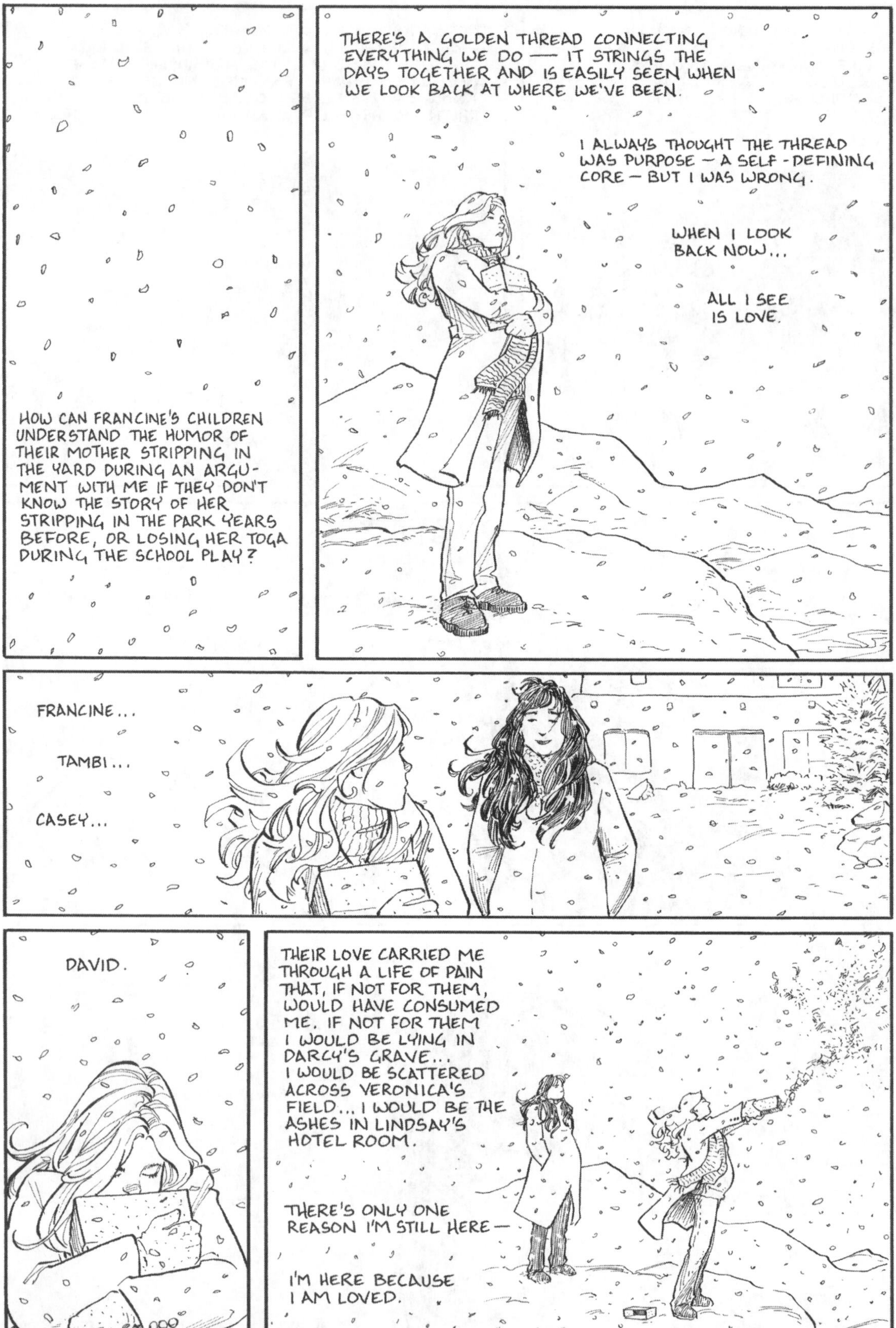
HOW CAN FRANCINE'S CHILDREN UNDERSTAND THE HUMOR OF THEIR MOTHER STRIPPING IN THE YARD DURING AN ARGU-MENT WITH ME IF THEY DON'T KNOW THE STORY OF HER STRIPPING IN THE PARK YEARS BEFORE, OR LOSING HER TOGA DURING THE SCHOOL PLAY?
THERE'S A GOLDEN THREAD CONNECTING EVERYTHING WE DO — IT STRINGS THE DAYS TOGETHER AND IS EASILY SEEN WHEN WE LOOK BACK AT WHERE WE'VE BEEN.
I ALWAYS THOUGHT THE THREAD WAS PURPOSE — A SELF-DEFINING CORE — BUT I WAS WRONG.
WHEN I LOOK BACK NOW...
ALL I SEE IS LOVE.
FRANCINE...
TAMBI...
CASEY...
DAVID.
THEIR LOVE CARRIED ME THROUGH A LIFE OF PAIN THAT, IF NOT FOR THEM, WOULD HAVE CONSUMED ME. IF NOT FOR THEM I WOULD BE LYING IN DARCY'S GRAVE... I WOULD BE SCATTERED ACROSS VERONICA'S FIELD... I WOULD BE THE ASHES IN LINDSAY'S HOTEL ROOM.
THERE'S ONLY ONE REASON I'M STILL HERE—
I'M HERE BECAUSE I AM LOVED.
DAVID WOULD WANT OUR CHILD TO KNOW THAT. I WILL TELL HER.

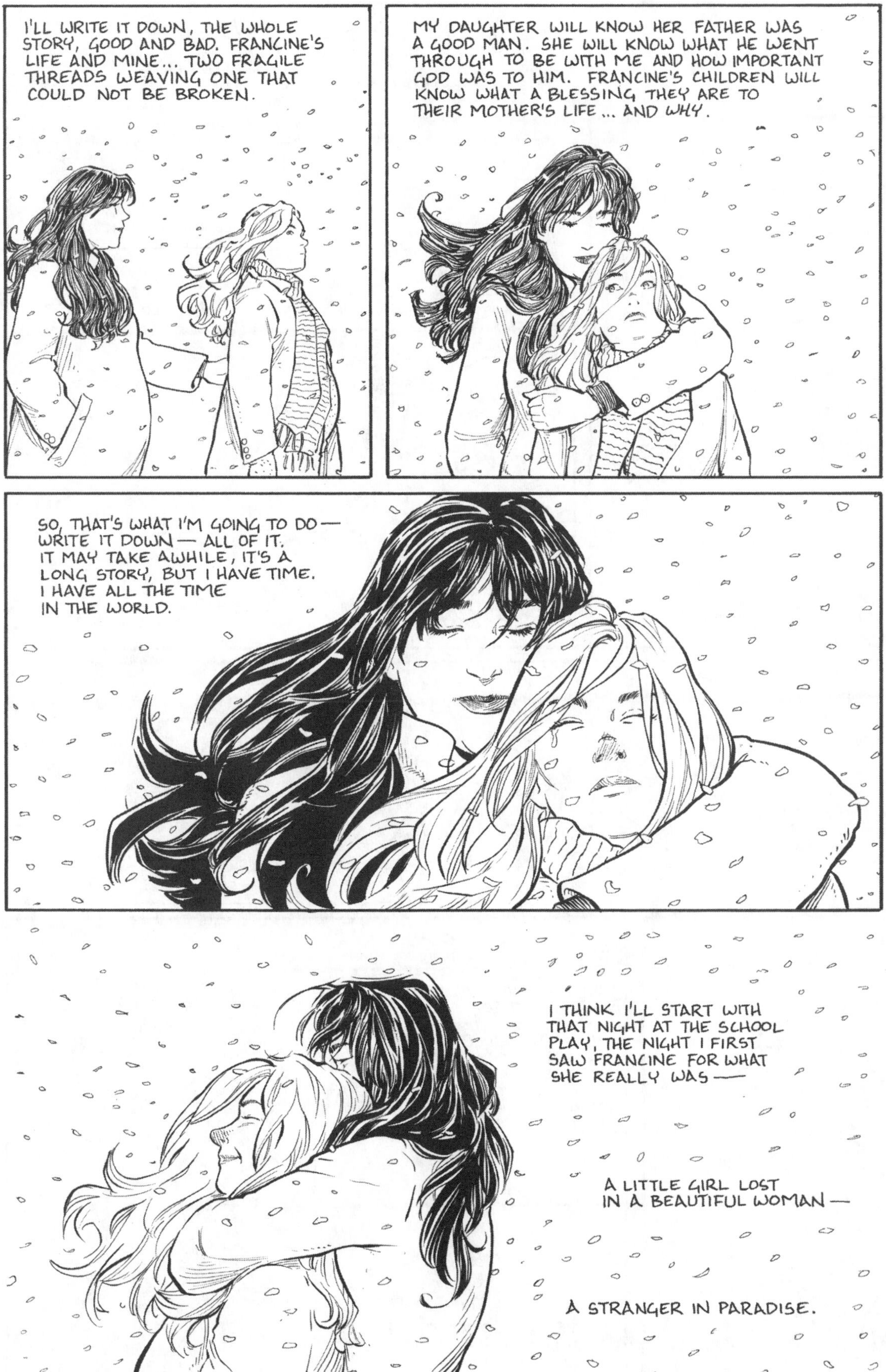
I'LL WRITE IT DOWN, THE WHOLE STORY, GOOD AND BAD. FRANCINE'S LIFE AND MINE... TWO FRAGILE THREADS WEAVING ONE THAT COULD NOT BE BROKEN.
MY DAUGHTER WILL KNOW HER FATHER WAS A GOOD MAN. SHE WILL KNOW WHAT HE WENT THROUGH TO BE WITH ME AND HOW IMPORTANT GOD WAS TO HIM. FRANCINE'S CHILDREN WILL KNOW WHAT A BLESSING THEY ARE TO THEIR MOTHER'S LIFE... AND WHY.
SO, THAT'S WHAT I'M GOING TO DO— WRITE IT DOWN — ALL OF IT. IT MAY TAKE AWHILE, IT'S A LONG STORY, BUT I HAVE TIME. I HAVE ALL THE TIME IN THE WORLD.
I THINK I'LL START WITH THAT NIGHT AT THE SCHOOL PLAY, THE NIGHT I FIRST SAW FRANCINE FOR WHAT SHE REALLY WAS—
A LITTLE GIRL LOST IN A BEAUTIFUL WOMAN—
A STRANGER IN PARADISE.